Reinventing the Library

FOR ONLINE EDUCATION

Reinventing the Library

FOR ONLINE EDUCATION

FREDERICK STIELOW

An imprint of the American Library Association
CHICAGO   2014

FRED STIELOW heads American Public University System's Classroom/ Research Information Services (CRIS). Dr. Stielow previously worked as director of the Amistad the Walter Reuther Labor Library at Wayne State University, Mid-Hudson Public Library System, Research Center at Tulane University, and Head of Special Collections at the University of Louisiana, Lafayette. He also held full-time professorial appointments at the University of Maryland and Catholic University along with visiting assignments at the University of Illinois and University of Puerto Rico. He has held major posts with the American Library Association and the Society of American Archivists. Stielow earned his bachelor's and master's degrees in history along with a dual doctorate in history and American studies from Indiana University, as well as an MLS from the University of Rhode Island. He has written ten previous books, including *The Management of Oral History Sound Archives*, *Creating Virtual Libraries*, and *Building Digital Archives*.

Printed in the United States of America
18 17 16 15 14   5 4 3 2 1

Extensive effort has gone into ensuring the reliability of the information in this book; however, the publisher makes no warranty, express or implied, with respect to the material contained herein.

ISBNs: 978-0-8389-1208-9 (paper). For more information on digital formats, visit the ALA Store at alastore.ala.org and select eEditions.

Library of Congress Cataloging-in-Publication Data

Stielow, Frederick J., 1946-
   Reinventing the library for online education / Frederick Stielow.
     pages   cm
   Includes bibliographical references and index.
   ISBN 978-0-8389-1208-9 (alk. paper)
   1. Academic libraries—Aims and objectives. 2. Academic libraries—
Effect of technological innovations on. 3. Libraries and colleges. 4. Digital libraries. 5. Libraries and electronic publishing. 6. Libraries and the Internet. 7. Internet in higher education. 8. Libraries—History. 9. Learning and scholarship—History. I.Title.
Z675.U5S77 2014
020.285'4678—dc23
                             2013028022

Book design by Kimberly Thornton in Charis SIL, Meta, and Verdana.

♾ This paper meets the requirements of ANSI/NISO Z39.48-1992 (Permanence of Paper).

What is more important in a library than anything else—
than everything else—is the fact that it exists.
—*Archibald MacLeish*

‹ contents ›

‹ figures ›

‹ *preface* ›

When it was proclaimed that the Library contained all books, the first
impression was one of extravagant happiness. All men felt themselves to be the masters of an intact and secret treasure. There was
no personal or world problem whose eloquent solution did not exist.
. . . The universe was justified, the universe suddenly usurped the
unlimited dimensions of hope. . . . As was natural, this inordinate
hope was followed by an excessive depression. . . . A blasphemous
sect suggested that the searches should cease. . . . Others, inversely,
believed that it was fundamental to eliminate useless works.
—Jorge Luis Borges, "The Library of Babel" (1941)

BORGES PRESAGES EXUBERANCE AND REQUISITE CAUTION
as libraries enter the teens of the twenty-first century. Some
remain optimistic about the prospects on the "information super-
highway." A counter-chorus grows wary. Economic crises threaten
financial underpinnings and the employ of librarians. World Wide
Web actively intrudes on traditional domains. The world's knowledge no longer fits neatly on library shelves. The need to travel and handle physical objects vanishes. Every area of library activity is fundamentally reordered.
And, as stressed in this book, a disturbingly different type of library setting
emerges for consideration.

An institution that literally defined human history faces existential tests. Can
libraries control their destinies in the web age? Could the Web subsume the
library as institution? Or, as featured here, are there redeeming and redefining
roles from online education?

PERSPECTIVES

The following chapters offer exploration through uniquely experienced and occasionally provocative perspectives. Though the book is of value for a variety of settings and library school students, the locus is higher education. Rather than a top-down research institution or consortial approach, dialog is from the bottom up. The voice seeks to address, inquire, and empower at the level of the practicing repository for the new of a virtual campus.

VIEWS FROM THE VIRTUAL

Even the best of current commentaries reflect print-era biases. The reality of centuries of practice backed by millions of dollars in infrastructure remains hard to escape. The book continues as the defining trope. Instead of transformational embrace, defense and recodification of established practices naturally lurk beneath the surface. Discourse mirrors reluctant transit from paper to "blended" electronic operations.

These dialogues launch outside the book "box." Conjecture is replaced by postmodern commentary from a previously unheard setting. Rather than projections on what may be coming, discussion is from an already reinvented library. Origins lie in a rapidly expanding online library—one with some eight years of experimentation and successfully serving over 100,000 patrons in more than 120 countries. Analysis comes absent huge abodes, vested personnel, or even ownership of information assets. Metaphors are of the web and the cloud. Functions are predefined from the electronic with barely a thought of paper. Through such rarified air, nothing is assumed. All operations are subject to critical examination and rife with change.

FOR-PROFIT JUXTAPOSITION

The outsider viewpoint is accentuated by a first-time look through the lens of online, for-profit universities. Part and parcel of a rising global economy, these are uniquely web creations. They originate without deference to vested infrastructures or established practice. Planners consciously inveigle against land-based traditions. Competitive forces unapologetically scrutinize for advantage and market share. Rather than assume entitlement and value, the landscape turns capitalistic and decidedly entrepreneurial. It presupposes heightened accountability, including prospects for ROI (return on investment) and unseen levels of justification for the very presence of an academic library.

TECHNOLOGY NEXUS

The treatment presented here also draws on personal engagement inside the "technology box." Observations date to the late 1960s with the running of a data processing shop and systems analyst training prior to entering librarianship. Subsequent experience parlays web-era management in both academic and public library system settings. Knowledge is harvested from the past of an Internet services provider (ISP), successful automation of dozens of libraries in a multi-county system, and building a virtual library for an online university.

My views are also bolstered by employ as a professor in schools of library and information science. The inquiry benefits from the familiarity earned through decades of teaching, including classes that range from the history of the book and preservation to an introduction to automation and web-based archives. To those are added a myriad of professional committee assignments and consultations along with two earlier web-related books.

That combination informs an environmental scan across the jungle of onrushing encounters, threats, and opportunities. I give attention to practical work-a-day insights yet do not shy from surfacing atavisms, the realities of the consumer marketplace, or the potentials of a born-web generation. Emergent applications are queried from Web 2.0 to voice recognition, touch screens, and 3D imaging. These pages proffer search engines as a new type of audience and service determiner. Libraries are invited to exit campus comfort zones for online classrooms and automated learning management systems (LMSs). Librarians are asked to step to the forefront, to engage and compete for new web-based roles within the university.

TOWARD AN IDEA

Reinventing the Library for Online Education moves between practice and theory—the classical blend of *praxis* and *techne*. The ultimate pretense is to advance a web-age library component within the critical baseline launched by John Henry Newman (1858) in the classic *The Idea of a University*. The practical orientation mirrors the Toronto School of Harold Innes, Marshall McLuhan, and Walter Ong. A "medium is the message" and global village orientation continue to offer predictive and crucial perspectives for transiting the web revolution.

Like Newman and the Toronto School, this book relies on a dose of historical analysis. It suggests that the allure of new technologies can prove dissembling. Naïve instrumentalism lends to overlooking the power of the library narrative.

Yet library genealogy continues to play its defining role within the university, even an online university. History remains differentiating bedrock for survival and success.

> ### › Thinking Web
> Aside from trust that the reader will credence views from the fringe and blatantly economic positions, this book's most daunting quest is an altered type of thinking. Not unlike the postpress rise of Cartesian modes and individualism, the new medium is transforming thought and how people approach information gathering. How then should the library and librarians respond in rewiring practice, service, and terminology?

Academic libraries also have lessons to learn and economic prospects to uncover from their past. An understanding of an originating mission of student service proves pivotal for the future. The field can draw too on previous encounters with communications revolutions to address the web phenomenon as something in midstream. Final answers at this stage would be presumptuous—but delayed response fatal.

Related influences. Management and economic theory come to the fore. Approximation-based planning and change management inform a complex transition. The implications of a global information economy merit special consideration. Acknowledgment is given to rising managerial trends but leavened by doses of Sun Tzu's military, Machiavelli's political, and Max Weber's bureaucratic awareness.

The treatment reflects a variety of other theoretical components as well. Contemporary commentators and futurologists influence near- and long-term projections on the fate of university libraries. Linguistics and literary theories pepper this book. Indeed, much of challenge resolves to the evolutionary nature of language and grammar in revolutionary flux.

Ultimately, the narrative is bookended between two towering figures from the 1940s.

- **Jorge Luis Borges.** As already seen, the commanding Argentine librarian/ author sets the stage with insightful jolts of caution, respect, and awe for the complexities that we now face.
- **Vannevar Bush.** This leader of the wartime science community helped inspire the Web and much more in the landmark "As We May Think" (1945). His *memex* concept remains a humbling reminder of still unachieved benchmarks for virtual libraries.

LAYOUT AND SUBTEXT

This book's design pays subtle homage to McLuhan. Echoing his landmark *Gutenberg Galaxy* (1962), it reflects the Web's unfolding impact on written communication. Print composition is augmented by electronic consciousness. Core chapters invite random access through a wiki-like encyclopedic framework and "stub" commentaries. Periodic "Readers' Advisories" invite "hopscotching" within the text. Footnoting is deprecated. The semistandard bibliography is altered, with URLs preferred. Citation leans away from pagination in deference to the utility of simple string searches. End matter extends to a "Webliography" of sites consulted.

Visual components also emphasize what McLuhan termed "gravitational" effects on composition:

- Bulleted or enumerated lists with boldface and italic trimmings are frequent features.
- Author-date (parenthetical) citation style replaces footnotes.
- Multilevel headings are far more frequent than in the past. Rather than boldface type, they began with underlying HTML coding (e.g., h1, h2 . . . h5) and design for search engine discovery.
- Information boxes/sidebars are frequently inserted for digressions and conversations that were previously relegated to footnotes.
- Paragraphing and sentence structures are deliberately shortened from scholarly norms.
- Type font for headings is Verdana—the first font designed for the Web. Released in 1996 from Microsoft's typography group, Verdana offers a sans serif face for enhanced online viewing and better transition from inking to pixelated representations on the computer screen.

The results are admittedly attenuated. The product is still framed as a standard book and unfolds through monographic chapters. It has to meet publisher demands rooted in print that strip off the structures and embedded metadata in the production process. The work is inherently "time stamped." Input and considerations are largely fixed by the draft's November 1, 2012, dispatch to the editors. Equally important, a book in hand cannot include hyperlinks. Ink on paper lacks the ability to repurpose resources automatically in multiple locations—or to add flourishes like automated references, glossaries, updating, videos, and external commentary.

CONTENT OVERVIEW

Reinventing the Library for Online Education unfolds in two major sections. Part A, "Preparing within a Revolution," spotlights a set of knowledge arenas to guide the construction of a virtual academic library. Three background chapters proffer top-down overviews:

> Chapter 1, "The Narrative," glosses the powerful story that is library history. Discussions promote an origins myth along with lessons from a series of technologically related paradigm shifts, which demark the evolution of the university library.
> Chapter 2, "Web Technology and Libraries," provides technical background on the Web and its first-round effects on academic libraries.
> Chapter 3, "Disruptions on the Long Tail," brings economics firmly to the fore. The library is set as a cog within a new information economy—one that includes unprecedented competition, added government oversight, and the disruptive forces of online universities.

Part B, "Virtual Campus Discourse," immerses the reader from the bottom up in an onrushing reinvention of the library. Discussion emanates from a critical era at the start of the second decade of this century. Questions are implicit and explicit. How can a library control its destiny with collections that are no longer owned or physically housed? How do academic libraries reverse current trends and prove their worth in a highly competitive atmosphere?

Explorations are based on practical experiences and a virtual campus-based classroom/research information services (CRIS) model. In this setting, library theory is redefined for librarian-centric services and demonstrations of value. Chapters engage as a series of applied exercises:

> Chapter 4, "Setting the Stage," juxtaposes a mainstream validation crisis and opportunities against a proposed remediation model from the virtual campus.
> Chapter 5, "Elimination Commentaries," strips away superfluous library practices for print-based artifacts and storage needs.
> Chapter 6, "Redefinition Commentaries," deconstructs remaining library functions for virtual operations.

Chapter 7, "Construction Commentaries," the final set of commentaries, is immersed within a growing array of concepts, tools, and services being wrought by the medium.

Chapter 8, "Rewiring Online Librarians," hypothesizes an elevated role for librarians. Librarians replace collections as the centerpieces for a new type of academic library—but they require rewiring.

Chapter 9, "Managerial Strategies," offers concluding analysis that draws from the previous discussions. It provides pragmatic suggestions for the implementation of an academic online library with emphasis on a for-profit virtual campus.

A speculative epilogue looks at prospects for empowering a higher-education economic zone along with a multilayered concept for the virtual academic library.

The text closes with a ceremonial colophon. Dating to the preprint era, such "final strokes" were once used to identify the source of handwritten compositions. The device reappears with background on the author and the electronic scriptorium that birthed the study—library operations on the virtual campus of the fully online American Public University System (APUS).

‹ *acknowledgments* ›

THANKS FOR FEEDBACK FROM LIBRARY SCHOOL STU-
dents at the University of Wisconsin–Milwaukee and University
of Rhode Island as well as attendees at the 2012 HELIN Conference. Several colleagues also wittingly or unwittingly contributed to this manuscript, especially those at APUS. Carol Gilbert
and Wallace Boston enabled opportunity at a rare moment in
history. My brother from another mother Frank McCluskey played a unique role
in fostering experimentation, and Karan Powell followed his tolerant practices
as APUS provost.

The bulk of accolades are reserved for "my folks"—the best group of online
librarians in the field—and their compatriots in electronic course materials and
APUS ePress. Appreciation goes in particular to Susan Hyland, Lydia Crawford,
and Andrea Dunn. They stood with me from the start in rewiring a different
vision of service. Finally, to wife Susan Rosenfeld and son Thane goes the grudging thanks for putting up with me. ☺

PART A

PREPARING WITHIN A REVOLUTION

Gaining understanding within a revolution is perforce daunting. Basic assumptions and the underpinnings of the field are being ripped away. Legacies from the past intrude. The library struggles for solutions while accommodating at breakneck speed. Unprecedented competition and financial strictures emerge. The hunt is on for guidance and models, but where is the experience—especially for smaller and midsize facilities?

This initial section of *Reinventing Libraries for Online Education* proffers insights from history but moves quickly to background and questioning from web technology and for modern economic considerations. The intent is a "view from 30,000 feet" to better guide practical choices for chaotic and threatening times.

> **› Readers' Advisory**
>
> Although interlaced, the book's sections may be read independently. Part A offers general background fodder, including philosophical and theoretical contents. Those bent solely on practical applications may jump ahead to part B's "Virtual Campus Discourse."

1

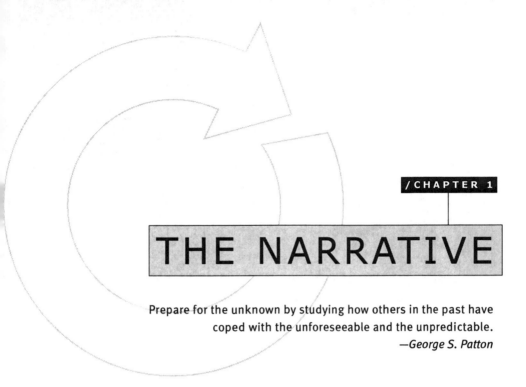

THE NARRATIVE

Prepare for the unknown by studying how others in the past have
coped with the unforeseeable and the unpredictable.
—*George S. Patton*

ENERAL PATTON'S ADVICE HOLDS FOR THE WEB. HIS-
tory is too valuable to ignore—or leave solely to historians.
Whether learning from success or tribulation, the past remains
a precious tool. This is especially so for libraries. Their narrative provides an unparalleled baseline for future sustainability. Historical understanding and methods offer the manager
valuable counterpoint and distance. Factual background and nonlinear evaluation help balance against the blinding allures of technology and latest business
fad. Rather than awakening to unpleasant hindsight, foresight based on the past
sharpens awareness for

- **Atavisms.** Tradition and allegiances to established practice can be dissembling for coping within a revolution. What should be discarded or at
  least questioned? Are there related lessons for bringing change to staff,
  operations, and audiences?
- **Functions and structures.** History helps avoid reinventing the wheel and
  clinging to presentist biases. What components from the past to use, not
  use, or—perhaps—resurface or furbish?

3

- **Image/prestige.** The library goes beyond physical services. What are the potential and responsibilities from its historical legacies, allegiances, and symbolic values?
- **Technological perspective.** The Web is not the library's first encounter with a transformational technology. What are applicable lessons from earlier communications revolutions?
- **Threat response.** The ivory tower is being assaulted. Marginalization again rears, and any sense of entitlement must be obviated. What are the threats from both external competition and internal acquiescence?
- **Strategy and tactics.** In General Patton's terms, what is the appropriate mix of defense and offense—of strategy and tactics—for sustainability and advancement in the web era?

> **› Readers' Advisory**
>
> This chapter offers a highly abbreviated overview. Those with developed awareness of the library's place in history may wish to jump ahead to the next chapter. Those with historical animus or narrow applied focus, however, are advised to still hopscotch to the "Sorbonne and the Invention of the University Library" then "The University and Education Reordered" in this chapter.

PROLOGUE

The idea of library is inherent to civilization, but its meaning varies with time and circumstance. This book's context is the library as stand-alone entity or branded subset of an institution—such as a university library. In addition to intellectual and civic context, I add stress for often underplayed ties to technology and pedagogy. Such tradition dates to the invention of writing at the literal dawn of history. Working as party to emergent political/religious systems, castes of priestly scribes developed groundbreaking technologies. These first technocrats engaged in two overlapping zones:

- **Religious/state services.** Writing transcended divination. With it, scribes could capture and reuse the words of their deities in a displayable and inheritable fashion. With it too, governments and religions were legitimated.
- **Notarial services.** The same skill set supported administrative controls and government bureaucracies. Governments could institute regularized

taxes. Laws and commercial transactions could be captured in reproducible form for verification.

The science of writing did not stand alone. Efforts bridged into education and knowledge building. They stimulated companion skills in mathematics along with investigations of the heavens and natural events. Such directions necessarily brought forth a subsidiary institution that would give name to their underlying enterprises.

Birth of the repository. Scribal functions naturally extended to record keeping. The storage and retrieval of content gave birth to the library/archives as institution. Care and growth of collections eventually called forth specializations. Those in charge needed expertise for different types of materials, storage units, and access. They had to handle museum-like artifactual collections, including sanctified objects. Preservation and copying functions entered. Over time, sacred and commercial realms would be augmented by educational materials, scholarly observations, and even a bit of pleasure reading/literature.

CLASSICAL PORTFOLIO

The democratic crucibles of ancient Greece and Rome fostered a remarkably mature form of library. Their institutions were a concrete manifestation of the doctrine of the "Good." In keeping with Plato's articulation for his philosopher kings, the library was a realization of the state's duty to its people. Establishment would come from an informed polis and required citizens' embrace as stakeholders. Temple traditions blended into a lasting duality:

> ### › Hydraulic Societies
> Western writing traditions date to Sumer and Egypt in the fourth millennium BCE. These were early agricultural civilizations beset by annual floods and also characterized as "hydraulic" societies. As proposed by Wittfogel (1957), writing and the parallel development of number systems provided the practical modus for the formation of sophisticated government. Recording authority was needed to deal with washed-out boundaries and water distribution.

- **Information services.** Temple and state duties extended to an enlarged clientele and enhanced services:
    - » *Public access.* Access to information was extended to the citizenry—the *polis*—as a democratic right.

» *Publication controls.* Responsibility for the provision of information extended from self-publishing to collecting from external sources.

» *Education/scholarly operations.* The library supported education along with creation/distribution of secular knowledge.

» *Stewardship.* Priestly responsibilities for the words of the gods transited toward the secular and preserving the documentary heritage for future generations.

- **Monument/cultural symbol.** The institutions became a civic statement somewhat independent of their religious placement. Beyond active services, the library signed:

  » *Legitimacy.* Political, cultural, and business bodies basked in the propriety wrought by the presence of the institution. Like a monument, the library helped affirm tradition and an establishment's right to exist.

  » *Scholarship/science.* Thanks to its educational overlap and holdings, the institution became a recognized signpost of wisdom, scholarly studies, and advancement.

  » *Prestige.* Whether altruism, duty, or conspicuous consumption, the library conferred respectability and social status. It readily became a locus for charitable contributions but also periodically an enticing fashion statement. As Stoic philosopher Seneca lamented over Roman values in the middle of the first century CE:

You will find, then, in the libraries of the most arrant idlers all that orators or historians have written—bookcases built up as high as the ceiling. Nowadays a library takes rank with a bathroom as a necessary ornament of a house. I could forgive such ideas if they were due to extravagant desire for learning. As it is, these productions of men whose genius we revere, paid for at a high price, with their portraits ranged in line above them, are got together to adorn and beautify a wall.

Unfortunately, the same prestige, legitimacy, and religious factors made for a tempting target. Positioning within wealthy temples to other gods was certain to draw the attention of invaders and rebels—doubly so when financial and property records were present. The past and present of libraries thus remain all too replete with demonstrations, destruction, and looting.

Alexandrian Museum, the Proto-university

Classical formations reached their epitome in the fourth century BCE. In keeping with Aristotelian precepts, the Ptolemaic city of Alexandria in Egypt founded a temple to the muses. The creation remains a transcendent statement. The Alexandrian Museum emerged as a trailblazing knowledge center—the world's first university before there was a word for university.

The museum articulated space for science and education. A lyceum offered teaching and public forums. The *peripatos,* a colonnaded walkway and gardens, were part of a grand design. They supported contemplative reflection—"a place for the cure of the soul." Amenities were specifically dedicated by subject, from astronomy and anatomy sections to a zoo of exotic animals. Over time, this creative confluence would be the fount for the "fathers" of math, engineering, physiology, geography, and medicine.

The academic library. Space and Aristotle's literary effects manifested through a groundbreaking library. The Alexandrian version was integral to the museum's operations but achieved its own fame and lasting legacy. Rather than part-time task, librarianship ratcheted into a full-time occupation. Practitioners became known and even gained a bit of celebrity. For instance, we can point to Zenodotus, the library's founder; and Callimachus, the first bibliographer and inventor of the *pinakes,* or library catalog.

Alexandria fully embodied what became a continuing ideal. In addition to a precedent-setting drive to hold all of human knowledge, operations fostered experimentation and development of a new auxiliary discipline or science. Alexandria pioneered trappings that continue to define and grace modern establishments—along with intriguing extras:

- **Acquisitions.** Alexandria reveled in the first transnational knowledge collections. This forerunner of modern research libraries forged the first mandate to collect the world's written information.
- **Cataloging.** The earliest known dedicated department for the bibliographic control of materials also included the first recorded use of alphabetic ordering.
- **Education.** The library boasted its own educational facilities with designated lecture halls.
- **Entrepreneurial center.** The Alexandrian Library augmented its state support by serving as an international hub of the book trade. It also stimulated nearby economic endeavors, such as the production of papyrus.

- **Public presentations.** Space was set aside for public and scholarly declamations.
- **Preservation.** A basic responsibility was ensuring the survivability of key texts.
- **Publishing.** Copyists put forth editions of classical works for internal use by scholars but also for sale and export.
- **Reading rooms.** Functional spaces were designed for scholars to unroll and compare materials efficiently.
- **Mass storage.** The library featured specialized shelving for the world's largest *bibliothekai* of papyrus and an assortment of parchment scrolls.
- **Scholarship.** Staff developed and used the skills of critical bibliography to determine the authenticity of texts.
- **Showcase.** The library's monumental presence made manifest the state's responsibility for the advancement of knowledge.

DARK AGES

Although the Camelot-like legend of Alexandria survived, the original was doomed. It fell to a prolonged series of Roman, Christian, and Arabian attacks. The halcyon era of librarianship followed a similar path to destruction with the downfall of Rome. By the sixth century CE, a mélange of depredations decimated literacy. The Roman Empire's "pagan" temples with their libraries were being destroyed or left to fall into disrepair. Centralized state recording/depository functions were eliminated. The public library impulse fell into abeyance. The library as urban monument along with its authentication studies, publication duties, and mass storage drifted into the dustbin of history.

Religious retreat alone avoided total destruction. Isolated and defensible monasteries sprang up in the face of waves of invasions and civil disorders. These refuges offered a lifestyle of contemplation along with defensive bulwarks against barbarian hordes and internal marauders. In a manner that defies modern comprehension, monks committed to encompassing communal religiosity. Even work should entail devotional value.

Enter one Cassiodorus Senatorus. In the aftermath of the Gothic Wars, this Roman statesman and cleric offered an Edenic alternative at Vivarium (*vivaria*—a place of fishing ponds):

> Its waves threaten no danger, but neither is it despicable for its size. It flows
> into your precincts, channeled artificially where it is wanted, adequate to

water your gardens and turn your mills. It is there when you want it and flows on when no longer needed; it exists to serve you, never too boisterous and bothersome nor yet again ever deficient. The sea lies all about you as well, accessible for fishing with fishponds to keep the caught fish alive. We have constructed them as pleasant receptacles, with the Lord's help, where a multitude of fish swim close by the cloister, in circumstances so like mountain caves that the fish never sense themselves constrained in any way, since they are free to seek their food and hide away in dark recesses. We have also had baths built to refresh weary bodies, where sparkling water for drinking and washing flows by.

As indicated elsewhere in his famed *Institutiones* (circa 562), Cassiodorus sought to extend the Opus Deum, or "work of god." He devolved scribal/library duties into high forms of devotion. Such labors demanded an elite corps of literate monks. The *Institutiones* announced a special calling: "in his hand preaches to men, with his fingers loosens their tongues, . . . with pen and ink fights against the unlawful temptations of the devil."

Retrenchment spreads. In keeping with the later medieval adage *Claustrum sine armario, castrum sine armamentario* (a monastery without a book locker is like a fort without an armory), Cassiodorus's model set the stage for almost a millennium. But the dictum was also indicative of losses. Massive reading rooms and colonnaded galleries were not needed. New publications were not considered. Rather than the Alexandrian model of tens of thousands of volumes, the library in the Dark Ages would be proud of a few hundred in a large container or two. A survivalist mindset narrowed what amounted to librarianship toward:

- **Preservation and copy cycles.** Approaches regularized the reproduction of key religious treatises and a selection of classical literature on expensive parchment or vellum.
- **Illuminations.** A new skill set added artistic flourishes. Illustrations facilitated praise of the Lord, assisted illiterate penitents in their devotions, and—incidentally—added value to what were already extremely expensive artifacts.
- **Codices.** This essentially Christian format supplanted the rolled papyrus volumes that had dominated classical libraries. Scribal librarians produced illuminated, handwritten manuscripts, which tended toward large formats.

- **Loans.** The monasteries instituted interlibrary loan among themselves. Patron borrowing was expected and remains one of the few lasting legacies of the Dark Ages.
- **Reading controls.** As indicated below in the sixth-century Monastic Rules of Cassiodorus's contemporary Benedict of Nursia (circa 530), practices were deliberately ordered to the overriding purpose of the monastery and entertained discipline:

> Above all, let one or two of the seniors be appointed to go about the monastery during the time that the brethren devote to reading and take notice, lest perhaps a slothful brother be found who gives himself up to idleness or vain talk, and does not attend to his reading, and is unprofitable, not only to himself, but disturbs also others. If such a one be found (which God forbid), let him be punished once and again. If he does not amend, let him come under the correction of the Rule in such a way that others may fear. And let not brother join brother at undue times.

A SAGA IN FIVE STAGES

Though reminiscences to the Dark Ages may surface periodically, planning is best prefaced through forays into the next phase in library history—the story of the university library. The lineage proves surprisingly uneven, but of singular importance. Repeated struggle for identity and recognition followed in fits and starts along a rough set of trend lines: from religious setting and content toward the secular; from the care and handling of high-priced treasures to ever more affordable commodities; in broad reflection of swings in the political economy and government interests; and through a series of reinventions in response to advances in communications technology and university pedagogies.

STAGE I. SORBONNE AND THE BIRTH OF THE UNIVERSITY LIBRARY

Western civilization began slowly to crawl its way back after the dawn of a new millennium. Security and with it European populations began to expand in the years after 1000 CE. Educational enterprises blossomed outside monastic respites. Cathedral schools began to sprout as a feature of renewing urban areas. Educational endeavors expanded beyond narrow clerical training to meet demands from the nobility and a burgeoning bourgeois. With possible envy of Arab learning centers, newly literate cohorts pressed for more. Their calls resulted in a lasting and new type of institution in the West.

Birth of the University

In the eleventh and twelfth centuries, small groups of interested students and faculty united into educational guilds. Their initial goal was a *studium generale,* or "School of Universal Learning." It arrived with disruptive intent. The guilds sought to escape local government limits and controls. In the mid-twelfth century, Emperor Frederick Barbarosa codified such directions with his charter for the University of Bologna. The university would be a distinct type of institution and independent polity. The Catholic Church followed for its own political and educational reasons and as a purported response to student rowdiness.

Universities joined the church and Holy Roman Empire as the trio of medieval transnational institutions. Rather than locals, the schools sought geographically dispersed students. They came for collaborative pursuit of knowledge as well as the financial advantages wrought by international contacts and friendships. University studies also earned lasting cachet as a rite of passage and place of diversion for the young elite. Despite such secular tendencies, training was typically aimed at clerical advancement. Success was signaled by the award of the baccalaureate. Studies were themed under a two-part liberal arts framework—one that continued to dominate in various shapes into the nineteenth century: the *trivium* (grammar, rhetoric, and logic), and the *quadrivium* (arithmetic, music, geometry, and astronomy).

A select few pushed beyond bachelor's robes into those of the "Master" teacher or pursued specialized faculties in law, medicine, and theology. Personal accounts of the early years are rare, but John Henry Newman recaptured a part of the continuing ethos. His famed *The Idea of the University* (1858) lamented the modern research university and Germanic reforms. It harkened to earlier times and special drives:

> The general principles of any study you may learn by books at home; but the detail, the color, the tone, the air, the life which makes it live in us, you must catch all these from those in whom it lives already. You must imitate the student in French or German, who is not content with his grammar, but goes to Paris or Dresden: you must take example from the young artist,

who aspires to visit the great Masters in Florence and in Rome. Till we have discovered some intellectual daguerreotype . . . we must come to the teachers of wisdom to learn wisdom, we must repair to the fountain, and drink there. Portions of it may go from thence to the ends of the earth by means of books; but the fullness is in one place alone. It is in such assemblages and congregations of intellect that books themselves, the masterpieces of human genius, are written, or at least originated.

Reading Services and the Medieval University

A formal library was tangential to the original universities. The scope of study and available literature were perhaps too limited. In the beginning, students apparently copied their own *reportata,* or course materials. The presence of the new institution and lure of disposable income soon had predictable effect. Entrepreneurs opened bookstores "stationed" near university meeting places. Stationers with their *librarii* (copyist staffs) provided practical alternatives to student copying or the occasional borrowing of illuminated codices from monasteries. Students could rent or buy *exemplars* (excerpts) of assigned canonical texts for study and subsequent declamation.

In a lasting theme, some students objected to the costs. Not all could afford to buy from the stationers. Poor transportation precluded regular retreat to monasteries as study halls. Only the richest of professors could have afforded to lend treasured manuscripts. Instead, students and instructors logically pooled funds for their own collections. Informal dormitory-style libraries helped distinguish colleges. They also set the stage for institutional response.

Sorbonne

Alexandrian designs returned and our continuing narrative arrives in the second half

> Enter Paper Making

As one might expect from the age of Marco Polo, contacts introduced products. The mid-thirteenth-century arrival of paper and paper making in non-Arab Europe was among the first concrete differentiators for a "renaissance" of knowledge and trend setter for the history of academic libraries. Mills and water power entered and in effect launched early European industrialization. Their product quickly impacted education. Paper proved a relatively standardized and accessible substitute for parchment or vellum. It offered a breakthrough with lowered costs for students. Affordability assisted with the spread of universities and suddenly expanding canon of knowledge.

of the thirteenth century. The university library emerged from a remarkable confluence of economic and pedagogical opportunities. The downturn of the Crusades enabled international commerce and banking. Newly opened trade routes exposed long lost Greek and Latin classics. Their presence in turn stimulated a collecting and educational craze. The materials provided an enticing draw for students and heady times for scholarship. Intellectuals struggled to rationalize the knowledge of the ancients with established church doctrine. The scholastic methodology of a Peter Abelard sharpened with Thomas Aquinas to deal with exciting discoveries and reappearances from the powerful pen of Aristotle.

The Sorbonne model. Chaplain to French king Louis IX, Robert Sorbonne entered the scene at roughly the same time as paper. His papal charter in 1252 helped recast the University of Paris and college education in general. The prelate revamped away from Bologna's student-driven model. Faculty leadership arose to become the dominant model for future universities. Sorbonne also presented an elegantly democratic and egalitarian vision. Higher education must be extended to the less wealthy—a place where students and faculty would proudly proclaim allegiance to *pauperem nostram Sorbonem* (the poor [students] of our Sorbonne).

Given the expense and expanding body of knowledge, a library flowed logically into Sorbonne's reforms. Operations would be decidedly communal. They were designed for the economic and scholarly benefit of faculty and students.

Like many to follow, the first university library embarked by donation of books. Growth continued in that direction and through the sale of excess materials. According to library rules from 1321, the Sorbonne's head librarian was to be appointed annually "for the benefit of the house and the better care of the books," with three major responsibilities: supervising the loans and care of the circulating collection; enlarging the fixed collection of chained volumes; and making a new catalog of the whole collection.

Library expansion. Although rudimentary, Sorbonne's library model left a lasting mark. Libraries became expected signs of a university. They were a vital detail in establishing a school's legitimacy and prestige. The library signaled permanence and was often the university's first visible capital investment. Library collections provided a treasure chest of portable wealth. They took on the attributes of a fashion statement and as point of attraction for external support. Richard de Bury, for example, paid homage to the Sorbonne as inspiration for his fourteenth-century plans and library rules to start Durham College at Oxford. As he detailed in the famed *Philobiblion* (1345):

Imprimis, we give and grant all and singular the books, of which we have made a special catalogue, in consideration of affection, to the community of scholars living in Durham Hall at Oxford, as a perpetual gift . . . to the intent that the same books may be lent from time to time to all and singular the scholars and masters of the said place, as well regular as secular, for the advancement and use of study. . . .

Each keeper shall take an oath to observe all these regulations when they enter upon the charge of the books. And the recipients of any book or books shall thereupon swear that they will not use the book or books for any other purpose but that of inspection or study, and that they will not take or permit to be taken it or them beyond the town and suburbs of Oxford.

Library keepers. The arrival of the university library marked the end of eight hundred years of darkness, but that fact should be kept in perspective. Publishing functions and systematic acquisitions were not fully embraced. Collections remained small—typically in the hundreds—and collection development typically a by-product of donations. As de Bury's comments reflect, those in charge of the collections were hardly what we might call librarians. They were "keepers" or stewards—distinct from the production motif of monastic scribes and *librarii*. Nevertheless, these academic library fathers produced a lasting ethos and functional responses, including:

- **Client services.** The service orientation should not be ignored. Students and faculty were guild members and viewed as special clientele, but the library also acted in the collective pursuit of knowledge with loans to outsiders.
- **Institutional framework.** In a split that continues today, proto-librarians had to cope with differences between individual departmental facilities and a central repository.
- **Chained books.** As seen in Sorbonne's library, new security technology and collection management techniques appeared in the late thirteenth century. These reflected the first discernible advance in librarianship in almost eight centuries. College collections would be divided. In continued support of the collective duty to advance knowledge, some volumes remained free for circulation, including external loans. Those in heavy demand, however, were chained to ensure availability for members.

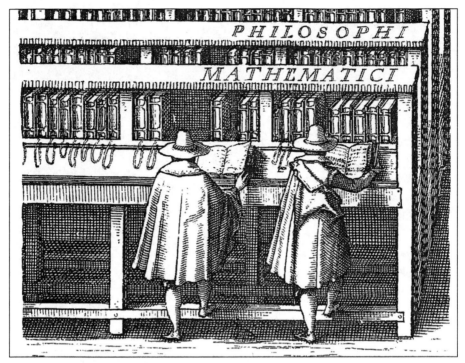

figure 1.1 Chained books, University of Leiden, sixteenth century (From Wikimedia Commons, http://commons.wikimedia.org/wiki/File:Libraries_in_the_medieval_and_Renaissance_Periods_Figure_5.jpg)

Chaining stations developed over time (figure 1.1). Subject classifications and labels entered the scene. Space was functionally differentiated, between standing sections for casual browsing and seated carrels.

STAGE II. PRINT AND THE RENAISSANCE UNIVERSITY

Timing for the second stage is easy to guess but came with less than positive results for university libraries. In keeping with Elizabeth Eisenstein's (1979) magisterial *The Printing Press as an Agent of Change,* the new medium proved transformational. The arrival of the press was like nothing before it. Print separated poetry from music and launched new forms of expression. It stimulated an age of discovery and opened a global earth. The press catalyzed revolutionary change, from the rise of capitalism to the disruptions of the Protestant Reformation. The new communications technology accelerated a renaissance in the West and let loose forces of modernization that continue today.

With foreshadowing for the Web, the power of print to compose, preserve, and extend access penetrated thinking modes. Prior community-centric embrace of declared "truth" opened to individual introspection. In McLuhan's (1962:138) analysis, the aural and communal gave way to the overwhelming "gravitational" pull of the visual:

> Print is the extreme phase of alphabet culture that detribalizes or decollectivizes man in the first instance. Print raises the visual features of alphabet to highest intensity of definition. Thus print carries the individuating power of the phonetic alphabet much further than manuscript culture could ever do. Print is the technology of individualism. If men decided to modify this visual technology by an electric technology, individualism would also be modified. To raise a moral complaint about this is like cussing a buzz-saw for lopping off fingers.

> **› Collective vs. Individual Thinking**
>
> With the exceptions of religious cults and other strongly fundamentalist groups, contemporary thinkers are hard pressed to understand the communitarian worldview. In such a perspective, group allegiance trumps individual analysis. Truth is defined for you. Carlo Ginzburg's (1992) *The Cheese and the Worms: The Cosmos of a Sixteenth-Century Miller* provides a convenient view of the convoluted impact of print and concomitant mental transitions, which may prepare for analysis of parallel effects with the Web.

Publishers Enter

Enter the most complicated and conflicted element within the library spectrum. Among the first modern capitalists, printer/publishers concentrated on duplicating large handwritten codices and capturing the canon of classical literature. Competitive drives for market share and the zeal of a revolutionary technology soon let loose a wave of innovation. The cumulative effects removed librarians as determinant factors. Printer/publishers delineated the framework for the next reinvention of librarianship, which included:

- **Book formats.** Publishers not only replaced the handwritten codex, they eventually refurbished it into a new format. Colophons gave way. Title pages entered as the first systematic form of international advertising and the library world's lasting descriptive touchstone. They were joined by such now-defining characteristics as indexes, paragraphing, and tables of contents.
- **Portable reading.** Venetian printer and humanist Aldus Manutius played a pivotal role. With him, huge lectern volumes gave way and the

typographic promise extended to the people. Manutius's Aldine octavos marked the start of the second phase of the print revolution at the turn of the sixteen century. His invention of relatively affordable pocket books created portable reading—a singular contribution for the ages.

- **Personal authorship.** The role of the author was reborn. Departing a fixed universe with narrow focus on uncovering and preserving a canon of classical authors, print spawned a renaissance with growing numbers of inquisitive writers.
- **New genres/subjects.** Scholars moved from uncovering the classics to writing commentaries about them and then contributing their own tomes for study. Over time, new formats made their appearance. By the seventeenth century, philosophical treatises could be joined by scientific reports, early journals, diurnals/newspapers, and so on eventually to encyclopedias and new forms of literature.
- **Vernacular outputs components.** The drive for expanded markets expanded beyond scholarly Latin, Greek, and Hebrew into commonly spoken languages. This powerful switch was far from benign. It stimulated the Protestant Reformation and set the stage for nationalism.

Humanists and the Renaissance University

Humanistic scholars also played a role in academic library directions. They were prime beneficiaries of print technologies and the rebirth of personal authorship. Humanists reformed Scholasticism. Their approaches and critical apparatus morphed into the reformed Renaissance, or humanistic, university. With it, academic studies extended beyond classics and rationalizing church doctrine. Personalized introspection and secular questioning slowly entered. By the seventeenth century, the likes of a Bacon, Galileo, and Newton contributed to the

> **> Terminology Note: Era of the Incunabulum**
>
> Historians and rare book specialists divide the development of print into two periods:
>
> - **Incunabulum.** The initial fifty years after Gutenberg led to a transformation away from the norms of the codex. The latter focused on lectern readers and reprinting the corpus of classical literature. The resulting products form a distinct class for book collectors and library special collections.
> - **Post-Incunabulum.** Formative development away from the scribal codex required from the tradition also continued for another forty years to reach fruition.

dominance of the "scientific method." Descartes could recognize a transformational assertion of self under "cogito ergo sum."

The printing press quickly reached into university instructional operations. Exercises moved from short *exemplars* of classical texts toward complete books and new forms of commentary. Humanists, like Manutius's ally Erasmus, joined publishers to hone the reformed universities and in the process perfect the new media. In addition to evolving new genres, scholars contributed such familiar library features as:

- **Bibliographies.** The deluge of new materials from widely ranging presses proved a significant problem. Swiss humanist Conrad Gesner was among the first to bring intellectual order to the burgeoning output of the printing presses. His mid-sixteenth-century *Pandects* and *Bibliotheca Universalis* set the stage for future bibliographies but, like book fair catalogs, proved difficult to maintain.

- **Classification schemes.** Renaissance humanism fomented a crucial switch from Platonic categorization into the more secular and relativistic Aristotelian. The father of the scientific method and inductive reasoning, Francis Bacon provided the essential framework for most modern schema in the early seventeenth century.

- **Footnotes.** This late seventeenth-century innovation acted in support of the scientific method and as a de facto replacement of the marginalia and emendations of the manuscript age. Over time, this element would evolve with peer review to help define monographic and journal scholarship as distinct genres.

> Analytical Bibliography

Lorenzo Valla's uncovering of the fraudulent "Donation of Constantine" in the fifteenth century prepared the way for "scientific" examinations of printed books. Gesner and other scholars followed with methods for the physical description of printed books and valuation of books. Analytical or critical bibliography includes the history of the printers and booksellers, description of paper or bindings, and the transit from manuscript to published book—as well as physical bibliography descriptions. The last embraces collation formulas, which may play an increasing future role as metadata, such as in declaring the proximate authenticity/financial value of a text—for example, Text Encoding Initiative's header has a `<collation>` in the `<msDescription>` or `<bookDescription>` elements of the `<sourceDesc>` section.

› Vatican Library

Although tangential to the print narrative, the Incunabulum period includes a major library landmark—the refounding of the papal library. Former librarian and humanistic scholar Pope Nicholas V took the initial steps to reclaim a legacy lost in the Dark Ages with a small donation of codices. Sixtus VI, another scholarly pope and originator of the Sistine Chapel, followed with a formal library suite around 1475. By 1481 the holdings expanded into one of the world's largest libraries—albeit with a mere 3,500 volumes. Continued growth eventually mandated a separate building, which appeared in 1587.

Papal action also stimulated a rage in manuscript hunting. The buccaneering book hunter and Vatican librarian Poggio Bracciolini scoured the monasteries of Europe to populate his new facility, occasionally stealing what he could not copy. The Vatican Library stimulated a rebirth of the cataloger's art as well as new types of scholarship, like Valla's paleographic and protodiplomatic studies.

Libraries and the Press

Although some may have been complicit in providing materials, libraries were relatively passive in early print development. The field missed the opportunity to engage the shift from codex to printed book. Publishers not only took those responsibilities but, as indicated, would subsume and effectively redirect the future of libraries. Book fairs, like Frankfort, and publisher catalogs replaced library listings as information centerpieces. Most important, library practice was reinvented in response to the new medium and manufacturing order.

Printing fostered the most momentous changes in library history. By the seventeenth century, the nature of the library was fundamentally different. Manuscript holdings were denigrated. Archival functions were abandoned or shifted to separate institutions. Internal production, copyist traditions, and codices were eclipsed. In their place arose the reinvented book library. Scribal arts that had defined the field for millennia were doomed. Monasteries bore the brunt in the struggle against the forces of print. With religious fervor and a sense of preservation far beyond today's norm, Abbot Johannes Trithemius's (1492) *De Laudem Scriptorium* (In Praise of Scribes) thus famously lamented:

> The printed book is a thing of paper and in a short time will decay entirely. But the scribe commending letters to parchment extends his own and the letters' lifespan for ages. And he enriches the Church, conserves the faith, destroys heresies, repels vice, teaches morals and helps grow virtue. The devoted scribe, whom we intend to describe, praises God, pleases the

angels, strengthens the just, corrects the sinner, commends the humble, protects the good, defeats the proud, and condemns the stubborn. The scribe, distinguished by piety, is the herald of God. . . . What is healthier than this art, what is more commendable than this piety which delights God, which the angels praise, which is venerated by the citizens of heaven?

Societal Challenges and Controls

Church and state also factor into print-era changes and the subsequent direction of academic libraries. Religious and government authorities had limited initial interest with the printed word. They were jolted awake by the onset of vernacular literature and economics of personal authorship. Popes and rulers realized they could no longer control the press as they had monastic copyists. Authoritarian reactions mounted against new-found freedoms of expression and demands for religious liberties. The state encountered monetary demands from a burgeoning new class of authors and publishers in search of a different type of property right. A combination of censorship and protocopyright financial drives began to emerge:

- The Catholic Church turned to a refurbished Inquisition and counter-reformation forces. Resort was strengthened for an approval process that ran from passing the censor's *nihil obstat* (no religious objection) to the bishop's okay with an *imprimateur.* Indexes of prohibited works were issued with some regularity—although, as the story goes, only to rebound into best-seller lists.
- England responded with exclusive registration permissions through the Stationers' Company.
- France set the somewhat less threatening precedent of legal deposit in the royal library with the Ordonnance de Montpellier in 1537.

States continued their piecemeal responses to the challenges of the press. Copyright and access moved forward fitfully through state and royal library participation. In England, John Milton's *The Areopagitica* speech to Parliament in 1644 on unlicensed printing also fostered a lasting debate on the people's right to free expression. Such discussions would lead by stages to the elimination of the Stationers' monopoly and England's first copyright law in 1710—the Statute of Anne, "An Act for the Encouragement of Learning, by vesting the Copies of

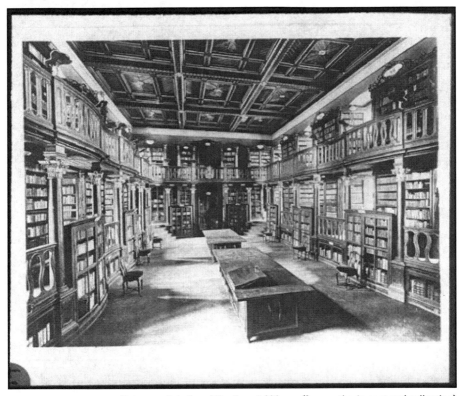

figure 1.2 Interior of the Escorial library (from author's postcard collection)

Printed Books in the Authors or purchasers of such Copies, during the Times therein mentioned." In France, the Royal Library made a major statement by opening its doors to the public in 1692.

The Golden Age. Church and state left other imprints on the future of libraries. An expansive age of scientific discovery coupled with an influx of wealth from the New World to produce a fad—the Golden Age of Libraries. During the seventeenth century, small individual rooms gave way to imposing self-standing library buildings. Conspicuous consumption induced such illustrious structures as the Mazarine Library in Paris and the National Central Library in Italy. In reflection of the Age of Discovery, Phillip II of Spain topped the field. He memorialized his colonial domains with the magnificent Escorial library (figure 1.2). A private 40,000-book collection was fitted into specially redesigned architectural space. The Escorial set the ideal for academic and other library buildings for centuries to come.

Academic Libraries in the Seventeenth and Eighteenth Centuries

The Golden Age seems a misnomer for academic libraries. They appeared as afterthoughts in the educational reforms of the humanistic university. The communitarian ideal of student support gave way. Prior concerns for the care of manuscript treasures entered a period of decline and reported neglect. Focus was given to less costly printed books. Libraries grew largely by happenstance and donation. University collections trended small, typically fitting into a room or small suite of rooms and rarely commanding a separate building. Rather than a librarian, the job remained a "keeper" and was normally filled by a junior faculty member or senior student. The idea of the university library was largely downgraded into a storage center and isolated professorial haven for another three hundred years.

Yet the academic situation was not wholly bereft. Academic libraries remained expected trappings of a university. Use of such space extended beyond holdings to the locus of intellectual discourse and the formation of scholarly societies. The switch from library-supplied codices to publisher-printed books was also less painful than for monasteries. Academic libraries had begun as consumers. They had fewer spiritual ties to their holdings. Though the treasure chest concept held for a time, chained books were destined to be unloosed. Increased size of collections and lower costs led to advances in storage as well as enhanced physical marking of bindings for retrieval. Most important, the number of academic libraries continued to grow apace with the spread of universities.

> ### > Librarians of Note
>
> Around the seventeenth century, library practitioners began to leave lasting impressions. Hence, we know of Thomas James at the Bodleian. Gabriel Naudé was confident to Cardinal Richelieu and later Cardinal Jules Mazarin. His 1627 book *Advice on Establishing a Library* argued for prestige and noblesse oblige. One's highest honor was building a library open to the public. In the eighteenth century, Johan Gessner had the unique opportunity to devise a library three years before the founding of Göttingen University, which became the West's leading academic library for over a century.
>
> A more lasting pattern arose with support and sinecures for famous individuals and scholars under the title of librarian. Selectees ranged from Giacomo Casanova to David Hume. The polymath Gottfried Leibniz offers an interesting example. Called the father of information theory, he contributed advanced concepts that remain valuable today.

American collegiate pattern. Experiences in the English colonies bring the topic closer to home and the next reinvention. Although libraries for private individuals and religious groups remained in fashion, English universities faced a special set of challenges. Libraries had been severely damaged under Henry VIII, who included them in his confiscations of church property. Edward VI's Royal Commission followed with destructive purges at Cambridge and Oxford—even to selling their shelving. Fortunately, Thomas Bodley and James reversed the trend in the early seventeenth century. Bodley's relaunch of the Oxford central library reestablished the presence of the academic library for England and soon its colonies.

In the New World, Protestant commitment to literacy and education spawned an educational ethos at the start of what would become the American dream. Library prospects were confirmed in 1636 in Boston, Massachusetts. Barely six years after the town's founding, John Harvard bequeathed several hundred volumes to initiate a new college. American colleges would presuppose a library, however small.

Although Harvard and a few other institutions subsequently added book funds, collections remained dependent on gifts or exchanges. The library could expect little or no direct support from the administration. These were small college operations. The librarian remained part-time—often a junior faculty member. Student access and external users appear to have been diminished from late medieval practices. Facilities were open on a few days at best. Precedence was afforded the faculty, then upper-division students, but rarely those in the lower divisions. Indeed, many students may have had more recourse to their own literary society or residence libraries.

STAGE III. MASS PRESS AND THE RESEARCH UNIVERSITY

The stage was set for a different layer of history. In the nineteenth century, the pattern of *longue durée*, or slow ebb and flow of history over centuries, gave way to rapid change. Modern civilization appeared in the guise of a rapidly evolving and tangled blend of political, industrial/technical, financial, educational, and cultural forces.

Industrial Revolution

The nineteenth-century narrative engaged a switch from agrarian and rural to industrial and urban. Time, distance, and government systems accelerated via advances in communication and transportation. Electricity conquered the night.

The telegraph brought instantaneous communication. Mechanized steamships mastered the oceans and railroads the land. Standardized time zones emerged as by-products of a new industrial order.

Publishing revamped. Industrialization left early marks in the publishing world. The prime determiner of library activity dramatically expanded in response to an interlaced series of technological advances:

- **Wood pulp paper.** Paper remained the most expensive element in book production until the Fourdrinier paper-making machine in 1799 and affordable wood pulp paper.
- **Binding.** William Pickering's Diamond Classic series in 1825 marked a significant switch from leather to lower-cost cloth bindings. It was joined by industrial versions of Isaac Howe's 1845 invention of the sewing machine.
- **Press.** Mechanization with rollers was enhanced with the letterpress. Production exploded and cost dropped significantly with Richard Hoe's rotary press in 1843.
- **Images.** In 1879, Karl Klic industrialized Fox Talbot's photographic process for intaglio engraving on copper in keeping with rotary press applications.
- **Typesetting.** Mergenthaler replaced hand composition through his 1884 invention of the keyboard linotype machine and hot metal casting.

Rise of the mass press. The move from hand art to automated production fomented an explosion in affordable materials and an allied communications revolution. The rise of the mass press produced effects on a scale with Gutenberg and Manutius. Reading was enabled for all classes. The bulk of today's genres would be put in place and with concomitant alterations to the nature of the library. In a circular fashion, the appearance of McGuffey Readers and other grammar school texts enabled an eager mass of readers and expanded marketplace. Novels achieved widespread distribution but also morphed into the inexpensive dime variety

> Romanticism

The romantic movement reacted against industrialization and the loss of agrarian values—something that one could predict rising again with the Web. Reflecting the seminal influences of Jean Jacques Rousseau and Johann Gottfried von Herder, romanticism lent support to nationalistic identities. Drives extended into building national literary sensibilities and recapturing the folk heritage.

> Literacy Elevated

Although the ability to read and write had long been seen as a good, the spread of compulsory education in the nineteenth century produced a new consensus. For the first time in history, illiteracy would be seen as bad. The state had incurred the duty to correct the situation. That change was also a vital precursor for the rise of a mass press, the development of an industrial workforce, and the rise of libraries.

and soon other genres with thrilling tales for children and adults. Affordable daily newspapers replaced weeklies and by the end of century had turned into the yellow press of Pulitzer and then Hearst. Comics appeared and eventually comic books. Images moved from line drawings to photographs. Illustrated magazines and paperbacks would arise.

The combination of the new print technologies, modes of distribution, low costs, and attractive applications had other implications. As reflected in the late nineteenth-century term *Comstockery,* censorship initiatives arose from concerned moral arbiters. Advertising and marketing emerged. Moreover, the forces of propaganda were set loose. For good or ill, a new world of popular culture and mass culture had entered the scene.

Nationalism

The mass press joined with eighteenth-century Enlightenment sensibilities and revolutionary drives for popular sovereignty. Nationalism, the most significant political force in history to date, also entered the picture. The nineteenth century was its crucible. Instead of "subjects," people became "citizens." Germany, Italy, and Norway reforged from a variety of polities and in the face of regional/tribal sensibilities.

Though sometimes initiated by force of arms, nationalism always employed the legitimating forces of culture and education. What began as Enlightenment and revolutionary drives for the people's right to know was enhanced by romanticism. With the French leading the way, countries articulated an interwoven fabric of secular identity building—as well as an occasionally unfortunate bent toward xenophobia:

- **Monuments and civic celebrations.** Supporting events, like the 4th of July and Bastille Day, appeared on the annual calendar.
- **Cultural sphere.** States similarly encouraged a wave of cultural institutions as concrete representations in support of the legitimacy of the new order. As evidenced by a preponderance of Roman and Greek architectural

designs, symbolic values were intended. In the process, archives, libraries, and museums divided into specialized fields.

- **Compulsory education.** The role of the state cannot be overestimated in its use of propagandistic materials to foster education and literacy.

Library Renaissance

Libraries were significant participants in the birth of the cultural sphere but were also enveloped in parallel movements that made modern education a mainstay of the state. After some 1,500 years of semioblivion, the educational ferment of the eighteenth-century Enlightenment and nineteenth-century revolutions coalesced on fertile grounds. As in ancient Greece, democratic people came to embrace their inalienable rights to information, and governments embraced responsibility to provide access.

The times left other crucial marks. The secular rose in prominence, at least on the educational scene. Religious drives were at least somewhat subsumed under civic and educational motifs. The close of the nineteenth century witnessed a wave of new college-dependent professions, including librarianship. The latter embraced the era's bureaucratic tendencies along with a scientific penchant for taxonomies. Rather than serve as journeyman "keepers," librarians sought new skills to meet the information demands of an industrial age and educational reforms.

National libraries. The French revolution took symbolic leadership. The opening of the Bibliotheque Nationale and Archives Nationale stimulated a fad across the Western world. A national library became an expected presence. In addition to subliminally legitimating the state, such facilities addressed practical needs for copyright deposit. They offered a response to the mass press and democratic

› Germanic Precursors

If France led on the cultural side, Germany would set the pace for education—including our new "scientific" discipline. In the first decade of the nineteenth century, Martin Schrettinger coined the term "library science" (*Bibliothekswissenschaft*). With the help of Frederick Ebert and Scandinavian support from the Dane Christian Molbech, he pushed for the specialized training. "Librarian nurseries" or training facilities began to appear within the various German state libraries at the time. Leipzig librarian Robert Naumann followed this line in 1840 with the Serapeum—the field's first scholarly journal.

> ## > Catalog Card Emblem

Although their origins can date to the eighteenth century, catalog cards and their furnishings were effectively a product of the late nineteenth and early twentieth centuries. In the United States, such elements came to prominence with the Library of Congress's promotion of printed card sets under Herbert Putnam. Their replacement of centuries-old notebook catalogs proved emblematic of a union of progressive mindset and industrial-age order.

access to government documents. State facilities would also serve within state-supported research activities in agricultural and engineering.

National libraries provided a significant source of leadership for the proto-profession. Thanks to the Antonio Panizzi, the library of the British Museum rose to leadership in the mid-nineteenth century with new cataloging arts. In the early twentieth century, the United States joined at the Library of Congress under Herbert Putnam. He launched projects such as the National Union Catalog, which systematically charted the nation's book holdings, and the famed Library of Congress Classification System. Under Putnam too, the Library of Congress joined the British Museum at the forefront of an international move to standardize library practices under the Anglo-American Cataloguing Rules.

American public libraries. In the mid-nineteenth century, the United States emerged as the main author for the period's key civic contribution. The public library movement also reflected Roman traditions and German theories along with architectural contributions of Henri Labrouste in France. Yet it took hold as a practical American extension of Horace Mann's educational reforms and concrete manifestation of Jeffersonian ideals. Conceived as "people's universities," these institutions were promoted as self-help extensions to the new school systems. The public library could enable adults in pursuit of the American dream. In addition, the institution played a little understood role in the national "Search for Order" and end of the frontier. The institution reflected a move beyond mandatory schools and defensive respite in the form of new police and fire departments. It became a genteel place of refuge for women and children. Arrival of a public library offered an iconic symbol of civilization and demonstration of a "progressive" community.

State libraries. State libraries entered the scene in the nineteenth century. In addition to government duties, they were significant in fostering public library development. This include interlibrary loan coordination and as a source of supplemental funds as well as cooperation with academic establishments.

› Library Subeconomy

Although overlooked in many discussions, the library movement fostered a subsidiary economic engine:

- **Construction.** Thanks to the research university movement and Andrew Carnegie's largesse, academic and public libraries stimulated specialized construction. Classical facades blended with state-of-the-art functional interiors. Industrial-age motifs, scientific arrangement, and the mass press deluge combined into dramatic fashion. The Escorial model was replaced with formal separations between reading and storage areas to accommodate the growth in books.

- **Furnishings and supplies.** Companies took the opportunities to produce catalog cards, book stamps, book pockets, and so forth as well as circulation desks, map cases, and innovative card catalogs with separate tops. The intrepid Dewey played his own part. According the Library Bureau website, he founded the company while still a student "for the definite purpose of furnishing libraries with equipment and supplies of unvarying correctness and reliability."

- **Reading materials.** In addition to purchasing the works of mainline and scholarly publishers, libraries stimulated specialized genres. Pioneering public librarian William F. Poole, for example, began his *Index to Periodical Literature* in the 1850s. In 1876, Dewey joined R. R. Bowker, the founder of *Publishers Weekly* and library supplier, to begin the *Library Journal*. The market space expanded to a wide array of dedicated reference tools and abstracts such as Chemical Abstracts. Library binders stepped to the fore to handle serials and, not unlike stationers in the Medieval era, also joined typists in university library–driven thesis production.

Professionalization. Library proselytizers deliberately aligned their vision to a late nineteenth-century penchant for professionalization. They relied on several familiar tactics in keeping with mid-Victorian penchants:

- **Professional association.** With all intended symbolism, the American Library Association (ALA) was born in the centennial year of 1876 in Philadelphia. Slightly more than one hundred movers and shakers attended, including Justin Winsor, Charles Ammi Cutter, Samuel S. Green, Fred B. Perkins, and the precocious Melvil Dewey.
- **Education and reform.** Dewey guided the crucial establishment of a specialized library undergraduate degree. By the close of the nineteenth century, librarianship had joined nursing and primary school teaching as pioneering "women's professions."
- **Specialization.** Professionalization was further signaled in two predictable arenas: functions increasingly differentiated into distinct job categories, such as cataloging, children, and reference specialists; and types of

libraries blossomed into a recognizable quartet with their own associations—public libraries, college and research libraries, school libraries, and special libraries.

The University and Education Reordered

Universities engaged in their own dramatic redefinition. Enlightenment ideals and revolutionary times synthesized with the drives of nationalism and industrialization. Rather than the liberal arts and religion, pedagogies turned to the secular. Practical concerns and scientific agenda emerged on the scene as nations sought to bolster internal allegiances, build prestige, and expand their domains.

France. As with so many other advances, Napoleon took center stage. Extending from the mandatory education policies of the revolution, he systematized teaching with model classrooms and curriculum at new *écoles normale*. Napoleon instituted the *baccalauréat*, or *bac*—a test that continues to determine French collegiate placement. Higher-education legacies from the Ancien Régime were reformulated to center on city universities. He also promoted scientific research, but in separate institutes that were housed in conjunction with a university.

Germany. With the goad of Napoleonic conquests, education minister Wilhelm von Humboldt extended Prussian educational reforms and mandatory education. He required teacher training and enhanced pedagogies with the seminar method at universities. The Prussians pushed a divorce from the Renaissance university through a practical marriage for the training of government bureaucrats. Their reforms spread by right of conquest during the unification of Germany, but also across the Western world. The German "New University Movement" became a model for most of Europe and extended into the United States.

United States. Matters changed quickly as the forces of nationalism entered American higher education. Perhaps befitting the other "New Romans," the United States looked to German reforms—but with a uniquely American stamp. Thomas Jefferson and the founding fathers had given symbolic approbation for education. It would be a touchstone for democracy and the American dream. In the early nineteenth century, Mann and other reformers stepped forward to engage that promise fully. They crusaded for mandatory grade schools and mass literacy in a time of growing consensus for the country's manifest destiny. By the Civil War, their efforts had succeeded across the northern states and would culminate by spreading to the South during Reconstruction. Literacy was established as an expected societal norm.

Post–Civil War effects extended upward. Before the conflict, the United States boasted a small assortment of normal schools and a couple of hundred colleges.

Studies remained ensconced within the classical liberal arts and were aimed at gentlemanly skills or clerical training. The war, nationalism, and western expansion forged the reforms into the modern university system.

- **Land grant universities.** The Morrill Act of 1862 catalyzed the movement from college to American university. In the midst of the nation's greatest tragedy, the government fostered a lasting educational legacy and model for the world. The new format was politically centered in individual states. The American approach to Germanic reforms was a progressive agenda to advance the nation on industrial and scientific forefronts. The quadrivium and trivium were diminished. New "scientific" departments with research agenda were to take their places and redefine the university. The American model was launched with an emphasis on schools of engineering and agriculture along with such now familiar, but then exciting, new units as history, psychology, and sociology.

- **Private university movement.** The scientific mindset of "ag schools" soon spread to other public and private institutions. The Gilded Age had arrived with heightened entrepreneurial spirit, robber barons, and what Thorstein Veblen termed "conspicuous consumption." Wealthy of the era sought prestige and approbation. They displayed a sense of noblesse oblige and social responsibility, reflected in Andrew Carnegie's Gospel of Wealth. Not surprisingly, many of America's best-known national universities developed under the auspices of industrial giants: Duke, Johns Hopkins, Stanford, Vanderbilt, University of Chicago (Rockefeller), and, of course, Carnegie Mellon.

- **Professional degrees.** Validation even extended to new curricula and departments. These combined with Gilded Age interest to foster the stamp of professionalism and an enlarged middle class. The latter

> **Accreditation Factor**
>
> In keeping with the American penchant for associations and partial reaction against fly-by-night competitors—especially the mail-order variety—American universities voluntarily pushed their movement into regional compliance arrangements. Regional accreditation was originally designed to help regularize college entrance requirements and standards for secondary schools. It continues as a major force for quality assurance. This includes the recognition of undergraduate and graduate programs but also continues to act as the main guarantor of a place for the academic library.

provided the main source of students and alumni to feed a growing number of universities. As seen from dentistry and business to librarianship and social work, the college degree became a distinguishing mark for entry into a host of new Industrial-Age professions. In a continuing trend, universities responded by expanding beyond law and medicine to ever more specialized offerings.

Academic Libraries Reinvented

As exemplified by the University of Illinois and other great land grant universities, the American university library was reinvented in the late nineteenth century. A research library became the hallmark of a great university. Implementation followed an Alexandrian vision—the ideal of universal scientific reading laboratory. Buildings tended toward the prepossessing, replete with classical styles and a featured location on campus. The library thus symbolically reaffirmed its university's acumen. To Professor Hiram M. Stanley (1889):

> The position of the library should be as central as possible. The library is the heart of a university, and should be so placed as to be in closest connection with each department. . . . The ideal university on the circular

> PhD Effect

The doctor philosophiae holds a vital place in the lore of academic librarianship and its overriding research mission. During the late nineteenth century, American universities turned to the PhD as suitable added distinction for scientific disciplines. The degree became an expected requirement for teaching at universities, especially in graduate schools.

More important for libraries, the PhD brought demands to "publish or perish." Expectations and growing choruses of experts jump-started scholarly publications and provided a new opportunity for academic libraries. Libraries were provided with justification for expanding from exchanges and donations into purchasing. In a circular process, the academic library fostered university presses, then became the major purchaser of their monographs along with the spate of scholarly journals emanating from an increasing number of scholarly associations. Aided by the technologies of the mass press, a deluge of specialized materials appeared and called forth ever larger storage systems. The era's Linnaean penchant for taxonomies led to elaborate control systems to bring order, and complications from library science contributions produced their own instructional needs for students and faculty.

plan would embrace a library building and a building for heat and power at the center, immediately surrounded by professor's houses and cottage dormitories, and in the outer portion of the circle by the buildings for the several departments.

Although far from complete and with faculty recognition often lagging, the academic library entered an unprecedented development for its "professional" staff. Images of the aging scholarly caretaker or callow junior professor waned before the arrival of college-educated librarians. In 1902, Ohio State University president James Hulme Canfield summarized the rapid advances:

> The changes which have come in all phases of college life during the last half-century constitute almost a revolution. But of all these, the changes in library constituency and in library management are most notable. Fifty years ago the college library was almost an aside in education. Indeed, it was like the sentence which we enclose in brackets: to be read in a low tone, or to be slurred over hastily, or even to be entirely omitted without making any serious change in the sense. With rare exceptions, the position of the librarian was a haven for the incompetent or the decrepit. The appropriations for maintenance were pitifully meager. The expenditures for expansion were even less worthy. The efficiency, or the inefficiency, was, naturally, quite proportionate.

By the early twentieth century, academic libraries had become a fact of life. Although nationalistic imperatives withered over time, the institution was no

> Documentalists

In the early twentieth century, a portion of the library field pushed beyond book-based approaches into document analysis. Special librarians, science librarians, and documentalists tunneled into the burgeoning sphere of scholarly journals to lay the foundations for what would become the field of information science. The Belgians Paul Otlet and his Nobel Prize–winning partner Henri La Fontaine led the way with the Central Office of International Associations in 1907—the same time as the arrival of the Special Libraries Association. Otlet found his intellectual inspiration not in Europe but in Melvil Dewey and the decimal classification system.

longer an afterthought and minor presence. The library engaged as a growing presence with a voice. Growing acquisition budgets and physical spaces testified to a vital cog in the research milieu. Librarians promoted their own advanced practices and standards. Landmark taxonomies appeared to unify across institutions and enable powerful browsing stratagems. Technical processing and cataloging rose to the fore. Librarians actively pushed the scholarly publications sphere with university presses and controlled embrace of peer-reviewed serials.

figure 1.3 Book cover, Snead's *Library Planning . . .* (1915)

In keeping with industrial-age and bureaucratic mindsets, internal space was functionally defined. As the output of the presses grew, special collections, reading rooms, periodical rooms, government document units, and circulation stages emerged. The redesign featured separate and often mass "stacks" of shelves (figure 1.3). The newly flourishing service ethos even helped extend such space for undergraduate exploration, albeit with unintended student social consequences.

STAGE IV. PROFESSIONALIZATION

The fourth stage of this history continues mass press technology but is distinguished by the emergence of librarians to power. Over time too, early visionaries with their proselytizing and entrepreneurial energies were replaced by college-educated specialists with an applied vision of service and vested interest in professionalization.

All was not immediately well in the new field. Almost two generations after the start of collegiate training in 1887 at Columbia, the Carnegie-sponsored *Williamson Report* (1923) revealed disappointing levels of preparation and service. The document spurred improvement. Programs were upgraded toward the master of library science, and the Carnegie Foundation underwrote a library PhD at the University of Chicago. Such changes and commitment helped set in place an eager crop of specialists in time for far more significant involvement.

World War II mobilized the library mission and different directions. The field embraced identification as an "Arsenal for Democracy." At the Library of Congress, Archibald MacLeish offered an unprecedented combat-support bridge. He even assigned an entire floor to "Wild Bill" Donovan's Office of Strategic Services for military intelligence purposes. Librarians—Mortimer Taube and Jesse Shera, for example—would go on to make significant postwar contributions, including drives for automation and information science.

At ALA, director Carl Milam wasted no time offering wartime services and leveraging the legacy. He deliberately extended to the national political scene by opening a Washington office in 1945. Library schools took their own opportunities to advance, including additional PhD offerings. More important perhaps, massive overseas destruction and internal advances left American libraries as world's leaders. The stage was set for sustained professionalization.

Postwar Government Involvement

The United States provided an occasionally underacknowledged force behind research library success. By the end of World War II, the nation was irrevocably changed. The federal bureaucracy had dramatically expanded and the country assumed its own mantle as head of the free world. America had its prestige and scientific leadership to protect as well as citizens to serve. Universities and their libraries not only merited attention, they were demanding it.

GI Bill. The World War II GI Bill reset the higher-education stage. The bill and postwar fervor ignited an unprecedented rush to higher education. In short order, the number of colleges and universities purportedly rose from the prewar 1,800 to over 3,000, all featuring academic libraries. Equally important, university education was democratized with a flood of new students. For the first time, those coming from the lower financial strata had reasonable expectations of going to college. A university education became firmly part and parcel of the American dream. The sheer number of returning military would also guarantee adaptation. Large lecture halls and teaching assistants were institutionalized. Community colleges and regional campuses expanded as commuting alternatives. As discussed in chapter 3, the college textbook industry, which had been a minor player with only Macmillan on the scene, provided an institutional-strength teaching remedy—albeit one that envisioned little library participation.

> **Regulations Arises**

Government funding seems inevitably to come with regulation and accountability. Wartime enthusiasm and an underformed federal bureaucracy, however, delayed the onset of GI Bill intrusions until 1952 and its extension for the Korean War. In 1953 education was elevated to cabinet status within HEW, a move that also brought increasing involvement in college accreditation. Research libraries were brought firmly into the government sphere. In addition to expected accountability for grants and contracts, for example, scrutiny expanded under the 1976 U.S. Copyright Act. Visible federal presence arrived in the guise of official notices for photocopy along with exemptions for preservation and a set of new prospects under fair use doctrine.

University libraries joined the response in their own fashion. Returning servicemen did not fit the previous pattern of callow 18- to 22-year-olds living in campus dorms. Libraries stepped forward with enlarged study areas and extended hours. Growing awareness of service to students engaged internal scholarship. In the 1960s such concerns stretched to user studies. The field experimented with innovative undergraduate libraries. These targeted social and study spaces in conjunction with tailored holdings for direct classroom support versus research needs.

Financial support. If World War II established the government/university research nexus, the shock of Sputnik in 1957 pushed matters to new heights. It set the stage for a new age. In 1958 the Department of Defense replied with DARPA (Advanced Research Projects Agency), which added intense focus on information services. DARPA partnerships with universities and defense contractors proved a major source of funding and advances, including the TCP/IP protocols for the underlying framework of the Internet.

Federal grants became a part of the university economic fabric. Entrepreneurial libraries strove to become part of that support mix. Libraries were also singled out for the first time for ongoing federal concern with the 1956 Library Services Act, but funds were more forthcoming with the 1962 Library Services and Construction Act. Interests turned more to academic libraries in 1965 with the Higher Education Act under Lyndon Johnson's Great Society initiatives.

Government resources. The United States recognized its responsibility to make information available to the public as early as 1811 but lagged behind Europe in some respects. The Government Printing Office (GPO) was founded only in 1860, and it took Franklin Delano Roosevelt into the 1930s to establish the National Archives and his presidential library.

Postwar drives and Sputnik-era responses were destined to accelerate the trend. The Depository Library Act of 1962 authorized the Federal Depository Library Program through the GPO. This step initiated the spread of significant resources across the nation as well as fostering government document specialists in the hundreds of cooperating academic libraries. In 1968 the Education Resources Information Center (ERIC) played a smaller but similar clearinghouse role. And, in 1970, the National Commission on Libraries and Information Science (NCLIS) was commissioned to deal with national plans for library services.

National libraries. Leaving aside the rudimentary National Library of Education, three sister research libraries added significantly to library professionalization and resources for academic libraries:

- **Library of Congress.** Although technically the library for the U.S. Congress, the Library of Congress became the de facto national library. Moreover, it assumed a mantle as the titular head of the world's libraries and quiet leader of American advances. Following Putnam's lead, the institution entered into partnerships with a range of international and American research libraries. It was pivotal on the cultural side of the ledger with the Center for the Book, American Folklife Center, and poet laureate appointments. Technical leadership covered the spectrum—including automation, copyright law, handicapped services, information science, preservation, and standards.
- **National Agricultural Library.** This library became "national" in 1962 but dated to 1862 and a shared spirit with the Morrill Act. In arguably the first American application of information science methods, Ralph Shaw pioneered Otlet's document delivery services and microfilming

› National Archives

Today's NARS (National Archives and Record Service) appeared in the mid-1930s along with the first in what has become a growing list of presidential libraries. Charged under federal law as the keeper of the records of the executive branch, the agency was deliberately kept separate from libraries in its early years. It was more the place for primary documents and male historians. That has changed. In the 1970s, distinct American archival education began to take root largely under the aegis of library schools. Automation in the 1980s and the Web in the 1990s continued to push toward cooperative endeavors, especially in the realm of digitization and digital preservation. A looming web-era contradiction between it and the outputs of the GPO, however, remains to be addressed.

applications there in the early 1930s. The National Agricultural Library entered partnerships with most of the libraries at agricultural schools and maintains AGRICOLA, the world's largest agricultural-oriented bibliographic database.

- **National Library of Medicine.** The Library of the Surgeon General of 1836 was elevated to national library status in 1956. It remains a major source for partnerships and information for medical school and public health collections and has risen to a position of leadership in information science with its Medical Subject Headings. MEDLARS (Medical Literature Analysis and Retrieval System) appeared as early as 1964 and sourced the online MEDLINE database in the 1970s.

Academic Library Maturation

The maturation of the academic library in the postwar decades is manifest in hindsight but a rolling tale for those immersed in the process. New grantmaking potential registered within research universities. As they came on the scene, development and alumni offices could also see the library's symbolic powers for endowment campaigns. As sampled below, academic and government research libraries entered their own sustained period of technological experimentation and advancement, one that would culminate in the automation of their systems and our fourth reinvention.

> Database Precursors

As with other innovations, the library marketplace stimulated external entrepreneurs, from equipment makers to research resources. In 1938 alone, Kodak's Recordak division began offering the *New York Times* on film, and UMI (University Microfilms International and the origins of ProQuest) launched dissertation microfilming near the University of Michigan's campus.

- **Microfilm.** A legacy of the prewar years, microfilm was the futurist delight in the pre–hard disk era. Many envisioned the medium as the solution to the unbridled space needs of academic libraries. The technology itself dated to the late nineteenth century. By the early twentieth century, Otlet and the documentalists foresaw a microfiche World Center Library of Juridical, Social and Cultural Documentation with print-on-demand functionality. The National Agricultural Library implemented a portion of that approach with pioneering document delivery services in the 1930s. Belief in microfilm as a savior, however, waned in postwar decades. Users were simply uncomfortable with the reading experience. Yet the technology continued, and the microfilm reading room became a staple in academic libraries.

- **Photocopying.** The advent of xerography joined with affordable cassette recorders in the 1960s to help precipitate a crisis that led to the 1976 U.S. Copyright Act. Academic libraries were among the first to respond to the new document technology. Many turned to centralized copy centers, which would defray the costs of expensive machines. Although some persist, such facilities eventually trended away to self-service machines. As one might expect, they were joined by commercial competition. In a manner familiar to the medieval stationer, Kinko's (now part of FedEx) was set in motion in 1970 to address student business at the University of California, Santa Barbara.

> Advocacy and Activism

I would be remiss without an aside from the sixties. In keeping with those heady times, reaction against racism and the Vietnam War galvanized the youth of the profession—including future publisher and ALA president Patricia Schuman. A field numerically dominated by women awakened to feminism. Activists embraced the symbolic legacy of libraries to instigate along two broad fronts that would become institutionalized within ALA: intellectual freedom and the Office of Intellectual Freedom under Judith Krug took what has proved a lasting place in the forefront of the people's right to information and privacy, and the Social Responsibilities Round Table extended to consideration of a full range of progressive social issues.

- **Preservation.** The 1970s featured the effective rediscovery of preservation and stewardship. Events began in 1966 with Italy's Florence flood, which damaged hundreds of thousands of works and engendered worldwide reaction. "Mud angel" volunteers included librarians such as the Library of Congress's head of conservation Peter Waters. His *Procedures for Salvage of Water Damaged Library Materials* (1975) proved a landmark in the reawakening. Waters was joined by the likes of George Cunha's New England (now Northeast) Documents Conservation Center. Librarians responded to the "slow fires" of acidification destroying the books on their shelves. Federal, state, and foundation funding appeared, standards were promulgated, and academic libraries replaced binderies with preservation officers.

STAGE V. COMPUTERIZATION

Wartime experiences prepared the way for another seed change. Thanks to their information science forebears, visionaries such as Vannevar Bush, and government support, research libraries arrived at the ground floor of applied computing. Postwar experimentation turned to planning and laying groundwork. Such efforts were framed within the pioneering atmosphere of mainframe computing, early computing languages, and the batch systems of the 1960s. An intertwined set of computerized developments followed to redefine the operational nature of the field.

> **> Readers' Advisory**
>
> This section is abbreviated. The time span is the shortest and of such recent vintage that historical perspective is hard to achieve. Like me, a portion of today's readers are more likely to be familiar and report from personal experience in the era. They are direct recipients of a continuum that flows into contemporary events and the Web.

Bibliographic Groundwork

Mainstream library automation revolves around automating bibliographic records. Its cornerstones were laid in the 1960s.

Library of Congress. The Library of Congress asserted the underlying leadership role and worked with other research libraries on an international basis. The collaboration produced two interlaced baseline contributions:

- **AACR2.** The second edition of the Anglo-American Cataloguing Rules was designed with computerized data elements in mind.
- **MARC.** Harriet Ostroff and her fellows followed with Machine Readable Cataloging standards (Z39.2) protocols for the machine exchange and interpretation of those data elements.

Bibliographic utilities/consortia. With the notable exception of interlibrary loan, academic libraries had retained a modified monastic ideal. The drive was individualized; each institution strove to hold the knowledge of the world. The federal government helped change that pattern. The impetus of World War II incentivized cooperation among research libraries for scientific and military advancement.

By the 1960s, the lure of automation and the economy of shared cataloging was increasingly evident. An unprecedented drive for associations and needed economies of scale emerged under the guise of "bibliographic utilities."

In addition to the Western Library Network and University of Toronto Library Automated Systems, two major operations rose to ongoing prominence in the 1970s:

- **OCLC.** Emerging from a catalog cooperative, this Ohio-based library consortium burst on the national scene in 1972. It would evolve into a worldwide electronic union catalog and fount for numerous advances.
- **RLG/RLIN.** In research library minds, OCLC and its public library component initially seemed insufficient. They banded together in 1974 into the Research Library Group (RLG), which maintained its own shared cataloging system in the form of the Research Libraries Information Network (RLIN) until revisiting and folding with OCLC in the web age.

> **Index Thomisticus**
>
> In the late 1940s, IBM founder Thomas Watson lent support to Roberto Busa and his *Index Thomisticus*—a key landmark in the early movement of the computer into the humanities. The Jesuit Busa used Watson's machines to automate the semantic lemmatization of the words and phrases of Thomas Aquinas. The decades-long effort resulted in a thirty-volume set that since 2005 appropriately resides on the Web.

Digital Publication Base

Bibliographic approaches morphed into rudimentary digital publications in the 1960s and 1970s. The stage was moving for fundamental change in the nature of library collections. Readers' guides and abstracting legacies of the mass press era provided the basis for automated entries:

- In the early 1960s, government libraries engaged action in support of scientific currency. The National Library of Medicine led the way with the groundbreaking *Index Medicus*. The database offered a solution to difficulties in updating library bibliographic and abstracting accounts. The National Aeronautics and Space Administration followed in related fashion with the *Scientific and Technical Aerospace Reports*.
- In the 1970s, commercial forces followed the line of opportunity. Westlaw and Lexis-Nexis, for example, arrived on the legal scene in the forefront of a sector-driven marketplace for research detail. Such products typically make a living mining and repackaging publically available materials.

- In the 1980s, journal database aggregators made their parallel appearance. What would become ProQuest emerged from university microfilm activities with library-oriented indexing and abstracting services. It would be joined by EBSCO. These operations joined with research databases to fundamentally reorder the library research process.

1980s: The Integrated Library System

The final pieces of the pie arrived in rudimentary form during the 1970s and would take hold in the 1980s (see chapter 2). The library and its "dumb" terminals played a transitional role in providing college students their first exposure to computing. Early access to ARPANET/Internet facilitated networking. Research approaches for users and internal technical services were turned on their head from manual to automated. The economic nature of the library was altered in the process. For instance, with the integrated library system (ILS), a variety of vendors took the opportunity offered by automated cataloging records to create a new market. They built software and hardware for new online public access catalogs (OPACs) and circulation controls. Over time, integrated modules expanded across the face of operations into acquisitions, interlibrary loans, serials management, and other functions. At the same time, library computer departments made their entrance in organizational charts and joined computer infrastructure as significant budgetary elements.

In the exuberant words of John Kountz (1992) within the then relatively new *Library Hi Tech,* a campaign had been won in remarkably short order:

> The Great Library Automation War has been won! The electronic future for libraries has never looked better. The backbone of library automation— backroom activities such as classification, cataloging, public catalogs, shelflists, serials control, and circulation—for all but the least endowed libraries is now so pervasive that few librarians can (or care to) recall the manual world of the past.

Automation Reinvention

The academic library of the late thirteenth century would be largely unrecognizable to the mid-1980s college student or faculty. No longer would one need be a cleric or scholar with Latin and Greek for entry. Small rooms with several hundred chained codices would vanish within a modern mega-library and its millions of volumes. The computer had irrevocably entered the academic library. For the first time in history, eyes alone would not suffice; a machine had to interpret first.

In addition, the machine fostered a fundamentally different presence beyond the bibliographic. The library building was penetrated by electronic information. Research libraries had been present and active in the arrival of the information highway from the early days of ARPANET into the Internet. E-mail, electronic discussion lists, and related tools were embraced almost as a matter of course. Indeed, the library world boasted development of its own Internet protocol with Z39.50. In theory, the standard offered shared controls for searching, browsing, sorting, and retrieving bibliographic data across different institutions and ILSs.

By the end of the decade, academic library operations had been forever altered. Users grew to rely on machines for locating their reading and research materials. Microcomputers and a new consumer marketplace were leaving their own mark in furthering tech-savvy students and faculty. Internal operations transited from the manual and handcraft arts to computer dependencies. Academic libraries were positioned for their next stage of development—the elimination of walls with the Web.

> Note on Sources and Historiography

The history described in this chapter came to me through professional work and teaching, including courses in the history of the book and libraries. The latter involved exposure to a variety of standard fact-based studies, such as Jackson's *Libraries and Librarianship in the West* (1974) and Schottenloher's *Books and the Western World* (1989). Michael Harris's *History of Libraries in the Western World* (1995) lent a different influence, moving toward the inclusion of roles in society and as an apparatus of the state. Comments on academic library professionalization, activism, and World War II intelligence activities are drawn from my publications and primary research.

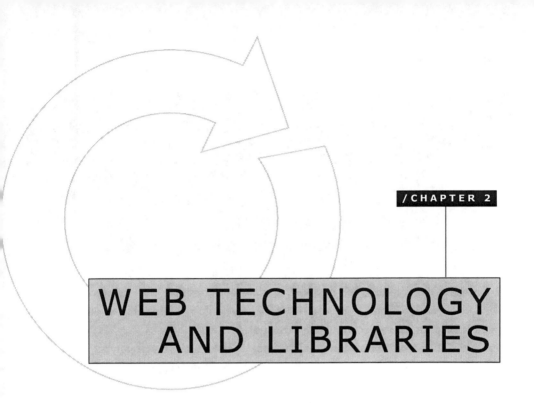

CHAPTER 2

WEB TECHNOLOGY AND LIBRARIES

E NTER THE WORLD WIDE WEB AND A SIXTH STAGE OF library reinvention. History can only partially inform such a dynamic atmosphere. Strategic responses demand constant attention from the midst of a communication revolution. As in previous communications revolutions, the library's fate is entangled with external technological factors, now set within a confusing and fluctuating arc of web development. This chapter follows with a modicum of background on the Web and its constituent parts, as well as the early phases of its revolutionary impacts on the academic library.

INTERNAL INFRASTRUCTURE

The World Wide Web (WWW) project aims to allow links to be made to any information anywhere. The address format includes an access method (=namespace), and for most name spaces a hostname and some sort of path. We have a prototype hypertext editor for the NeXT, and a browser for line mode terminals which runs on almost anything. These can access

> **Considering a Hyper-Incunabulum**

The reader is asked to recognize that the Web is only twenty years old at the time of this writing. Like print, it is engaged in a multigenerational evolution—a hyper-Incunabulum. The first phases are in, but much remains in transition. Ubiquitous computing and the personalized Web are only beginning to emerge. Extant capacities in voice recognition, touch screens, 3D projections, and augmented reality have barely been touched. Ever more tempting applications and unavoidable updates pour in daily. Above all, the "born web"—those who natively learn how to absorb information through clicking and scrolling—have barely entered what will be their scene to define.

files either locally, NFS mounted, or via anonymous FTP. They can also go out using a simple protocol (HTTP) to a server which interprets some other data and returns equivalent hypertext files. . . .

If you're interested in using the code, mail me. It's very prototype, but available by anonymous FTP from info.cern.ch. It's copyright CERN but free distribution and use is not normally a problem. . . .

The WWW project was started to allow high energy physicists to share data, news, and documentation. We are very interested in spreading the Web to other areas, and having gateway servers for other data. Collaborators welcome! I'll post a short summary as a separate article.

This summer invitation from a particle physicist in Switzerland (Berners-Lee 1991) presaged the most dramatic confluence in the history of communication. Tim Berners-Lee's World Wide Web began as a sidebar, an informal communications project for the scientific community. Within two years the creation had gone "scholarly" viral. Thousands of sites sprouted a variety of academic wares, locations, and collaborators, albeit in mere prelude to the millions that would soon follow.

INITIAL FORMULATION

The launch was well-timed. Implementation came together easily in the summer of 1991.

> **Readers' Advisory**

This chapter should be read in juxtaposition to chapters 6 and, especially, 7. The "Initial Formulation" section of the present chapter offers technical depth and jargon by way of basic grounding in the logic of the Web as medium. Though useful for those in need of background, such detail is no longer necessary for the construction of a virtual academic library. Informed readers may wish to skip ahead to the "Worldwide Web Consortium" section.

It engaged through the confluence of three components. The Internet, as adoptive parent, was joined by Berners-Lee's twin creations of the HTTP server protocol and HTML word processing/presentation format.

Internet

Berners-Lee sought a communication system to link cooperating sites in the research community. The Internet provided a familiar and ready-made backbone. In addition to word-processing exchange, this selection would facilitate the integration of nonweb components from e-mail and electronic discussion lists to instant messaging and voice over Internet protocol (VOIP).

Roots of the information highway lay firmly in the U.S. military research community. In the 1960s, the Defense Advanced Research Projects Agency (DARPA) sought to enhance the exchange of project information among universities and research laboratories. The task devolved to the daunting "internetworking" of dozens of nonstandardized, time-sharing mainframe computer systems in that era. Results evolved in stages into the Internet.

> **E-mail**
>
> Ray Tomlinson contributed what became the Internet's main user application as a by-product while working on a DARPA communication project in the early 1970s. His effort benefited from notice of the elegant "@" symbol sitting largely unused on his teletype.

The technical solution arrived in the form of packet switching. Messages could be broken and enveloped into small transmission-size units, or packets, with their own addresses. Instead of permanently dedicated and, hence, vulnerable circuits, virtual routing platforms could be created on the fly. Packets could then be independently dispatched across a maze of cooperating routers for reassembly in remote computers.

Development proceeded apace, including the steady expansion of complicit sites, inexorable march to formal guidelines, and notable applications. By the mid-1970s, physical tentacles had extended across the oceans and into a global ARPANET. The prototype had gone worldwide but could be represented in a simple half-page schematic (figure 2.1).

Telecommunication standards fell into place in the early 1980s. They arrived under the guise of two defining protocols or set of shared rules—TCP/IP:

- TCP (transmission control protocol) provides transit information and monitoring of packeted data as they pass from originating to receiving machine.

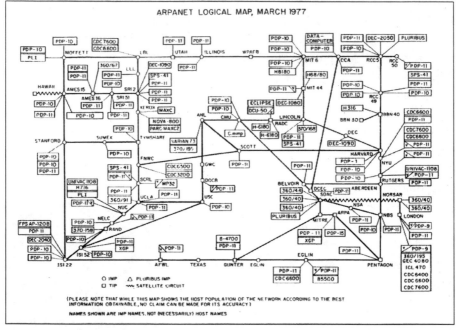

figure 2.1 ARPANET early configuration (from Wikimedia Commons, http://upload.wikimedia.org/ wikipedia/commons/thumb/b/bf/Arpanet_logical_map,_march_1977.png/300p_Arpanet_logical_ map,_march_1977.png)

- IP (Internet protocol) controls the fragmenting and reassembling of data as well as the unique machine locations (IP addresses) for system recognition. The IP version 4 32-bit approach currently dominates. Its "dotted quads" array in a top-down fashion from the high-level network to subnet to host address. The four parts render in a dot-decimal fashion, such as 186.17.263.1 or my home's 69.255.58.186.

The Internet cometh. With the arrival of TCP/IP's Internet control suite, DARPA had done its seed work and began to segment away from academic partners. The agency looked to "civilianize" the technology and

> ## › IPv6
>
> IP version 4 is destined to be supplanted by version 6. In the early 1990s, the Internet Engineering Task Force initiated work in anticipation of exhausting addresses—an eventuality that looms large in 2013. The updated protocol employs 128-bit addresses and an eight-position schema. In contrast to version 4's 4.3 billion limit, the resulting 2^{128} possibilities are what the Wolfram Alpha engine terms a "transcendental number." Unfortunately, compatibility problems between the two promise a bumpy transition.

> ## › Usenet
>
> An early "Netizen" and prelude to web culture developed around the sharing of information through usenets such as the WELL. Such exchanges fostered the ideals of the free interchange of information.

initiate a monumental drawdown toward the eventual disestablishment of ARPANET. In 1983 the .mil domain entered the scene. The agency also decided to limit underwriting costs for linking and registration to the military. Infrastructure control was passed to the National Science Foundation. By mid-decade, ARPANET was spun off into the "Internet"—a semi-independent entity for university and research laboratory exchanges and soon in a hunt for underwriting.

The Internet took a tentative but ultimately significant turn toward the commercial. Internet service providers (ISPs) began to creep into the picture. The High Performance Computing and Communication Act of 1991—or Gore Bill—confirmed the direction. Private enterprise was destined to replace government support. A new economic engine had been set in motion. The Internet itself was fully opened to commercial development, underwriting, and partnerships in 1995. By the end of the decade and thanks to the spur of the Web, Internet access would even emerge as the country's newest general consumption utility.

Technically, the Internet is a cooperative and voluntary network of TCP/IP-compliant networks. Activity takes place through an informal conglomeration of government, industry, nonprofit, and for-profit interests. Satellites and cell towers join dedicated cables along with repositioned telephone and power lines in a transmission's mishmash. Traffic is routed through a few hundred top-level nodes in self-sustaining and unmapped concert with thousands of subsidiary ISPs. The conglomeration almost magically provides access to hundreds of millions of receiving/sending stations around the world.

› National Science Foundation and National Center for Supercomputing Applications

In the 1980s, the National Science Foundation (NSF) began to replace DARPA as the player of main interest for computerized communication. As the Internet moved to generalized use in mid-decade, the NSF stepped forward with NSFNET and operations such as the National Center for Supercomputing Applications (NCSA) at the University of Illinois—a major player in the early Web. NSFNET provided a dedicated channel among universities and laboratories with supercomputers; it was disengaged in 1995 as part of final opening of the Internet to commercial forces.

In the mid-1990s, the NSF's interests extended instead toward "very-high-performance Backbone Network Service." Such directions evolved into the Internet2 project under EDU-COM/EDUCAUSE.

Internet governance. Since late 2005, the IGF (Internet Governance Forum) has assumed titular lead of what translates as Internet governance. Reality remains with consensual controls in a loosely configured assortment of voluntary task forces and working groups, with DARPA lurking and the United Nation's International Telecommunication Union trying to break into the action. Activities break into two broad arenas:

- Name spaces: ICANN. The Internet Corporation for Assigned Names and Numbers works under contract from the U.S. Department of Commerce. ICANN controls the registries for IP addresses in coordination with the Domain Name System (DNS). The latter aliases IP's numerical addresses into recognizable name structures—URLs (universal resource locators)— which have been subdivided into different domains such as .mil, .edu, and .com.
- Technology development: IETF. The Internet Engineering Task Force is the most visible agency developing the Internet. It works in consort with the Internet Architecture Board (IAB), the Internet Engineering Steering Group (IESG), and the Internet Research Task Force (IRTF). A self-organized international assortment of volunteers, the IETF concentrates on advancing voluntary standards through its "working groups."

HTTP

The hypertext transmission protocol (HTTP) is Berners-Lee's quiet twin. As specified under RFC 2616, HTTP is the daemon or protocol in the TCP/IP suite that declares a web session. Though awkwardly designated, the "http://" indicator enabled transcendent hypertext advances—as well as ongoing confusion between the Internet and Web. With it, the Web seamlessly moves from its HTML setting to embrace a range of operations on the host information highway.

The protocol proved remarkably stable. It remains largely as first envisioned:

- The requester sending a TCP knock with a "handshake" offer to the receiver's IP address at the HTTP-server door (normally the computer's port 80).

> **> HTTP 1.1**
>
> Tweaking aside, the only significant upgrade to HTTP was finalized in September 2004. Version 1.1 worked around 1.0's "stateless" mode of individual requests. It allowed for persistent connections with multiple actions in a session.

- The receiver's HTTP server sends back a rejecting status message or launches a confirming handshake to initiate a session.

Although deep understanding of HTTP is not vital, some is helpful in tuning thinking for the medium. The protocol shapes within a two-part header and body message frame. Contact between machines alternates as "handshakes" between request and response:

- **Request.** Depending on the server's abilities, requests may entail as many as nine types of commands, but four are key:
  - » *Get.* The first and for a time only command or HTTP "verb," Get remains a required server feature. It is used to retrieve specified resources—for example, Get the HTML page at *xxx* IP/URL address.
  - » *Head.* Similar to Get, Head is aimed at retrieving metadata from the header—for example, Cookies, (DNL) do not list, Location (rerouting), Referer (where the visitor originated).
  - » *Options.* Highly recommended for HTTP servers, Options requests a display of the methods supported; hence, functionality checks for the type of request.
  - » *Post.* The central command for web interactivity. Post involves a query [?]. It is used to submit information for processing at the receiver, such as a search request, entering data on a form, or updating Facebook status.
- **Response.** Replies can be acknowledged under five statuses:
  - » *100s—Informational.* Under HTTP 1.1, these indicated provisional status, such as continue or switch protocols.
  - » *200s—Success.* The request was received, understood, and being processed—especially the standard 200 OK.
  - » *300s—Redirection.* Requester may need to take additional steps—for example, 301 Moved Permanently, 303 See Also (of great interest for Semantic Web operations), 305 Use Proxy, 307 Temporary Redirect.
  - » *400s—Client error.* These messages include 400 Bad Request, 401 Unauthorized, 404 Not Found (may be available later), 405 Method Not Allowed, 407 Proxy Authentication Required, 408 Request Timeout, 410 Gone (resource permanently removed), 423 Locked, 426 Upgrade Required, 429 Too Many Requests, 450 Blocked by Windows Parental Controls, 451 Unavailable for Legal Reasons, and 418 I'm in a teapot (lingering April Fool's Day joke).

» *500s—Server error.* The receiver is aware of a problem on its side. These may involve timeout or authentication issues along with 500 Internal Server Error (generic), 501 Not Implemented (server cannot handle the request type), 502 Bad Gateway, 503 Service Unavailable, 505 HTTP version Not Supported, 508 Loop Detected.

HTML

The twin would undergo more frequent changes. HTML was an extended form of word processing. As reported by the World Wide Web Consortium (November 3, 1992), it started with a mere eighteen tag elements. These featured then radical notions of hypertext linkages (HREF) to anchors (name) within a document and out to other HTML and Internet addresses. Initial interest in textual document exchange quickly expanded. The forum resolved into a presentation medium. Images would vie with text. Sites frequently emerged more akin to highway signs, rife with institutional announcements and bulletin board displays.

The technology enabled in simplified reflection of SGML (standard generalized markup language) syntax and < tag > structures. These rendered through a two-part electronic document:

- Head section facilitates the transfer of information between computer servers. Such information is typically delivered as metadata, including a Title tag that automatically populates the top of the web browser.
- Body followed as a word processor composite. It holds intended visible contents along with their markups for interpretation and display in a browser.

› SGML Background

In a now somewhat alien concept, computers were once almost exclusively dedicated to computing; they crunched numbers and did that largely in isolation. Human communication was an afterthought and idiosyncratic to individual systems. According to the International SGML Users' Group (1993), generalizable respite appeared in 1969. Then, Charles Goldfarb, Edward Mosher, and Raymond Mosher invented generalized markup language (GML). Like other advances under discussion, it began as an offshoot or aside—in this case to an IBM project for law office systems. The approach drew upon established editorial markups to printers. Design and layout instructions were announced through bracketed closed tagging structures, ‹format› narrative ‹/format›. These methods took hold to underlie text editors in the 1970s and microcomputer word processors in the 1980s.

By 1986 informal practice also pushed into a formal SGML meta-language (ISO 8879:1986). The standard articulated within document-type definitions (DTDs) (subsequently enhanced into "schema"). The declaration ‹!DOCTYPE . . .› of a form (article, book, report) was linked to a rigid set of individualized rules for layout to mark up into electronic presentation for the computer screen.

Heading Levels & Simple Formatting

Structure: Heading levels add valuable structure for document analysis and retrieval.

Text Components

Basic format tags feature **bold face**, *italics*, and underlining.

Unlike SGML, paragraph tags do not require an end or closing tag.

Hypertext Considerations

This crucial advancement involves setting internal anchors (name) and hypertext reference (href) links to those or externally held sites on the Web.

Return to Top of Page

```
<html>
   <head>
      <title>Basic Web Coding</title>
   </head>
   <body>
      <h1>Heading Levels & Simple Formatting</h1><a
      name="top"></a>
         <p><b>Structure:</b> Heading levels add valuable
         structure for document analysis and retrieval.
         <h2>Text Components</h2>
            <p>Basic format tags feature <b>bold face</b>,
            <i>italics</i>, and <u>underlining</u>.
            <p>Unlike SGML, paragraph tags do not require an end
            or closing tag.</p>
      <h1>Hypertext Considerations</h1>
         <p>This crucial advancement involves setting internal
         anchors (name) and hypertext reference (href) links to
         those or externally held sites on the Web.
         <p><a href="#top">Return to Top of Page</a>
   </body>
</html>
```

figure 2.2 Basic HTML coding and browser display (Courtesy of author)

Figure 2.2 serves to illustrate a raw HTML page and the resulting browser presentation. In such an application, the external site sends an HTTP Get request to a designated IP address. If accepted, the owning site dispatches its packages through the Internet. Material arrives and is assembled at the requesting IP address for transmittal to a software browser, which interprets the markups and renders the body for display.

WORLDWIDE WEB CONSORTIUM

The World Wide Web quickly outgrew its birthright. Berners-Lee's invitees and related parties brought other topics to the CERN table. In the most important of these, 1993 reactions against the commercialization of the University of Minnesota's Gopher pressured for a crucial determination. CERN followed to abandon any pretense of copyright ownership. The Web and its underlying codes would be open source—available to anyone for development.

Ad hoc arrangements inevitably frayed in the face of financial and political realities as well as the interests of a particularly powerful player. By early fall of 1994, CERN and Berners-Lee were ready for change. The former divested leadership to concentrate on its scientific mission. DARPA and a new Worldwide Web Consortium (W3C) body stepped forward. The main seat of operations and infrastructure development moved to the Massachusetts Institute of Technology, with Berners-Lee in the leadership role.

W3C governance evolved into an occasionally contradictory mixture of scholarly and commercial interests. The consortium committed to standards and an enhanced technical vision, including a crucial stance to go beyond word processing into computer and financial operations. The communitarian bent toward an Open Web and royalty-free development remained, but fiscal realities could not be ignored. In keeping with parallel development on the Internet, commercial players were admitted. They would prove crucial to the Web's advancement, but they also engendered a conflicted hunt for profit-making methods.

> Tuning the Web Page: Basics

Berners-Lee's original conceptualization of HTML added structural features that pushed beyond the visual results of word processing toward computer recognition. Two remain particularly crucial for relevancy and retrieval by search engines:

- **Title.** The only visible part of the head is a major element for discovery. Consider the wording carefully and concentrate on the first sixty or so characters.

- **Headings.** What you see is not all that you get. Headings bring internal structures. They are vital for computer and search engine interpretation through Bayesian and artificial intelligence applications. Think of H1 as a chapter title. The computer can weigh the words for relations to the contents that follow. The H1 owns and further defines the H2 main subdivisions within it. Those H2s own their H3s so on in a cascade of related context. Again, carefully consider word selection, and be sure to replicate the terminology in the narrative to ensure validation.

W3C and HTML

Berners-Lee's original version of HTML arrived with a mere handful of commands. Core formatting (bold, italic, underline, paragraph), hypertext, and structural (h1, h2 . . .) continue. Specific codes from formulation on a NeXT computer quickly gave way. The machine-agnostic wisdom of the Internet took hold. The march toward related standards advanced with semiformal embrace of SGML in a 1993 HTML DTD and formal alignment under HTML 2.0 in 1995.

Produced in cooperation with IETF, the new specification proved a definitive guide for future iterations. W3C with its allied commercial interests stepped in to take charge of subsequent versions. With the final release of HTML 4.01 in mid-2001, W3C effectively walled HTML development from outside influence.

Specifics on elements and timing between HTML 2.0 and 4.01 are beyond the needs of this text. One merely notes a move away from browser defaults and toward design specificity—for example, color palates, font choices, and other stylistic determiners replaced browser defaults. Forms, frames, and tables added different structures. As that complexity increased, W3C looked to ease the coding burden in the body. Moreover, the consortium and its business partners had already committed to another direction.

XML

The answer for design dilemmas and migration to non-microcomputer screens was the separation of content from layout. Layout controls could be removed from the body for detail in the head through cascading style sheets (CSSs). The solution came as almost a sidebar to W3C's main commitment for computerized operations, financial enablement, and long-term drive for ubiquitous computing with the Web at its center. The modus vivendi arrived in the form of XML (extensible markup language).

XML's quiet underwriting from Microsoft is illustrative of the Web's seed change toward the commercial. W3C's push beyond human comprehension to computer manipulation established the technological basis for a global financial engine.

The new standard employed a reduced tag set but required rigid adherence to SGML orthodoxy. Unlike HTML, XML must be "well-formed" or will not function. SGML syntax rules, for example, demand that capital letters mean something. Only proper Unicode characters may be used. Formal tagging procedures must be engaged, such as beginning and end tags in place and elements within properly nested.

> **> XHTML**
>
> A separate, compromise language arose to prominence in the early twentieth century. XHTML reformulated HTML within XML's strict adherence to SGML rules. Such directions are being supplanted by the rise of HTML5.

XML called forth SOAP and related standards for fiscal operations. It also eased SGML's requirements for preexisting ontologies in the form of DTDs or web schemas. With XML, DTD-like declarations could be made on the fly. The language allows for delineation of a term such as <book> as an object, which can then be parsed by self-created structural tags <title_page>, <front_matter>, <chapter>, <quotation>, <end_matter> until </book>.

HTML5

With HTML5, W3C proffers a saving grace and likely point of concentration for the rest of this decade. Although continuing SGML-like syntax, the new standard has abandoned slavish adherence to the rule set. HTML5 restores the flexibility and forgiveness of HTML, but with significant advances. HTML5 comes enabled for the embrace of media and interactive applications as well as delivery on mobiles or other Internet devices. It subsumes reliance on externally delivered capacities of Flash or other external apps and scripts (document object models—DOMs).

Other W3C Initiatives

In the late 1990s, W3C committed to two other major continuing initiatives, universal access and the "semantic web." As discussed in chapter 7, both are of high interest to librarianship but may be judged differently from a virtual library perspective.

Universal access. W3C embraced a call to make the Web the "universe of network-accessible information." Its intention was to reach every device and cut across cultural, language, and national boundaries. The medium would be intertwined across the full range of human activity with machinery. Initial concentration was given to the Web Accessibility Initiative (WAI), which extended universality as an entitlement or inalienable right to those with physical or mental handicaps. WAI's fourteen points (W3C 1999) are called to attention for any website:

1. Provide equivalent alternatives to auditory and visual content.
2. Don't rely on color alone.

3. Use markup and style sheets and do so properly.
4. Clarify natural language usage.
5. Create tables that transform gracefully.
6. Ensure that pages featuring new technologies transform gracefully.
7. Ensure user control of time-sensitive content changes.
8. Ensure direct accessibility of embedded user interfaces.
9. Design for device-independence.
10. Use interim solutions.
11. Use W3C technologies and guidelines.
12. Provide context and orientation information.
13. Provide clear navigation mechanisms.
14. Ensure that documents are clear and simple.

WAI would leave related imprint on the Americans with Disabilities Act in the Section 508 requirements for electronic material.

Semantic web: Web 3.0. The second drive reflects Berners-Lee's dream for a semantic web. As indicated in a *Scientific American* article (Berners-Lee et al. 2001) and elsewhere, the concept involves "a web of data that can be processed directly and indirectly by machines." Instead of display for human readers, information is cast for computer manipulation. Elements within documents are enhanced through metadata linkages to an external network of explanatory tools for machine analysis.

The semantic web reflects the taxonomies and subject tracings of libraries but relies on artificial intelligence and extensive construction for linkage and implementation. It is underpinned by two elements:

- RDF (Resource Description Framework) is an XML metadata specification. It provides the language structures for computerized parsing and evaluation. RDF resolves data into "triplets"—simple sentences hashed (#) with subject (the resource), verb (relationship between the subject and object), and object (resource's trait). Those elements are individually recognized with universal resource identifiers (URIs).
- Ontologies are commonly available formats to assist with interpretation. They involve the complex production of taxonomic thesauruses with inference rules to define the relationships among terms.

EXTERNAL DEVELOPERS

> The World Wide Web was designed originally as an interactive world of shared information through which people could communicate with each other and with machines. Since its inception in 1989 it has grown initially as a medium for the broadcast of read-only material from heavily loaded corporate servers to the mass of Internet connected consumers. Recent commercial interest [in] its use within the organization under the "Intranet" buzzword takes it into the domain of smaller, closed, groups, in which greater trust allows more interaction. In the future we look toward the Web becoming a tool for even smaller groups, families, and personal information systems. Other interesting developments would be the increasingly interactive nature of the interface to the user, and the increasing use of machine-readable information with defined semantics allowing more advanced machine processing of global information, including machine-readable signed assertions.

Berners-Lee's 1996 report underplayed the transformation. The Web's scholarly purity joined the Internet in a commercial seed change. Businesses were given entrée. Such directions flowed logically from financial realities, government pressures, and the 1998 Open Source Initiative. An array of interested parties took the opportunity to advance toward a new global economy (see chapter 3).

The process was not immediate. It took time, experimentation, and ongoing compromise. Activities were engaged through two overlapping zones.

- **Generic support.** Building from a bed of inquisitive—and occasionally entrepreneurial—scientific minds, pioneering developers looked to enhance access and the display capacities while remaining in rough conformity with open-web principles.
- **Commoditization support.** Entrepreneurial forces were determined to find ways to employ web infrastructure for profit making. Baseline extensions transited into a promotional vehicle and delivery mechanism for services and digital products.

ENABLING COMMERCIALIZATION

Once freed of the hint of CERN copyrights, tinkerers blossomed, universities explored, and commercial forces emerged. Such external involvement enabled

› Open-Source Continuation

Although the focus in this section is on commercial applications, scholarly contributors continued as a force in expanding the usability of the Web—as well as through open-access publications (see chapter 3).

the revolution and would leave direct impact on library operations.

Killer Apps

1994 was the "Year of the Killer Apps." Non-W3C actors helped democratize the scholarly reserve into a people's forum. The specialized niche market was transformed into a consumer zone. Two seminal contributions proved vital to the shift, browsers and search engines.

Browsers. The Netscape browser was the first of the "Killers." It grew from the National Center for Supercomputing Applications' Mosaic interface, a 1993 Gore grant product by Illinois student Marc Andreessen. The product was remarkably simple to engage. Instead of tabbing from hyperlink to hyperlink, it provided a graphical user interface (GUI) with mouse controls. Taken commercial, the slightly more refined and transparent Netscape quickly became the world's most popular doorway to the Web—but significantly retained open-access tradition as a free download.

Netscape's success instigated the "browser wars" of the late 1990s. Microsoft battled forth with its Explorer alternative. The craze catalyzed a related rush for products to simplify and enhance the production of web pages. Institutional websites became the norm. Office suites converged into automatic connectivity and web rendering. Rounds of improvement ensued in never-ending fashion. The Web grew from sidelight into the central element for modern computing.

Search engines. The Web was born without effective searching. In the early years, librarians and subject specialists often stepped into the breach with referential websites. But technologists were also eager for solutions. Led more by university students than faculty researchers, opportunities cascaded into 1994's second Killer App. Products such as Lycos and WebCrawler were followed by AltaVista and Yahoo. As exemplified by front-runner Yahoo, the first trend involved human-mediated directories. Search engine software spiders crawled the Web and returned information to the search engine's catalog or index, which then resolved requests through the directory's classification system.

Although deep technical nuance is beyond the needs of this text, the net effects were crucial in popularizing the Web. Not unlike library taxonomies, search engines brought order to a seemingly uncontrollable mass of information.

They enabled the average person to locate desired sites almost instantaneously. With somewhat disturbing facility, one could bypass set navigation paths and hunt for information within a site. Instead of complicated searching through legacy tailored bibliographic indexes and catalog cards, users gained the luxury of searching full text and even being directly connected to the data.

Applications underwent transcendent advances in the early twenty-first century. Google burst on the scene with enhanced full-text prospects and a multiplicity of relevance weightings. Its PageRank algorithm provided a breakthrough crowd-sourcing method, and the company continues to fine-tune on a daily basis. In short order, the product came to dominate the market—its name transformed into a synonymous verb for conducting a web search.

Enhancing HTML

Though perhaps removed from library implementations, other nonprofit and for-profit players helped enhance the display potential and power of HTML:

- National Center for Supercomputing Applications and the common gateway interface. The Center was a World Wide Web partner in several web advances, especially in the free-flowing communications of the early days. Its HTTPd, for example, provided the software core for today's dominant Apache web server. That landmark server also launched the common gateway interface (CGI). In a major move beyond word processing, a CGI script post to a CGI-bin allowed for the engagement of executable files.

› Mind Rewiring

In keeping with McLuhan's predictions (1962), the Web is impacting human cognition. Those who learn to absorb information in a clicking and scrolling medium differ from those who learned to read ink on paper. Betsy Sparrow et al. (2011) push the effects further. As indicated in their preface, researchers quantified shifts in memory and "Googlization" effects with a developing machine symbiosis from search engine use:

> These results suggest that processes of human memory are adapting to the advent of new computing and communication technology. Just as we learn through trans-active memory who knows what in our families and offices, we are learning what the computer "knows" and when we should attend to where we have stored information in our computer-based memories. We are becoming symbiotic with our computer tools, growing into interconnected systems that remember less by knowing information than by knowing where the information can be found. This gives us the advantage of access to a vast range of information, although the disadvantages of being constantly "wired" are still being debated.

- DOMs (document object models). Private industry stepped forward during the browser wars with lightweight programs to interact with objects within web documents, including the creation of dynamic pages. Netscape led the way with JavaScript in 1996. The enhancement pushed W3C's open-standards buttons toward ECMAScript, a common browser scripting language that enables application programming interfaces (APIs).

SUPPORTS

Web commoditization divides among several strands (see chapter 3). Here we concentrate on library-directed products to make money from the Web as "platform."

Access

ISPs were the first on the scene. Site hosting and development services entered in mid-decade. People proved willing to contract for assistance in producing sites. Service providers American Online and CompuServe also found an ongoing market with those who pay for the convenience of access. Business information interests also intruded on scholarly domains. The rise of the Web readily led virtual private networks (VPNs) from frame relay and other networking options to TCP/IP on the Internet.

Advertising

In the early years, web denizens greeted commercial marketing with hostility. Browsers, search engines, and service providers were pivotal in preparing the way for commercialization beyond the Web's original scholarly and socialistic basis. Shareware tradeoffs ensued. The public at large was not as protective of the rights to free services. In exchange for free software,

› Web 2.0/ Social Networking

Social networking sites offer the most recent expression of the open-web ethos. Tim O'Reilly took the Web 2.0 sobriquet away from W3C's semantic web. The implementation is less about technological innovation than a different way of using the medium. Instead of the one-way broadcasting channels that came to dominate the early medium, social networking returns to the concept of an information interchange. The original idea of a scholarly forum has been augmented by "an architecture of participation" that invites collaboration for a more popular range of groups. Facebook and LinkedIn extend human communication beyond mail and the telephone. They can embrace an ever-widening array of blogs, chats, geographic location identifiers, multimedia displays, RSS feeds, tagging, and wikis.

users learned to tolerate newspaper-like banners and boxes. This synthesis produced arguably the Web's first revenue streams.

Apps

Garnering profits from software applications offered unique challenges for the consumer marketplace. Entrepreneurs had to bridge from shareware expectations. Advertising worked in some instances. Others could be enticed to pay or license DOM software to enhance sites that retained free viewer access. Another tactic involved staged product lines. A free teaser would be piggybacked with a more powerful, professional version. As in many other ways, Apple helped bust open another line of attack. Its App Store provided enterprising software developers with a publically acceptable marketing venue.

Deep/Invisible Web

In the mid-1990s, Mike Bergman of Bright-Planet described the increasing presence of an invisible, or "deep," Web. As opposed to the open or surface Web, these were resources not available to web search engines. That distinction is no longer fully valid. Instead, the largest accumulation of holdings on the Web is roughly categorized by these types:

> Pay-per-Click and Other Enhancement

Gauging the impact and, hence, costing models for advertising were a significant challenge in the early web years. In the late 1990s, Overture (originally Goto.com) innovated a major new form of advertising: pay-per-click would provide a major source of income for search engines and other commercial sites. Google subsequently tweaked the approach with relevance rankings. Amazon took a different internal marketing approach with profiling and "push" methods mapped to user preferences. Processes have now advanced toward ubiquitous computing. Much to the chagrin of privacy advocates, GPS and usage tracking applications can deliver messaging dynamically as one walks down a store aisle or drives along a city street.

- **Authentication required.** Our main arena of concern—those free or pay-for sites that require logons, proxy, or other forms of verification for entry and retrieval of resources.
- **Computer/spam sensitive.** Those sites using robot exclusion protocols or requiring human-sensitive engagement, such as Captchas.
- **Dynamic pages.** Sites based on entering a form or created on the fly in response to a query.

Software as a Service (SaaS)/Cloud Computing

"Cloud computing" has become the buzz phrase for web services in the 2010s. The idea is rooted in time-sharing systems of yore. Instead of the 1980s transition into loading software and performing operations within a microcomputer, we return to dumb terminals. Software and data storage services are outsourced to agencies on the Web. An institution's desktops, laptops, and mobiles work as web browsers to engage operations remotely.

The cloud offers distribution benefits and lifts the need for hardware capitalization, but it brings forward complex staffing and identity issues. The term evolved from graphic representations (e.g., figure 9.1). It has been simpler to render the complex interplay of products, network, and users in an amorphous, heavenly setting.

LIBRARIES ENTERING STAGE VI

If the Open Web proffered the weapon for another reinvention of the academic library, commercial enterprises and the Deep Web provided the ammunition. That confluence also brought forth as yet unresolved issues. Its early phases flew in a convoluted mashup as high-minded scholarly traditions melded with unfolding commercial operations. As discussed in part B, these trends included the usurping of library functions and as yet unresolved applications for a new type of university education.

LIBRARIES AND THE OPEN WEB

University libraries were more than ready for Berners-Lee's initiative. Indeed, academic libraries were waiting for something akin to his web. Thanks to location on major research campuses, they were well ensconced on the information highway. The computer stage had firmly prepared the way. Libraries had prepositioned technically inquisitive specialists and automation facilities along with information literacy skills. Developments in this first prong emerged along three main strands.

> **> Readers' Advisory: Technology Teaser**
>
> This section illustrates general contours on the technological side of library rewiring during the first twenty years of the Web. The treatment should be understood in tandem with discussions of the new economy in chapter 3. The intent is not in-depth coverage but prelude and setting for virtual campus responses in part B.

Pioneering Times

Although prominently engaged, initial open-web participation was relatively minor for library reinvention. The medium was nonetheless inviting and World Wide Web's ethos congenial for several lines of innovating development:

- **ISPs.** A selection of academic and public libraries played willing roles as early ISPs. They facilitated the entrance of low-cost or free services that helped to popularize the medium.
- **Bulletin boards.** Libraries proactively engaged with their own sites, which were and often remain web landmarks. Announcements, contact information, and the occasional displays quickly became the norm—an expected marker for all libraries.
- **Organizing the Web.** As discussed in my now aging *Creating Virtual Libraries* (1999), libraries played prominent roles in the pre-Google days of search engines. Academic libraries had already committed to sharing subject knowledge and trusted site discovery through pathfinders, gophers, electronic bibliographic devices, and the like. Aided by "findable" title tags and built-in campus constituencies, library sites contributed many of the early "go-to" places in the pre–search engine period.

Bibliographic Exploration: The Dublin Core

The Dublin Core represents an innovative attempt to engage W3C at the start of the Web's commercialization phase. In the mid-1990s, OCLC and NCSA embarked on efforts to extend bibliographic controls to web resources. The resulting Dublin Core presents a set of fifteen repeatable data elements. These remain in keeping

> **Special Collections**

Academic libraries featured an overlooked component in their wings. Archivists and manuscript curators were outliers in earlier automation drives. Their unique collections were the obverse of library automation drives for shared resources and descriptive practices. Special collections, however, took the opportunity provided by the Web. In a significant and still intellectually unresolved inversion, the most traditional of arenas would come to command much of the future for academic library contributions on the information highway—including entrance into the realms of digital preservation.

with catalog card predecessors: Title, Creator, Subject, Description, Publisher, Contributor, Date, Type, Format, Identifier, Source, Language, Relation, Coverage, Rights. Those have been enhanced by a Qualified Dublin Core set of three more data elements: Audience, Provenance, and RightsHolders.

The scope goes beyond bibliographic origins. The Dublin Core offers generalizable metadata vocabularies. It seeks interoperability to enhance discovery and the management of a wide variety of electronic resources. As indicated on its "About" web page, the DCMI is committed to

- Providing open access to education, training and documentation resources related to innovative design and metadata best practices
- Supporting a worldwide community of people working with metadata to share experiences and find common solutions through collaborative tools, publications and meetings
- Promoting co-operation, and interoperability across standards and vocabularies, by engaging with other organizations and communities
- Developing and maintaining the DCMI metadata vocabularies and promoting their use in conjunction with other vocabularies for describing resources

Unfortunately, the Dublin Core's influence remains limited and the application largely ignored by current search engines. This inspiration for the semantic web was also overlooked in W3C's early efforts, but that may be changing. In 2005, DCMI sought closer conformity with W3C's plans through an RDF-compatible "DCMI Abstract Model." In May 2010, W3C belatedly recognized the obvious, then authorized its Library Linked Data Incubator Group (LLD XG). The massive treasure trove of library records was recognized as a ready-built proving ground for global interoperability with the semantic web.

Digital Preservation

Digital preservation represents one of the most significant financial investments and singular examples of library involvement. Whether sustainable in the long run, the movement has caught the fancy of the library field. Although tangential to the medium itself, these directions illustrate commitment to extend into a new role of information stewardship for the web age.

Research library locus. Despite early interest with serials and related storage issues, library alignment dates more properly to the close of the 1990s. As with many advances, the Library of Congress took the titular lead in coordinating the nation's leading research libraries and other federal agencies. Congress replied with $100 million in seed funds to orchestrate planning for a national digital preservation effort, which coalesced in 2000 as the National Digital Information Infrastructure and Preservation Program (NDIIPP). As indicated in that program's "About" web page, there are three areas of focus:

- *Capturing, preserving, and making available significant digital content.* Content under stewardship by NDIIPP partners includes geospatial information, websites, audio visual productions, images and text, and materials related to critical public policy issues.
- *Building and strengthening a network of partners.* The NDIIPP national network currently has more than 130 partners drawn from federal agencies, state and local governments, academia, professional and nonprofit organizations, and commercial entities.
- *Developing a technical infrastructure of tools and services.* NDIIPP partners work collaboratively to develop a technical infrastructure by building the information systems, tools, and services that support digital preservation.

> **Libraries, Archives, and Museums Converge**

Digital preservation has helped stimulate the reconvergence of libraries, archives, and museums. The component grew from the archival community. In the 1970s, Charles Dollar at the National Archives led efforts to manage the flow and continuity of electronic records. Born-digital applications in archives soon spread as alternative modes of access. These included the digitization of ink-on-paper records, photographs, and eventually three-dimensional objects. As discussed in my *Building Digital Archives* (2002), the field moved forward with expansive and increasingly professionalized intent in the web age. The National Archives was significant in the exploration of the now dominant OAIS (open archival information system) model from NASA along with METS and other metadata standards.

Globalization. The engagement of the Library of Congress also extended to the international scene. Don Waters and John Garrett (1996) provided an intellectual bridge for such directions with their "Preserving Digital Information: Report of the Task Force on Archiving of Digital Information." The results returned national involvements worthy of nineteenth-century romanticism. The European Union's *Committee des Sages* (2011), for example, envisioned such directions as the cornerstone in its *New Renaissance* report. As Nancy McGovern (2012:11) reports, internationalization appears to have reached a critical mass:

> Cumulatively, these indicators document the emergence, increasing cohesion, and ongoing maturation of the digital preservation community. Progress towards the terminology needed for developing digital preservation as a domain, the development and promulgation of standards and good practice, and understanding the nature of the sound investments of resources for sustainability are good indicators of the maturation of the digital preservation community. These results suggest that the community is ready to engage in the development of strategies for aligning national approaches.

LIBRARIES AND THE CONSUMER MARKETPLACE

The commercialization of the Web prepared the way for major transformation and a more significant trend in the library reinvention. In the second half of the 1990s, libraries extended from niche computer services to consumer applications. Entanglement within the budding web marketplace would inevitably engage the field in a new stage of development.

Enter the Web Marketplace

The idea of the library was about to expand beyond the building. Given their pioneering involvement, academic librarians shared in mental allegiances to the open scholarly traditions of the Web. Yet they also expressed early embrace of

› Commercial-State-University Partnerships

The movement to large-scale digital preservation initiatives exemplifies the different financial fabric of web stewardship. The blossoming scope of new media and ownership issues demands massive involvement beyond the solid efforts of Brewster Kahle and his Internet Archives. Individual libraries may join, but sustainability will rest on government engagement and that of major software and communications companies such as Google and Microsoft.

the commercial technologies that democratized the medium and converted it into a public utility—as well as threatened many of their prior roles.

Browsers and monitoring. Rather than systematic initiatives, many sites started as exploratory pilots from tech-savvy librarians. Commercial browsers opened the door for fledgling efforts beyond limited scholarly reserves to an unbounded audience. The technology enabled unprecedented visibility for participants, and a website for the university library quickly became an expected element.

Beyond site design and maintenance, browsers had limited effects on internal operations for most of the 1990s. As discussed in part B, that situation altered dramatically in the twenty-first century with the second stage of web reinvention. Browsers proved central in enhanced demands for metrics and access to electronic publications. In addition to collecting usage statistics and addressing bandwidth issues, the sophisticated library would need to engage in monitoring its patron's browser types and versions. Browser upgrades must be factored as a baseline for design consideration and delivery minimums. Online librarians have to be equipped with appropriates types of browsers to test database additions and troubleshoot service interruptions.

Search engines. Search engines represent arguably the Web's most disturbing element—one still in need of professional resolution. Their appearance significantly enhanced the librarian's researching potential but at the same time empowered users to ignore such skills. With search engines, ready reference collections become questionable and the basis for reference services redefined. Indeed, as indicated in part B, terminology and tactical switches may be in order. APUS, for example, significantly increased usage by merely renaming library "Reference" to the web "Help"—including strategic/tactical placement as the last button in the screen's upper right.

In effect, search engines should be recognized as a new type of audience. The library needs to account for their approaches and presence. Link exchanges should be

> ## > Search Engine Heuristics vs. the Semantic Web

Search engines and full-text analysis offer significant challenges to the semantic web. Google's success is undeniable. Bayesian mathematics, artificial intelligence, and other heuristics produce more than serviceable relevance without added descriptive apparatus. One may expect the rise of a blended approach with high priority. Yet, in keeping with Zipf's Principle of Least Effort (1949), to what degree is it justifiable to expend the effort/costs for ontologies and linked data structures?

encouraged, and recognition given to use patterns that no longer follow designated pathways. Site design must consider search engine expectations.

Search engines bring other professional issues to the table as well. The variety of vendor search engines has proved problematic for online operations. Internal site development should similarly consider these tools and their tuning for enhanced retrieval.

Commercial Services

The switch to web ILSs accelerated the pattern of revolutionary change. These systems, however, followed a natural line of transition. Products transited from campus-bound computer systems of the 1980s and were already sitting on the Internet. The Web pushed further with scalable opportunities that rebuilt the face of the catalog and circulation systems. In addition to significant enhancements to the look and feel of the library online, the web ILS and the arrival of electronic materials spurred advances in bibliographic description and retrieval methods. Library standards and infrastructure had to be reworked:

- **MARC and the 856 field.** The Library of Congress's Network Development and MARC Standards Office pushed on a number of fronts. Their "Guidelines for the Use of Field 856" (1999, 2003 revision), for example, relate evolving standards for the 856 field to retrieve full text and media:

  > Field 856 in the MARC 21 Bibliographic, Holdings, Authority, Classification, and Community Information formats is used for Electronic Location and Access information to an electronic resource and contains information related to the resource. The field may be used in a bibliographic or holdings record for a resource when that resource or a subset of it is available electronically. In addition, it may be used to locate and access an electronic version of a non-electronic resource described in the bibliographic record, part of the resource, or a related electronic resource.

- **Z39.50 updating.** Attempts to update database retrieval for the Web began in 1999 through the Bath Profile. The recommendation demands exact syntax in a hunt to regularize search results among different systems. The disruptive power of the Web, however, has pushed it further. ZING (Z39.50 International: Next Generation) has followed to maintain query strengths and syntax for bibliographic searching but comes with an admission of partial defeat. With it, HTTP replaces Z39.50.

> ## › Caution
>
> Though significantly enhancing the library presence on the Web, automation explorations would stealthily advance to the point of undermining or absorbing many professional librarian operations, especially in technical services.

The Web enabled unprecedented access to information and scaling services to the smallest of libraries. Spurred by federal, state, and Gates Foundation funding, the late 1990s and early twenty-first century witnessed the first stages of a virtualization of libraries. The Web and ILSs became the new norm. Vendors expanded options for HTML interfaces, branding prospects and automating all variety of services.

Electronic Publications

As discussed in chapter 3, a fundamental catalyst arose from revolutionary change to publishing and distribution channels. With the Web, users would no longer need to visit the library to read or take out desired materials. Such directions spurred opportunities and spurred new sectors of development within the library's supporting economy:

- Journals and databases led the way to dramatic conversions in library operations. The Web facilitated the appearance of database aggregators on the commercial side and the reactive rise of open-access journals on the scholarly side. Serials management and massive storage investments were overhauled in the process.
- E-books were somewhat delayed in reaching the scene but would take popular hold in the second decade of the new century.
- The Web pushed beyond print-based journals and books, opening the doors to multimedia delivery and new interactive formats.

CAMPUS AUTOMATION

One other potential reinvention trend needs to surface. The Web enveloped academic libraries in the onrush of campus computerization and a new era of

> **Tin Can API**

This interface is under development to extend SCORM beyond LMS confines. It alters dependency on shareable content objects (SCOs) for tracking individual performances within an assignment/activity. With Tin Can, the content exists external to the LMS in a type of "Learning Record Store."

accountability. 1980s automation fed into the ERPs (enterprise resource planning) systems and SISs (student information systems) of the late 1990s. Banner, Datatel, SAP, Ellucian, PeopleSoft, Jenzabar, CampusView, and similar products redefined university infrastructure and political power. Whether it chooses or not, the campus library is enmeshed in this new operational reality. Management can expect to deal with additional automation prospects and robotic ordering from financial and human resource systems.

As featured in the second half of this book, the Web also begat a revolutionary new space for engagement. The first decade of the twenty-first century gave witness to learning management systems (LMSs). Blackboard, Desire2Learn, Moodle, Sakai, and others arrived with transformative effect. With them, visits to the quadrangle could vanish from consciousness. The LMSs enabled online education—the most significant advance in higher education at least since the GI Bill and textbook model of the 1950s. Mail-based distance education was supplanted. Software could control student engagement from enrollment throughout the classroom experience. Student study was automated and made interactive. A virtual campus significantly redefined the meaning of going to college—and not necessarily to the advantage of the library.

The LMS significantly strengthened observational abilities. Classroom activities could be monitored as never before. Such prospects helped inform government and institutional drives for oversight and accountability. A new era of metrics and quantitatively driven management entered higher education.

The library must simply take interest and seek involvement in the campus LMS. Technological awareness includes acquaintance with such concepts as these:

- SCORM (Sharable Content Object Reference Model) set the scene for the mature integration of LMSs and web-based e-learning. Like much of the enabling technologies, this XML-based specification emerged under the aegis of the Department of Defense. SCORM allowed LMSs and e-learning programs to "play nice." Package interchange sequencing regulates such elements as fixed training paths, bookmarking progress, multiple user address/resetting of the same materials, and testing applications—that is, the QTI (question test interface). APIs (application program interfaces) are set in place to interface between add-on applications and the LMS.

- Common cartridge/learning technology interface (LTI). On the more speculative side, IMS Global is attempting to package SCORM-compliant specifications to simplify the creation and exchange of online educational activities and materials. Fortunately, the organization has proved amenable to academic library participation, with a dedicated subgroup formed in 2010. Its plug-and-play modular concept could obviate the need for APIs and thus facilitate the integration of library services on the virtual campus. As indicated on the LTI home page:

> LTI specification is to allow the seamless connection of web-based, externally hosted applications and content, or Tools (from simple communication applications like chat, to domain-specific learning environments for complex subjects like math or science) to platforms that present them to users. In other words, if you have an interactive assessment application or virtual chemistry lab, it can be securely connected to an educational platform in a standard way without having to develop and maintain custom integrations for each platform.

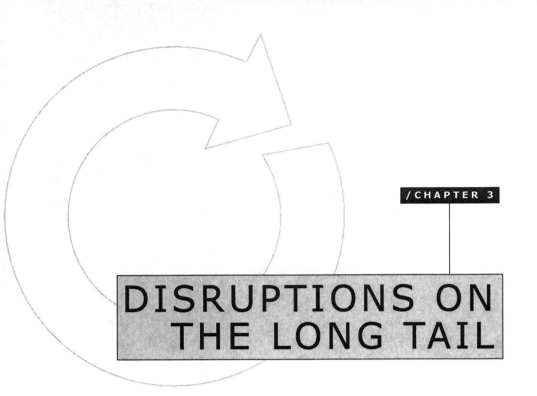

CHAPTER 3

DISRUPTIONS ON THE LONG TAIL

TO PARAPHRASE POLITICAL ANALYST JAMES CARVILLE, "It's the economy, librarian." Web reinvention on the technical side proves relatively straightforward, financial adaptation far more troublesome. Library mindsets rooted in communal and scholarly ideals engage at the dawn of a dramatically different era. Industrial-age commitments, nationalistic imperatives, and state support wither. Modern business models and government oversight increasingly intrude on the ivory tower. Like the printing press and capitalism, the latest communications revolution is transforming fiscal policy. Repositories must come to grips with a different and increasingly global economy, one that involves an elemental inversion:

- **From a public good.** In the old, information services were embraced as part of the public good or tolerated as overhead for doing business.
- **To a commodity.** In the new, information becomes "The" business. A revamping economy is based on intellectual property rights. Materials once relegated to libraries can be transformed into products for monetization.

A new global information economy thus joins technology and the historical narrative as discussion pilings within rough seas. The library as institution needs to be ready for a hard ride. The marketplace is unbelievably choppy. Academic library survival demands conscious engagement within economically perilous fiscal waters. Expect to encounter old and new forces. Each can be simultaneous friend, foe, and partner—but nothing can be ignored.

WEB MACROECONOMICS

Two post-McLuhan economic theories offer valuable insights to help transit as yet uncharted and developing macroeconomic oceans.

LONG TAIL

Chris Anderson, editor-in-chief of *Wired* magazine, authored his seminal "Long Tail" editorial on the heels of web commercialization in 2004. Anderson visualized the end sections of a Gaussian bell curve as a forecasting engine for a different type of economy. Thanks to the Web, geographic limitations elongated into a worldwide marketplace. Long arms stretched to vast and previously inconceivable buying power.

> ### ❯ Economic Theory of the Public Good
>
> Battlegrounds are being joined. Nobel laureate Paul A. Samuelson provides quantifiable fodder to better inform the debate. In 1954 he established the concept of the "public good" in economics through the landmark "The Pure Theory of Public Expenditure." As indicated in this chapter, the value of the concept is diminished by challenges from the external marketplace and internal changes in university administration. In *Under New Management: Universities, Administrative Labor, and the Professional Turn*, Randy Martin (2011) chastises the latter for an unsettling shift away from "public" to "private" good. In such environments, the value of education, information resources, and library-type services is juxtaposed against privatized returns and susceptible to marginalization. Education per se washes away in a narrow drive for trade school training. The essence of the university is threatened and the wisdom of Sorbonne ignored.

Anderson's approach rested on a corollary of "intensively interested" virtual communities. He contrasted Long Tail opportunities with the "hit-driven" of the music industry of the early 1990s. The Web proffered a game changer. With it, production, storage, and distribution costs became trivial. Moreover, the medium enabled globally-based audiences. Economies of scale were thus redefined. "Hits and misses" could ironically be placed on equal economic footing. Anderson (2004) readily extended this concept to the older book market:

> What's really amazing about the Long Tail is the sheer size of it. Combine enough nonhits on the Long Tail and you've got a market bigger than the hits. Take books: The average Barnes & Noble carries 130,000 titles. Yet more than half of Amazon's book sales come from outside its top 130,000 titles. Consider the implication: If the Amazon statistics are any guide, the market for books that are not even sold in the average bookstore is larger than the market for those that are. . . . In other words, the potential book market may be twice as big as it appears to be, if only we can get over the economics of scarcity.

DISRUPTIVE INNOVATION

Clayton Christensen, Clark Professor of Business Administration at Harvard University, promulgated the second idea—disruptive innovation. In a series of books beginning in the late 1990s, Christensen argues that the medium inherently upsets underlying assumptions in the extant economy. The Web is destined to open sectors that were previously isolated from competition because of their complicated, expensive, and relatively inaccessible natures. It enables the affordable dispersal of information products and services. New capacities foster innovation and invite entrepreneurs. With the Web, even the best run of the old economy faces serious pressures and potential obsolescence.

Christensen broadened his model to higher education from boots-on-the-ground exposure as a consultant for Southern New Hampshire University. As he and his collaborators (2011) warn in the introduction of *Disrupting College:*

> The theory of disruptive innovation has significant explanatory power in thinking through the challenges and changes confronting higher education. A disruptive innovation has a couple key elements or enablers that are particularly salient to the future of higher education.
> . . . The first is a technology enabler. This allows the innovation . . . by serving people—who were not able to be served or were not desirable to serve—to be "upwardly scalable" and improve year over year without replicating the cost structure of the old products and services it gradually replaces.

. . . The second element of a disruptive innovation is a business model innovation. Disruptive innovations are plugged into new models, which allow organizations to serve a job to be done in the lives of customers at this new lower price point or in this new, far more convenient fashion without extra cost. Plugging a disruptive innovation into an existing business model never results in transformation of the model; instead, the existing model co-opts the innovation to sustain how it operates.

PUBLICATION MARKETPLACE

The importance of library monitoring, engagement, and search for alternatives has not been greater since Gutenberg. Nowhere is interest clearer than with publishing—nowhere too is the market more confused or opposition more apparent. Despite inevitability and financial streams, today's Web continues to frighten and confuse publishers. As they recognize, the means of production and distribution have been thoroughly disrupted. Amazon and self-publishing threaten loss of control. Marketing tactics seem strangely conflicted. Traditionalists find it difficult to understand sales by "giving away" electronic content and relying on advertising to replace or augment sales revenue. Strange demands for web "discovery" and metadata vie for their interest. Narrow profit motives and shortsightedness continue to exacerbate.

CORPORATE BACKGROUND

Some publisher problems predate the Web. In the final decades of the twentieth century, the industry became enveloped in a series of corporate takeovers. These prefaced communication problems for academia. Newfangled media conglomerates inclined away from scholarly editorial delights and a shared sense of social responsibility. Financial accountability and unfettered profit pushed to ascendancy.

Number-crunching leadership seems to have defaulted with a conservative technological bent. In the 1980s, microcomputers and word processing were granted grudging entrance. The potential of SGML was ignored, as was recognition of the Web. The late twentieth century ended as a wash in terms of a digital book market.

Book publishers remained in denial into the middle of the first decade of the new century. Amazon and its Kindle e-reader altered their reality. On arrival,

› SGML: Lost Opportunity

In one of the earliest SGML DTD (document type definition) initiatives, the Association of American Publisher's (AAP) Electronic Manuscript Project engaged some thirty information-related organizations including the American Chemical Society, American Institute of Physics, American Society of Indexers, American Mathematical Society, Council of Biology Editors, Council on Library Resources, and Library of Congress. As indicated by the SGML History Group (Spiro and Henry 2010), "From 1983 to 1987, an APA committee, chaired by Nicholas Alter of University Microfilms, developed an initial SGML application for book, journal, and article creation. The application is intended for manuscript interchange between authors and their publishers, among other uses, and includes optional element definitions for complex tables and scientific formulas."

awakening came with paranoia firmly in evidence. Fears of piracy and desires for control led to a mishmash of electronic readers, high-level DRM controls, and distrust of standards. Despite the delay, positive financial impact soon proved undeniable. A minor $2.3 million proposition in 2005 exploded to $119.7 million in 2010. In that pivotal year, Apple's iPad tablet computer effectively sealed the deal. E-book reading became publically accepted and demanded. The promise is double- and triple-digit growth for years to come.

According to Aptara's annual e-book survey (2011), two-thirds of American publishing embraced e-books by 2010 with another 25 percent committed to join. Yet production methods remain strangely retrograde. PDF page-image files and basic word processors dominate the composition room. XML approaches from the late 1990s are a bit rare and often outsourced to such companies as Vital Source, CourseSmart, or CourseLoad. The budding HTML5-based EPUB 3 standard seems to be receiving more lip service than commitment.

Publishers, vendors, and copyright holders are in the midst of a massive web-induced shakeout—one replete with crucial subtext for libraries:

- Pricing models are in flux, with lower per-unit costs for individuals, higher library licensing, pay-for-view similar to the recording industry, and timed rentals among the options.
- Not unlike the music business, publishers are discovering Long Tail value in the conversion of backlists. Modern titles may never go out of print.
- In addition to Apple's hardware and Amazon, Wal-Mart and other web-based competition enter the scene with disruptive pricing pressures.

- Though Amazon remains by far the biggest point of sale, publisher financial interests begin to push toward their own distribution sites.
- Land-based bookstores—Borders, for instance—begin to falter and fail.
- Embargos on mass-market trade volumes and paperbacks are removed for e-books sales—but likely to play a role for library acquisitions.
- Texts are "decoupled" for chapter extraction and payment by segment.
- Electronic sampling and complete free versions of the text emerge as marketing devices for hard copy sales or with distribution underwritten by advertising revenues.
- Self-publishing rises along with innovative shorter-format firms, such as Atavist and Byliner, as well as alternative marketing/distribution approaches from booksellers and publishers.
- Brookings Institute and other think tanks extend from print to electronic publishing and are joined by a growing host of web offspring such as the Huffington Post news service.
- Open-access options become increasingly viable, often tied to print-on-demand for revenue prospects.

TRADE BOOKS

Popular-reading trade books reflect the largest and most problematic sector of the industry for the sister field of public libraries in terms of e-book access. Although publishers see lost revenues with each checkout, the libraries are on an access mission for their communities. OverDrive stepped to the front as a key intermediary agent, along with welcomed competition from services through Barnes and Noble's Nook reader. Despite those and library engagement efforts, publishers remained wary, boycotts threatened, and communications confused.

Globalization accentuated publishers' economic blinders. Modern trade publishing had evolved with a decidedly international cast—one without historical affinity to the legacy of the public library, the right of first sale, or understanding of fair use. Unlike the

> **> Public Library Buffers in the Web Economy**
>
> Despite the electronic access contretemps, public libraries are well positioned and provide object lessons to help weather the revolution. Rather than holdings, they trend toward the delivery of services and librarian-centric operations. The public library comes with a sense of client awareness, feistiness, and community involvement that is vital to future sustainability.

unity of purpose that arose after World War I, twenty-first-century American librarians encounter an internationalized "Big Six American houses":

- Hachette Book Group USA (HBGUSA) boasts a U.S. pedigree that dates to 1837 with Little, Brown and Company but is part of a French company of the same name.
- HarperCollins has become a subsidiary of Australian Rupert Murdoch's News Corporation. It appears among the most recalcitrant in terms of public library access to electronic versions.
- Macmillan is now owned by the German Holtzbrinck Company, albeit with its interesting origins from a post–World War II book club.
- Penguin Group is the second-largest trade publisher and a division of the British Pearson conglomerate, which is also the world's largest educational publisher.
- Random House of Bennett Cerf fame has become part of the German Bertelsmann firm and currently is the largest house.
- Simon and Schuster sits alone under American ownership, but it has also drifted from print origins into the media domain of the CBS Corporation.

ALA rose in defense. It dispatched a delegation to Penguin, Macmillan, Random House, and Simon and Schuster in January 2012. As indicated within American Libraries' "E-content: The Digital Dialogue" (ALA 2012) supplement, the association faced a daunting task. Initial negotiations in March under ALA president Molly Raphael broke down. Librarians and publishers were not speaking the same language. Publishers remained adamant about their right to profit, control of digital distribution in the face of an Amazon, and worries over their own continued existence. Yet ALA and public libraries persisted with sophisticated advocacy efforts. Publishers also appear to have realized the value of their traditional relations along with "Pay-to-Buy" buttons and other advertising opportunities from library partnerships. Compromises thus emerged in the five months since the November 2012 submission of a draft for this book. With Simon and Schuster's April 15, 2013, announcement, all the Big Six had agreed in principle to

> ### > Random House/Penguin News
>
> As this manuscript heads out the door to ALA Editions, news arrives of a merger of Random House and Penguin. Pearson will take the lead in the new partnership with Bertelsmann. The proposed union will produce the world's largest trade producer. Indicators suggest a combined effort in reaction to the Web and for bargaining leverage with Amazon.

the presence of electronic editions of trade books in public libraries, but implementation details still await.

Universities and trade publishers. With the exception of student pleasure-reading collections and respite for cost-conscious literature students, university libraries have heretofore maintained limited involvement with the trade press. The Web is changing such matters. Public and academic libraries are destined to overlap with electronic publications.

Electronic access to anthologies and modern literary works under study harkens to Sorbonne. As discussed in part B of this book, related opportunities arise through scanning/electronic publishing for materials out of copyright and the gray zone of orphaned works. The trade press itself takes the lead in terms of experimental offerings. It is a locus for development from shorter formats to media inserts and interactive scenarios. Trade publishers are also at the front in support controls and lobbying for extra protection under legislation, with such proposals as the Stop Online Piracy Act and the PROTECT IP Act. They are at the heart of the drumbeat for profits from copyright over the public's right to know. Keep in mind too their role as a trial horse for pricing—for example, Harper-Collins's efforts to set a limit on the number of e-book checkouts.

TEXTBOOKS

Textbook publishers merit enhanced attention and wariness. This sector adeptly expanded its presence from a base with the GI Bill. Publishers successfully nurtured textbook dependency as the teaching model for the second half of the twentieth century. Polished products and free review and desk copies with chapters mapped to weekly curricular calendars continue to entice a loyal faculty following.

Universities were complicit in the process. They blithely passed costs to the student. This process furthered their own bottom lines, with campus bookstore profits reportedly averaging over 25 percent. Academic libraries joined in self-destructive directions. Overwhelmed with their own challenges from the GI Bill and comfortable in research bents, they overlooked the legacy of Sorbonne. Repositories tolerated and lent qualified support to textbook implementations.

Enterprising students and bookstores found a way to intrude partially into publisher profit picture: the semester ritual of used book sales. Such endeavors erode over 60 percent of potential return from new books. Publisher concerns over that lost revenue remained vaguely complacent until the conglomerates arrived. Pricing increases would double the rate of inflation in the mid-1980s.

They spiked, however, with the Web. The millennium witnessed a pattern of ever faster editions updates, new features, and inflationary spirals.

Despite widely publicized student protests, congressional investigations, and a legislative mandate for transparency—companies persist in their right to high profits. Kelly Gallagher's (2011) presentation within the unsubtly titled "Making Information Pay for Higher Education" conference for the Book Industry Study Group confirms such directions. As seen in figure 3.1, transactions escalated from $5.7 billion in 2005 to a $7.3 billion dollar proposition in 2010, with dramatic lockstep price rises for both new and used books.

The gentleman's agreement appears in flux, and academic libraries should be on alert. Textbook publishers exhibit a well-meaning hubris and aggressiveness on their knowledge and ability to satisfy the information needs of college curriculums. They readily discount or overlook academic library resources. The Web drives this Big Four to compete unconsciously with academic libraries:

- Cengage's MindTap pushes toward the ideal of personalized learning environments. This cloud-based portal can integrate e-textbooks,

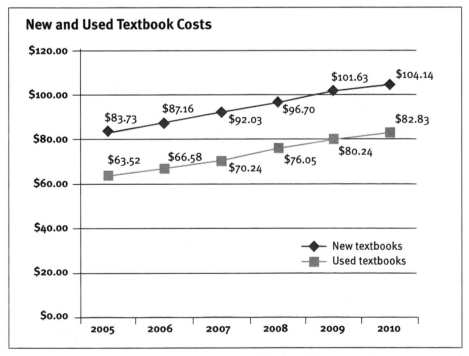

figure 3.1 New and used textbook costs, 2005–2010 (after Gallagher 2011)

homework help, media assets, and so forth into embrace of the six hundred library databases from the Gale division.

- McGraw-Hill has been active with Blackboard's LMS and as seen in figure 3.2 is making sure faculty have "trusted, relevant online and digital resources" in competition with academic libraries.
- Pearson's Aptara platform is arguably the most powerful current product. The company is involved in a push for industry-wide upgrades, including adoption of EPUB 3 and ADA 508 compliance measures. It also offers a library-like suite of materials and the digital repository prospects of

---

Enhance Teaching With Unlimited Access to McGraw Hill Content

Faculty have long complained about the difficulty in finding trusted, relevant online and digital resources. No more. Now, McGraw-Hill makes it quick and easy for ALL faculty to find just the right resource, at no additional cost.

See why over 100 schools have already signed up for McGraw-Hill's new digital resource platform.

Register for this webcast to hear leaders from Ohio University, Indiana State and Mt. Wachusett Community College discuss why they selected MH Campus to enhance teaching and learning on their campuses.

Don't miss this webcast to hear how you can:

- Streamline access to digital resources on your campus
- Support ALL your faculty, regardless of which textbook publisher they use
- Give unlimited resource access at no additional cost to your faculty, institution, and students
- Avoid any hassle for your technology team, with quick, simple connection into multiple learning management systems

Engage today's students and enrich your courses with McGraw-Hill content. See how MH Campus seamlessly connects with your institution to provide faculty one-click access to McGraw-Hill's vast library of e-books, associated slide presentations, test banks, multimedia tools and more.

Presented by:

- J. Brice Bible, *chief information officer, Ohio University*
- Kelly Wilkinson, *Ph.D., director, Center for Instruction, Research, and Technology, Indiana State University*
- Vincent Ialenti, *Ed.D., dean of academic and institutional technology, Mount Wachusett Community College*
- Isaac Segal, *president, McGraw-Hill Tegrity and MH Campus*

Moderated by: Matt Villano, *senior contributing editor, Campus Technology*

REGISTER NOW

figure 3.2 McGraw-Hill e-mail advertisement (E-mail solicitation received by author)

Equella: "One system to house your teaching and learning, research, media and library content."
- Wiley-Blackwell's Wiley Online Library includes access to its run of 1,500 scholarly journals and approximately 10,000 volumes. The Wiley Plus product links electronic texts with media resources and tools for instructors and students as a single-source classroom experience.

Other players on the textbook tail. The Big Four are not alone in meriting scrutiny. A variety of old and new players could threaten or assist library ends:

- **Copyright clearance.** Operations like the Copyright Clearance Center and CourseWare help simplify the organization and distribution of copyrighted materials in classrooms. These interests also gain vested interests in limiting fair use that extend to a willingness to go to court for enforcement and work against library budgets.
- **Distributors.** Follett and MBS have web initiatives that may compete with libraries. For example, MBS (Cormier 2010) ignored library holdings to announce the Xplana database as the "world's largest collection of online learning materials. . . . How does Xplana plan to conquer the world of online, social learning? Xplana will focus their efforts on content, the desire for students to connect with one another and provide a one-stop shop for a student's online learning needs."
- **Library database vendors.** As I write and in addition to pricing exploitation, Elsevier appears to be positioning its own LMS. EBSCO and ProQuest are well posed to also push forward into the classroom space.
- **Rental/library options.** CourseSmart and India's KopyKitab.com belong to a new sector of electronic rental and purchasing options that are independent of publisher controls. Such enterprises and a firm like Books24/7 are willing to break ranks and offer library packages.
- **Alternative textbook producers.** As also reported in the discussion of the open-access movement in this chapter, publisher dominance is under assault by new web-based entrepreneurs:

> **> Author's Disclosure**
>
> I engage in extensive and mutually beneficial transactions with each of the Big Four along with many of the smaller houses. Such activities include travel and entertainment encounters. Financial involvement also extends to a seat on the advisory board for Cengage's MindTap, as a Pearson author, and as editor for a Wiley journal.

Apple and Microsoft are bridging from their technological base to enter the textbook publishing space. Flat World is an interesting hybrid with commercialization of the open-access textbook market; the for-profit began free digital textbooks but pay-for-print options. (Note: Based on a phone call from the company in October 2012, the financial model appears to have run into difficulties and Flat World will be turning to low-cost pricing.) Kno is an electronically launched attempt in line with efforts by textbook publishers to push beyond the print model with encompassing layers of information.

SCHOLARLY PUBLISHING

Academic library involvement is clearest with this third sector. Scholarly publishing implies peer review and the doctoral-level research/publishing nexus. Engagement continues largely along a nineteenth-century divide between journals and monographic literature. Academic libraries remain the main customers and primary economic reason for the sector's existence. Herein lies a rub and roots of the current crisis in scholarly publishing. Budget woes mean libraries cannot afford to underwrite the sector. As sales retreat, presses cut back on the size of runs. That works to the detriment of their bottom lines but also endangers prospects for scholars.

Monographic literature. Technological confusion is greatest and web implementations the weakest in the scholarly book market. This arena is the provenance of a handful of commercial presses and myriad university-sponsored versions. Readers face a multiplicity of e-book readers or outdated PDF versioning. Pricing seems out of synch, especially for interlibrary loan (ILL).

Commercial presses. Such operations have been present on the monographic scene since its birth with Aldus Manutius and the humanists. Today's production is frequently funneled through smaller specialized houses—Scarecrow on the library side or boutique brands within larger conglomerates such as Palgrave

› Chegg: Social Education Platform

The highly successful web textbook rental firm has rebranded itself. Chegg went on a buying spree and accumulated a variety of companies that tune to the students and their learning experience with interestingly disruptive prospect. Its spiders crawl the Web to mine online course catalogs. The system tries to know what books will be required in advance. Its Cramster tutorial service retains a horde of on-call subject specialists in India. The Notehall marketplace facilitates the sale and exchange of notes or other course materials.

> **Web Mashups**

The Web threatens to splinter the book/journal order. Paper-based distinctions are now blurring. Praeger Security, Janes, and other specialized databases joined the like of Columbia University's CIAO with all-embracing electronic products. The future unfolds with information-driven mashups—knowledge centers of electronic articles, books, primary source materials, media, and Web 2.0 communications.

(Bertelsmann), Blackwell (Wiley), and Routledge (Taylor and Francis). As seen in figure 3.3, Long Tail differentiations are beginning to make inroads. Freed from the need for warehousing, distribution centers, and large print runs, startup e-publishing firms are taking an interest in reaching "a specific niche of people who have an intense interest in a certain narrow field of information."

University presses. Academic entanglements are centered on university presses. The most conflicted arena in publishing, they may be exacerbating the crisis. The library purchaser frequently encounters a sense of entitlement. University presses may instead need reminders of history. Libraries were seminal in their birth and in a few instances may continue to be in charge of operations. They share a joint mission in the hidden economy that emerged with the PhD and research universities. Libraries must be recognized as the major customers and a major reason for the existence—as well as the future—of university presses.

Specialized Publishing: Taking Hold of the Book Market and Taking Off

SPEAKERS

Tuesday, July 26, 2011
2:00 p.m. ET/11:00 a.m. PT

The word "specialized" applies to both ends of the equation: the information being published and the audience for which it is being published.

Whether it's NASCAR, art, or topics of a more professional nature (accounting, law, medicine) – specialized-information publishing is designed to reach a specific niche of people who have an intense interest in a certain narrow field of information.

The idea? The companies or individuals that make up these specialty markets are usually willing to pay more for highly targeted information that they want or, in some cases, need.

This webinar will explore the opportunities surrounding specialized publishing applications including:
- Defining specialized publishing products
- Finding your niche
- B2C and B2B opportunities
- New methods to monetize specialized publishing programs
- The changing print and digital landscape …

Dale Williams
Vice President, Operations & Technical Sales
SCI

Chris Greene
President
CGX Publishing Solutions

Andy Mclaughlin
President and CEO
PaperClip Communications

MODERATOR

Barb Pellow
Group Director
InfoTrends

figure 3.3 New methods to monetize specialized publishing programs (E-mail solicitation received by author)

With the notable exceptions of Cambridge and Oxford, university presses dug an early hole in the web revolution. They remain backward in terms of technology and marketing for the new age. Presses continue to cling to print formats even as readers move to the electronic. As late as the fall of 2010, a special edition of the *Journal of Electronic Publishing* on adapting to the Web resulted in defensive reaction and support of the status quo. Technophobia and over-commitment to the research monograph continue as operative in the face of declining fortunes.

External criticism has been sharp. Laura Brown et al. (2007) in *University Publishing in a Digital Age* see drift from the core mission. In *Planned Obsolescence: Publishing, Technology, and the Future of the Academy*, Kathleen Fitzpatrick adds perspective from her position as director of scholarly communications at the Modern Languages Association. She includes a pointed call for librarians in an interestingly titled "Academic Publishing and Zombies" interview for *Inside Higher Ed* (Kolowich 2011):

> To the university librarian: help fight for the acceptance of new modes of scholarly communication by collaborating on new digital publishing projects with the university press, by creating structures to support faculty experimentation with new modes of production and dissemination, and by helping gather the data about usage and response that will help faculty members demonstrate the influence of their work. Getting involved with faculty projects at the outset will also help you create a plan for their preservation. I'd also encourage the university librarian to open a frank conversation about the costs of resources and the limitations placed on their access.

University presses have appeared as blindly driven for returns as some of their commercial counterparts. For instance, the American Association of University Presses (AAUP) supported attacks against library course reserves in *Cambridge University Press, Oxford University Press, Sage Publications v. Georgia State University* (2012). The organization failed to recognize conflicts between its rights to profit and serving as part of the support mechanism for the university community. It persisted in this line even after the landmark decision in favor of libraries and fair use.

Yet hope exists. The AAUP demonstrates some awakening to its membership's cooperation with academic libraries and need for discussions. On their part, academic libraries have not been complacent. They have inserted reminders of

> **Research Works Act: Slamming Open Access**

Though progress can be noted, relations remain unsettled. In December 2011, university presses returned to their near-sighted way of a protectionist Research Works Act. The bill seeks to prohibit federal agencies and nongovernment contractors from publicly disseminating government-sponsored research findings. The agencies would be forbidden to build their own internal archives for such materials as unfair competitive practices.

their financial clout, but also to impart web savvy. In February 2007, the AAUP "Policy Brief on Open Access" offered hesitant retreat. Later in that year, the ITHAKA-sponsored *University Publishing in a Digital Age* by Laura Brown et al. (2007) ignited a minor cooperative spark. Several years later, the AAUP Task Force on Economic Models for Scholarly Publishing (AAUP 2011) acknowledged the dawn of a new market, one with undeniable impact on cherished gatekeeper functions: "When financial constraints are removed—when any and everything can be 'published'—different forces come into play. The challenge for the scholarly enterprise is to ensure that the best characteristics of selectivity, enrichment, authority, and imprimatur can be retained in the hyperabundant landscape, where market forces no longer dictate a particular kind of limit."

The Task Force report stresses renewed cooperation and communication. The AAUP followed to launch a directory service of collaborative publishing ventures among presses, libraries, and research centers. The document displays awareness of librarian drives for preservation, a noncommercial ethos, and the importance of unfettered access to materials. Previously decried open-access models are reexamined in cooperative spirit.

A selection of university presses has stepped forward with innovative self-preservation measures. The University of Rochester looks to prospects for translations in its "Three Percent" solution. The University of Northern Georgia embraces textbooks and even rental options. Copublishing with libraries emerges as a parallel interest, including advanced electronic production platforms:

- Rice University, which disestablished its press in 1996, returned a decade later with a fully electronic operation and Connexions e-publication services.
- University Press Scholarship Online made its entrance in the fall of 2011. This Oxford University Press e-book venture involves American University in Cairo Press, Fordham University Press, Hong Kong University

Press, University Press of Florida, and the University Press of Kentucky, and Edinburgh University Press.

- University Publishing Online from Cambridge University Press was scheduled at roughly the same time as the Oxford endeavor. It came with the announced participation of Foundation Books India, Liverpool University Press, and the Mathematical Association of America.
- Project MUSE Book Collection is in motion with plans for 14,000 titles from sixty-six university and scholarly presses. The press announcement declared searchable and downloadable PDFs with unlimited usage and no DRM.
- Books at JSTOR debuted in mid-2012 with perhaps thirty publishers and input from major libraries, including the latter's need for enhanced discovery to reach scholarly journals.

> ### › E-book Distributors
>
> E-book availability and potential competition come through new entrants to the library economy. Such companies as ebrary, NetLibrary, and Questia act as intermediaries to offer a wide range of web-based library e-books and e-book collections. These come with often highly sophisticated OPAC-like interfaces and cloud delivery. The new sector is being joined by tailored offerings from other sectors, such as ACLS's Humanities Library and Alexander Street Press. Their efforts manifest as a new type of independent library for web consumers.

Scholarly Journals

In what comes as no surprise, this part of the library-dependent economy has advantages and disadvantages. Due in no small part to the acumen of such aggregators as EBSCO and ProQuest, journal distribution is more technologically sophisticated than its monographic counterpart. Relations are enhanced by university underwriting of learned societies and their publications, such as Indiana University's ties to the journals of the American Historical Association and Organization of American Historians.

We arrive at a major fount for financial tensions. From the birth of scholarly journals in the seventeenth century and their nineteenth-century takeoff, library interests continued in the communal line of a Sorbonne. They committed to the precapitalistic mission for cooperative research and shared advancement of knowledge.

Matters turned entrepreneurial in the aftermath of publisher consolidations. Elsevier was among the early and most egregious entrants. It made a calculated and profitable push to grab control of major scientific journals. That move was followed by pricing at "disproportionally expensive" levels for the library community. Such practices earned the ire of universities from Duke and Harvard to Stanford. The company remained steadfast against such complaints, even threatening to sue libraries that did not subscribe to its journals and recently disengaging from prominent receptions at ALA.

Discussion should not be overly simplified. On one hand, the American Psychological Association, American Chemical Society, and a small selection of associations also appear entranced by monetary rewards for their publications. Monetary considerations increasingly seek to push beyond the base of library purchasing and into underwriting from authors. On the other hand, publisher underwriting remains important for sustaining quality and enhanced access to many scholarly periodicals. Even profitable commercial publishers can prove reasonable, and new players are emerging:

- Wiley, among the oldest commercial houses, partners with approximately 750 scholarly societies with some 1,500 peer-reviewed journals. In 2012, Wiley turned to open access for it electronic delivery component.
- Gale is a part of the Cengage brand and offers over 600 journals as well as a variety of reference works.
- Berkeley Electronic Press (bepress) represents a new generation of web-based journals. Founded by professors in 1999, it hosts approximately 150 titles on its open-access Digital Commons. Libraries and consortia such as Rhode Island's HELIN employ its services for their digital collections and the external storage and curation of electronic resources.

> Profit Margin Note

As seen with a number of closings, university and smaller presses struggle within the new economic climate. Despite their fears, the larger publishers and some of scholarly societies appear to have been doing very nicely. An examination of recent SEC 10-K filings and annual reports reveals:

- Reed Elsevier, academic and medical division, revenues of $3.16 billion with pretax profits of $1.3 billion for a gross profit margin of 36 percent in 2010
- Wiley, academic publishing division, revenues of $987 million with pretax profits of $405 million for a gross profit margin of 41 percent in 2010
- American Chemical Society, a not-for-profit, with 2009 publication revenues of $460 million

- **Nonprofit library economy.** As discussed shortly, the disruptive forces of the Web also enable the open-access movement as a counterweight to commercial presses. The library world's electronic preservation efforts (see chapter 2) spawned allied forces on the "semi-nonprofit" side. Enterprising agents within research universities and the library community took their stewardship responsibilities and web opportunities in hand:

- Project MUSE began as a joint university press/library initiative in 1993 at Johns Hopkins University under the innovative eye of James Neal. The Mellon Foundation provided seed funding along with support from the National Endowment for the Humanities. MUSE's hosting platform offers e-books and alternative journal subscription options.
- JSTOR similarly used Mellon Foundation support for its 1995 launch. Now joined with ITHAKA, the service responded to web-based demands from research libraries to address long-term storage and electronic access to journal literature. Its collections engage thousands of libraries across over 160 countries. A "moving wall" helps embargo newer materials from licensed archival contents. JSTOR also expanded preservation into cooperative agreements with a growing number of book publishers. Equally important, Google trawls its articles; the results heighten student requests and confusion for retrieval under the JSTOR brand.
- HathiTrust Digital Library began with a small group of leading research universities and libraries. They parlayed Google's interest in digitizing their massive collections as a mechanism to gain their own digital duplicates. The Trust also extended its digitization efforts and partnership opportunities in a variety of ways. The October 2012 announcement of victory in *Authors Guild v. HathiTrust* could indicate a seed change for the future of library engagement. The Trust has come away with distribution controls over the Google Book project's electronic legacy.

REFERENCE BOOKS

The Web is at its most menacing for reference publishing. University budgets are shrinking at the same time as demand for such material is decreasing and its prices escalating. Moreover, the Web intrudes with ubiquitous and free access. Search-engine driven discovery of Wikipedia and other open-source resources readily captures and satisfies most student and faculty interest. Can libraries continue in good conscience to underwrite this $3 billion a year industry?

The ABC-CLIOs, CQ Presses, Facts-on-Files, and other purveyors are well aware of possible obsolescence. In "The Future of Reference Publishing," Schlager's Blog (May 3, 2009) notes:

> For too long—decades now, really—reference publishers have pumped out a cascade of books (and now databases) but done very little to address a fundamental problem: discoverability. Reference books have always required a conduit—the librarian. . . . The familiar library convention discussion group topic—"Is Print Reference Dying?"—is both mordantly funny and also terrifyingly legitimate. The truth is that lots of print reference is still published and bought, but most of the new stuff joins its ancestors—it sits on a shelf, unused. . . . The situation is only modestly better with electronic reference.
>
> What have reference publishers done to address these longstanding problems? We've stuck our heads in the sand. As long as libraries were buying our products, we didn't worry our pretty little heads over something as pedestrian as usage. We may have spent ungodly amounts of time and money to produce one wonderful set after another, but as long as enough libraries bought our titles, we didn't care. We had decades to come up with user-friendly solutions to the problems of discoverability and usage, but we couldn't be bothered.

EMERGENT MARKET

The Long Tail economy bequeaths threats and publishing prospects beyond those mentioned above. Textbook publishers intrude with their own digital assets. Other entrepreneurs push library-type services. Search engines replace the reference core. Cloud-based operations remove internal housing for collections. New applications ingest digital copies and catalog personal libraries. Content farming and "scraping"—reusing information gleaned from earlier web postings—birth research business sites like eHow and WikiHow. Small startups vie with Apple and Microsoft giants in efforts that can cooperate with or adversely affect the library. In the words of Paul Courant (2006), the University of Michigan's innovative director of libraries:

> In the world of Google, we have an interesting challenge. We need to show
> the broader world, as well as our own communities, that our way of col-
> lecting . . . really is of value. Not only to scholars but to others who will
> care about the reliability and meaning of the cultural record. Only librar-
> ians know how to do this. One of our institutional imperatives is to make
> plain its value. If we fail, we are at risk for losing access to our own history.

Amazon joins Google as primary examples from the postprint, web economy
for library surveillance. Both web giants bring unquestioned excellence and
undeniable strength as allies. At the same time, they are worrisome predators—
competitors that have reached the status of world library.

AMAZON

Launching at the very start of the commercial web, Amazon has become the
world's top online vendor. A brilliant "my portal" site revamps the Web from
bulletin-board presentations to an interactive, personalized service zone. Amazon's profiling of users and proactive responses to their perceived desires offer
seductive power. Hampered by privacy laws and legacy software, even the best
of contemporary library systems can only struggle to match such a personalized
face of the future.

Amazon has also effectively conquered modern publishing. Its Kindle was the
major goad pushing publishers into digital realms. Given the company's market
share, almost all new offerings must now engage an electronic option. Despite
collusive efforts by Apple and mainstream publishers, recent court decisions
affirm its position as the major price setter for books. In addition, the company
offers competitive vanity press/print-on-demand services as well as its own publishing lines under Amazon Publishing operations.

Amazon's dominance foments challenges for libraries. On one hand, Amazon
extended library-based e-loans and Kindle downloads in 2011. Libraries must
thus consider loaning Kindle appliances and dealing with its proprietary reader.
On the other hand, the company announced the availability of its own competitive textbook and popular reading rental programs along with a personalized
cloud library. By January 2012, the lending program was engaging 300,000
volumes a month from a library of 75,000 titles.

GOOGLE

The mixed message and competition theme continues with one of the world's
most enlightened corporations. Following its 1998 start, the Google search

engine quickly took the world by storm. A deceptively simple query box, relevance metrics, and full-text coverage advanced library research methods. Users were also quickly spoiled. For them, "discovery" and the power of full-text searching natively outstripped library bibliographic methods.

The Google Books initiative provides a related example of transformative powers and contradictory complexities. Digitization negotiations with the lead research libraries helped birth HathiTrust, which would gain intriguing prospects from its control of a duplicate set of volumes. Yet historian and Harvard librarian Robert Darton (2010) proffers overriding dangers in a cautionary "Jeremiad":

> Google represents the ultimate in business plans. By controlling access to information, it has made billions, which it is now investing in the control of the information itself. What began as Google Book Search is therefore becoming the largest library and book business in the world. Like all commercial enterprises, Google's primary responsibility is to make money for its shareholders. Libraries exist to get books to readers—books and other forms of knowledge and entertainment, provided for free.

Despite legal setbacks on the Books project in 2011, Google continues to press on multiple fronts of library interest. Digitization ventures at the British Museum overlap with Google publishing and side agreements with publishers, such as the Hachette Group for French back titles. Libraries need to stay abreast of those and a seemingly ceaseless set of moves, such as:

- Google Correlate search option, which allows for comparison views of a term and phrases related to it by other searchers and joins frequency searching across the Google Books database as potential new areas of scholarship.
- Google Search Plus Your World, a major 2012 revamping of the search engine functionality that adds contextual searching options mapped to the individual.
- Ownership of YouTube and the provision of its massive media stocks
- Linking with leading German universities into a new academic research institute.
- WebGL Bookcase, with 3D imaging that can hold thousands of volumes in a personalized bookshelf of Google Books.

OPEN-ACCESS MOVEMENT

The Long Tail and disruptive nature of the Web enabled a countermovement that had begun with the Internet. By the close of the 1990s, American universities were adding a new approach in their struggle against the inflationary costs of journal literature. Why should they pay again for research conducted and financed under their auspices? Twenty-first-century universities reacted with requests and mandates for professors to retain copyright and share access for the school's educational purposes.

The U.S. government roused more recently to an expensive paradox and documentary responsibilities. Congress began to consider regulations to ensure that results of sponsored research remain available in the public domain. In February 2013 and after this text went to the editors, President Obama confirmed such directions in an order for open access with a one-year embargo for federally funded research.

International movement. Western governments and nonprofits followed parallel and overlapping paths toward open access. The influential Open Society Institute emerged from an international meeting in Budapest in December 2001 and the next year sponsored the Nordic Conference on Scholarly Communication, which in turn inaugurated the DOAJ (Directory of Open Access Journals) at the University of Lund in Sweden. In 2003 the British University of Southampton added ROAR (Registry of Open Access Repositories), with its fascinating charts on the growth of open access and a landing page declaring, "The aim of ROAR is to promote the development of open access by providing timely information

> ## › Publication Options

The open-access movement engages either as Gratis OA with no-cost online access or Libre OA, which typically involves some form of author underwriting charges. Libraries will want to differentiate based more on two types of approach:

- Green signals author-initiated, self-publishing ventures from blogging to monographs. This direction circumvents the normal rounds of scholarly vetting. It raises methodological issues for collection development and the long-dominant role of peer review.
- Gold involves institutionally-based publications. It is more in keeping with traditional scholarly standards, including peer review and refurbished publishing prospects for libraries. Examples of this growing option are on display in the Directory of Open Access Journals.

In late 2012, the Copyright Clearance Center attempted to reinject publishers in these domains. Its RightsLink platform includes management tools to help guide author productions. The toolset also provides fee mechanisms for such services and rights releases.

about the growth and status of repositories throughout the world. Open access to research maximizes research access and thereby also research impact, making research more productive and effective."

Creative Commons. Aided by the Center for the Public Domain, Lawrence Lessig, Hal Abelson, and Eric Eldred organized the Creative Commons in early 2001. Not satisfied with the protections offered by extant copyright legislation rooted in literary and journalistic financial concerns, they offered tripartite declarations with sections aimed at authors, lawyers, and search engines. The approach featured six categories with needed nuance, illustrated in figure 3.4.

Attribution—CC BY
This license lets others distribute, remix, tweak, and build upon your work, even commercially, as long as they credit you for the original creation. This is the most accommodating of licenses offered. Recommended for maximum dissemination and use of licensed materials.

Attribution-NoDerivs—CC BY-ND
This license allows for redistribution, commercial and non-commercial, as long as it is passed along unchanged and in whole, with credit to you.

Attribution-NonCommercial-ShareAlike—CC BY-NC-SA
This license lets others remix, tweak, and build upon your work non-commercially, as long as they credit you and license their new creations under the identical terms.

Attribution-ShareAlike—CC BY-SA
This license lets others remix, tweak, and build upon your work even for commercial purposes, as long as they credit you and license their new creations under the identical terms. This license is often compared to "copyleft" free and open source software licenses. All new works based on yours will carry the same license, so any derivatives will also allow commercial use. This is the license used by Wikipedia, and is recommended for materials that would benefit from incorporating content from Wikipedia and similarly licensed projects.

Attribution-NonCommercial—CC BY-NC
This license lets others remix, tweak, and build upon your work non-commercially, and although their new works must also acknowledge you and be non-commercial, they don't have to license their derivative works on the same terms.

Attribution-NonCommercial-NoDerivs—CC BY-NC-ND
This license is the most restrictive of our six main licenses, only allowing others to download your works and share them with others as long as they credit you, but they can't change them in any way or use them commercially.

figure 3.4 Creative Commons licensing options (http://creativecommons.org/licenses)

Lessig (2008) followed with calls for reinvention of copyright law. As he details, the
original idea for copyright came with print.
It helped ensure the author's rights to profit,
but in balance with the public good through
regulation of a thing called "copies." That
was fine for the analog world. In a digital
one, any use yields copies. The act of viewing through the HTTP protocol inserts a
"copy" in your computer. Is it time to add
a less profit-driven and technologically
suited approach to ensure scholar communications? As queried in the Epilogue of this
book, what about a distinct type of copyright
for education?

> NGOs

Several nongovernment agencies should also be cited as
overlapping in the government
arena. The Bill and Melinda
Gates Foundation is increasingly prominent in terms of
analytics and web-based
pedagogies. The Pew Trust,
MacArthur, Mellon, Sloan
foundations, and others serve
instrumental roles. They work
with the schools (occasionally
including the onlines), inform
the government, and support
both exploration and public
policy for higher education.

OER (Open Educational Resources). The
open-access movement also spun into the
classroom and the battle against textbook inflation. OER and its Open Textbook component are growing exponentially. In October 2012, for instance, the
State of California adopted an OER support policy. The implications spread with
worldwide appeal. At the close of 2011, UNESCO and the British Commonwealth of Learning promulgated *Guidelines for Open Educational Resources (OER)
in Higher Education* for governments and universities along with their faculty
and staff.

POLITICAL ECONOMY

The Web has spurred government intrusions and opportunities in higher education. The power of the narrative and common law tradition remains in favor of
the library. Nationalism and tradition continue to provide succor and the promise of ensuring engagement through public policy. The Library of Congress as titular leader and other national libraries provide crucial allies and major points of
entry to decision makers. Yet the global nature of the web economy also brings
unprecedented interest and demands on the academic library scene.

COPYRIGHT ZONE

The most obvious arena comes under the 1976 Copyright Act (Title 17 U.S. Code). In America, the unfolding scene engages through civil actions, court decisions, and interpretations by the Librarian of Congress; but events are complicated by globalization and U.S. embrace of the Berne Convention along with the involvement of the World Intellectual Property Organization (WIPO).

As indicated by ACRL's (2012) *Code of Best Practices for Fair Use in Academic and Research Libraries,* copyright has become an unavoidable concern in the web age. The area is a special and unprecedented minefield for for-profits and anyone engaged in virtual operations. For example:

- **Artistic works.** The United States continues to differ from international practices in favor of moral rights, which give the creative artist great control over the use of the materials. Such extensions can vitiate the doctrine of first sale and force author royalties for interlibrary loans.
- **Fair use.** Long an American tradition and formally ensconced in the 1976 legislation, fair use must be understood as uniquely U.S. and Israeli exemptions to Berne. Its loss could prove devastating for libraries, universities, and scholarly communication in general. Given financial interests, this international outlier is assured future controversy and litigation. Academic library monitoring and engagement become a professional requirement.

Fortunately, a string of successful defenses in 2012 offer powerful solace for the future of academic libraries. The historical narrative and creative inclusion of ADA 508 are gaining traction within the U.S. court system. UCLA prevailed on technical factors to continue its electronic distribution of videos in the classroom. *Cambridge University Press, Oxford University Press, Sage Publications v. Georgia State University* resulted in landmark support for electronic course reserves. In *Authors Guild v. HathiTrust,* a federal district court granted controls to the wealth of the Google Book project. Most recently, the Supreme Court's March 2013 ruling in *Kirsaeng v. Wiley and Sons* reaffirmed the first sale doctrine for lawfully produced overseas materials and thereby upheld ILL for foreign works.

- **World Intellectual Property Organization and Traditional Cultural Expressions.** The complexities and international nature of modern challenges are on full display in the ALA Presidential Traditional Cultural Expressions

Task Force Report (2011). The document shies from the originating request for endorsement of the World Intellectual Property Organization's (WIPO) initiative toward permanent and collective copyright protection for traditional cultural expressions, which refer not to the physical collections or archival capture of the events on film but the conceptualization that underpins those performances, traditional medicine, and art objects. From the perspective of a task force member, the action was put forward with the best of all intentions—to protect oft-abused intellectual property rights of native groups over their unique cultural conceptions.

Promised effects would be sweeping. The amendment enables extraterritorial extensions well beyond present American statutes. For the first time, a type of copyright would be permanent. Rather than award the individual artist, it proffers a new communal right. Moreover, an abstract tribal ruler would be empowered to censor use, to confiscate the notes of scholars, and to replevin materials from libraries—even if they had resided in the public domain.

EDUCATIONAL COMPLIANCE

A second and less apparent onus/opportunity set stems from government regulation and web-era interest in universities. Consider:

- **ADA Section 508.** One of the first web-based opportunities was codified by Congress in an amendment to the 1973 Rehabilitation Act in 1998. Section 508 (29 U.S.C. 794) requires that federal agencies take "reasonable" steps to make their electronic information universally accessible. The requirement extends to universities receiving federal student aid, including obligations for library materials.

› Berne Convention

With the 1988 Berne Convention Implementation Act, the United States ended a century of delay to become a signatory of the global Convention for the Protection of Literary and Artistic Works. The country initially took a decidedly "minimalist" approach, merely surrendering Librarian of Congress Putnam's requirement for a © symbol in the 1909 Copyright Act. Blending with World Intellectual Property Organization (WIPO) rules would take time. The Web and WIPO's affinity for DRM and profit protection began to emerge to prominence in the late 1990s. The 1998 Digital Millennium Copyright Act charged the Librarian of Congress with making biannual interpretations in response to the Web's moving impact.

- **Higher Education Opportunity Act.** This 2008 enactment has been barely touched in library literature, but comes with several areas of entrepreneurial interest:
  - » *Course materials.* Although the government has not been able to reduce costs, it does mandate transparency and price listings that include electronic options. These are useful points of comparison for collection development purposes as well as potential cost-saving ventures.
  - » *Credit hour determination.* Although competency-based options loom, universities have been required to display measurements of student activity in keeping with the Carnegie unit: "an amount of work represented in intended learning outcomes and verified by evidence of student achievement," establishing a "quantifiable minimum basis" and as a means to "quantify academic activity for purposes of determining federal funding" (CHEA 2010). Given the absence of classroom lectures and focus on course materials in online education, libraries could entertain a new type of quantification function.
  - » *Earned income.* The drive is on for metrics to check on salaries after graduation; hence a possible monitoring role for librarians along with the addition of job-hunting resources.
- **Technology, Education and Copyright Harmonization Act.** The TEACH Act of 2002 excludes for-profits but has significant implications on the use of media and other materials in the classroom.

UNIVERSITIES: MICROECONOMIC STAGE

The Web and times are resetting the stage for colleges and universities. Business-oriented forces remake universities in their image. Government and Long Tail economic factors disrupt the ivory tower. State financial support for higher education dwindles. Prior governance models and faculty dominance give way. All of this results to new trends for the new millennium:

- **Assessment.** Quantitative assessment and number crunching rise in prominence, whether or not proven.
- **Bottom-line factors.** Research and publication focus remain, but with accelerated concentration on financial returns, fund raising, and endowment building.

- **Curricular reordering.** Increasingly differentiated degree programs are born, with a trend toward technical skills at the expense of the liberal arts.
- **Employment training centers.** In keeping with John Henry Newman's fears (see chapter 1), education per se is being diminished. Government pressures drive toward secular practices and training. The centrality of teaching for thinking and research gives way to university accountability as job preparation centers.
- **Noneducational overhead.** The times have passed when faculty, laboratories, and the library defined the core of a university's finances. Instead, new administrations fashion new administrative offices and add their own salaries to the inflationary picture.

State Accountability

State-supported institutions bring demands for metrics-driven accountability. In August 2011, for example, the University of Texas Board of Regents approved a state-driven model to redefine the nature of higher education. The "action plan" was designed to "raise quality and productivity" as well as ensure that taxpayers are "getting their money's worth." It directs universities to create metrics for display through interactive web dashboards, which would provide students, parents, and legislators with measures of departmental productivity and efficiency.

Residence universities expand student services in felt need to compete for students. Sports take their own priority. College costs and loan debt swell in exorbitant fashion at the expense of student bodies.

ENTER ONLINE EDUCATION

While developing a strong presence on the Web, higher education was slow in engaging classroom extension. Although MIT, Cornell, Michigan, and a handful of other leaders sought early involvement, systematic implementation was delayed into a twenty-first-century proposition. Administrations failed to grasp the import of the coming tsunami. Early ventures were often ignored as fad or relegated as a toy. Pedagogical implications were left on the sideline to a few interested professors or the hands of technologists. LMS software arrived from the outside in the form of externally developed platforms like Blackboard and Moodle.

Like publishing, once allowed growth in online education was explosive. The first decade of the new century witnessed a somewhat incoherent fad of response. Mainstream universities (and their libraries) were hard pressed to get online education "right." Business forces repeatedly overestimated potentials and underestimated the nature of education. Even University of Illinois could fail in multimillion-dollar attempts. Enterprises were fated to clash with campus realities and entrenched teaching modes. Professors remained a force of intelligent opposition. They had traditional approaches to rely on along with few incentives to switch. Automated web classrooms and asynchronous methods were readily perceived as minor addenda or annoying threats.

Though grudging, adoption was nevertheless inevitable. From 2000 to 2008, the number of undergraduates taking online classes increased rapidly from 8 percent to 20 percent. By 2010 most American universities and many colleges would offer some form of web-based coursework. In late 2012 and early 2013, Multiuser Open Online Courses (MOOCs) became the new rage.

The Long Tail would not be denied. In keeping with Christensen's model, rising university costs, decrepit educational models, and delayed responses created an undeniable opportunity in the first decade of the new century. Online universities rested on LMSs but tapped a different and expectant market. By 2010 the NCES reported a five-year growth rate in student enrollment some 400 percent higher than public universities. Figure 3.5 illustrates the rise of for-profits from the ether after 2001. Within a decade, they commanded 12 percent of the market, and project enrollments surpassed that of private schools within a few years.

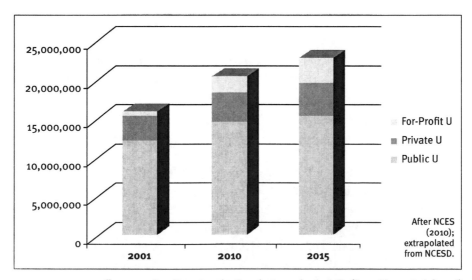

figure 3.5 Enrollment projections by type of university (From Phan, et al. [2011])

The virtual campus. As uncomfortable as it may be, a paradigm shift looms for higher education. As explored in the remainder of this book, the online for-profits employ different expectations than research universities—the dominant model of the past two centuries. Not only are they housed on virtual campuses, online universities embrace dissimilar demographics. Rather than a straight line from high school to full-time college study, those studying online tend to be older, working, and may have mobility issues (Bradford 2011). Odds are the online student, especially those in the military, will take classes at more than one university before graduating. In market terms, "nontraditional" students account for over 80 percent of current enrollments. According to Wallace Boston (2010), the nature of the virtual classroom can even lead to the chimera of color-blind education. In what I read as a disturbing challenge to mainstream orthodoxy, his studies show no statistical differences on race or gender in terms of student success or failure at the online APUS.

The new education model ironically contains echoes of the origins of the University at Bologna. In that seminal environment, students were in charge and catered to. Rather than exhibiting professors' convenience and industrial-era techniques, the virtual variant is similarly student responsive. In the new model, success devolves from client-based services that consciously remove entrenched barriers and faculty dominance:

- **Analytics.** On the back end, online programs have unprecedented abilities to monitor student and faculty activity. For-profits are especially able to marry inherent data-mining capacities to their financial metrics.
- **Asynchronous pedagogies.** Large lecture halls and face-to-face engagement largely vanish. Classes are more akin to extended homework sessions. They involve intense readings/assignments with electronic exchanges through the Web. In a subtle return to declamation and dialectical formats, there is no hiding in the back row of a virtual classroom. Everyone must participate.
- **Open admissions.** Similar to a community college, schools tend toward the model set by Britain's Open University in the 1960s. These are available to anyone with a high school diploma or equivalent, effectively removing the angst of letters of acceptance/rejection.
- **Scheduling.** Instead of the fall/winter/summer pattern, classes can start on a monthly basis. Courses are designed for availability and to ease student planning without the entrenched ritual of scheduling struggles.

- **Socializing.** Intramural sports, off-campus hangouts, and library study spaces are largely removed in favor of limited engagement through Web 2.0 applications.
- **Transportation and security.** The struggles and expenses of campus parking are no more. The absence of physical presence eliminates concerns over inclement weather and safety.
- **24/7 operations.** There are no set class periods. The ritual of attending importunely timed sessions (e.g., late Friday and early mornings) disappears. Students turn on their computers at a time and place of their choosing within the framework of the course.

In keeping with Frank McCluskey and Melanie Winter's (2012) introduction to *The Idea of the Digital University,* higher education has to accommodate a profoundly new component in order to preserve itself in the web age: "Our thesis is simple: The digital university is a fundamentally different institution from the traditional university. We are seeing the birth of a new kind of institution. We argue, however, that while much has changed in universities in recent decades, there are elements that need to remain the same for the university to maintain its 'heart.'"

FINAL COMMENTS: DISRUPTION

Transformation in higher education will not stop with online universities. Given notable exceptions for client-centric and asynchronous methods, their roadmaps follow the same path as the mainstream—a traditional accreditation route. The second decade of the twenty-first century remains in a hyper-Incunabulum, and the Web is forcing the way for disruptive change.

For-profits are not alone in an increasingly varied and uncertain terrain. Mainstream academia has joined the hunt to tame online education. MIT opens its syllabuses on the Internet. It joins with Harvard and other schools in a different type of educational consortium. MOOCs burst on the scene with particular alacrity. In late 2012, Stanford professor Sebastian Thrun uses a spectacular 160,000 enrollment to launch Udacity—an alternative, low-cost form of higher education. Coursera follows suit in concert with dozens of major universities. MOOCs in general proffer a massive "big class" and financially appealing alternative, but as yet lacking in final answers. Similarly, the online but nonprofit

Western Governors University pioneers self-paced competency programs. Classroom engagement readies for a seed change with individualized instructional approaches and personalized learning environments. Licensure and testing "badging" promise still another route to a college education outside prior admittance procedures.

The private sector has itself become active—and eerily competitive. Smarthinking's StraighterLine spinoff "backdoors" accreditation through licensing deals for its courses with universities. The Khan Academy appears, and other web-based study initiatives offer substitute models for college education. In late 2012, Blackboard joins a growing sector orchestrating online education for colleges along with Academic Partnerships, Bisk Education, Deltak, Embanet-Compass, Learning House, Pearson, and 2tor.

Barely acknowledged in the mainstream, major textbook publishers morph into "learning companies" and push toward universities on their own. Pearson, for example, launches classroom operations in conjunction with the University of London and goes forward to buy Embanet-Compass. Wiley invests in related courseware approaches. The list does not end there. Smarterer launches as an online assessment service with some eight hundred topics from C++ to Gothic architecture. It is joined by Skills.to and Degreed. Bloomberg enters with resume services for financial sector jobs and ACT with National Career Readiness Certificates that measure employability.

In sum, the future of higher education and appropriate pedagogies remains in flux. As seen in the remainder of this book, libraries cannot wait on the outcome. They must engage a vital mission to ensure sustainability.

VIRTUAL CAMPUS DISCOURSE

The Web has already wrought significant redefinition. Networking advances in the 1990s opened to the outsourcing and new economics of the twenty-first century. Yet reinvention is far from complete. Academic libraries cannot escape budding challenges from the Long Tail and evolving technology. Sustainability and success require adjustments for "disturbing" new entities—online education and virtual universities.

Here we explore such directions in a series of "grounded theory" exercises (Glaser and Strauss 1967). Our discourse is assisted by a web-based CRIS model. The view reorients concepts from physical artifacts and storage facilities toward virtual operations. In the process, a selection of previously sacrosanct functions effectively disappear. Remaining practices are streamlined and redefined. Long distinct activities "mash" together. New ones slide onto the scene. Management skills are redefined and reinvention presses forward on a fundamentally different plane.

Although rooted in practice, this book should not be confused with a full-blown "how we did it right" book. I acknowledge the impossibility of perfect or final answers. The market and technologies are moving far too fast. Rather, these chapters proffer a selection of coping strategies and a plethora of questions. Uniquely experienced perspectives propose counterpoint—a way to think from within the revolutionary environment toward a new form of library.

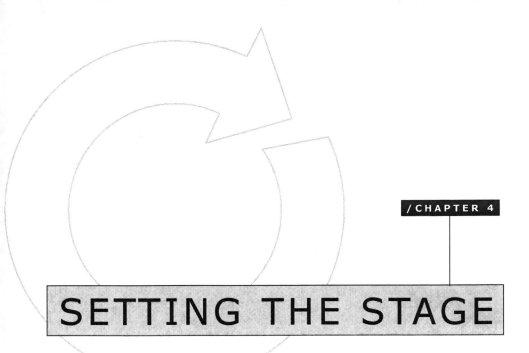

CHAPTER 4

SETTING THE STAGE

THE WEB HAS ALREADY REORDERED ACADEMIC LIBRAR-
ies. Changes wrought over the first 750 years pale against the
rapidity of effects in the 1990s and twenty-first century. Today's
facilities boast a look and feel unlike anything in the past.
From time immemorial, users were tied to a chain of physical
engagement—dedicated visits followed by catalog searches, to
a retrieval stage, and onto the handling of the materials for reading. With the
Web, travel and parking become optional. Automated access transits from bibliographic records to full text. Search engines replace the reference desk. Hours
of operation vanish. The library's walls are knocked down. Stacks reorder into
meaninglessness. In the new millennium, patrons anticipate anytime and anywhere access on devices from desktop computers to smart phones.

The shift, however, remains incomplete. University libraries are at a historical tipping point. Despite visible advance, the scorecard is distressingly mixed.
Beyond coping tactics for the early phases of reinvention, academic libraries in
the second decade of the twenty-first century are engaged in a struggle against
obsolescence and a hunt to establish themselves as value propositions for a new
age. They have yet to resolve fully for a very different educational crucible.

IN MID-PARADIGM SHIFT

A review of the literature suggests matters coming rapidly to a head at the second decade of the twenty-first century. Web-induced competition, economic pressures, and government interests have had time to interpose their wills. Past sureties of the ivory tower are recognized as under attack. A Web in hyper-Incunabulum continues to batter with ever newer applications. In *Trends in Academic Libraries, 1998 to 2008,* Denise Davis (2111) confirms the prefatory telescoping and conflicted nature of effects during the first decade of the millennium. Relying on data from the National Center for Education Statistics (NCES), she reports a staggering reordering. The nation's 3,911 academic libraries took a different face in short order. As Davis summarizes at the start of her work:

- Circulation decreased by 20.9 percent.
- Interlibrary loans increased by 62.9 percent, but the use of commercial document services declined from increased digital access to databases.
- Number of hours of weekly service grew, featuring a 90 percent-plus increase in those with more than 120 hours in coverage.
- While paper-based materials expanded only some 20 percent, the number of e-books jumped almost 900 percent and serial subscriptions 244.6 percent.
- Total expenditures went up 48.5 percent, with a significant shift as resource spending (56.5 percent) jumped by 20 percent to rise well above staffing costs; operational costs for consortial activities were up 27.3 percent, but computer hardware and software declined slightly (-2.9 percent).
- Electronic services increased. E-reference was up 52.4 percent and technology assistance for the

> ### > Hesitancies and a Paradigm Shift
>
> In keeping with Thomas Kuhn's (1962) famed *Structure of Scientific Revolutions and McLuhan* (1962), paradigm shifts inherently engender conservative reaction. Given the power of the print heritage, huge physical structures, established staff, and vast investments, library elements are naturally reticent. There is much to recommend or self-justify continuation of past practice. Despite existential threats, history predicts residual commitment to atavisms, deference to outmoded research models, and temporary communication problems.

handicapped up 27.2 percent. Electronic theses and dissertation applications grew 140.7 percent, but digitization efforts appear to be waning from their peak, with a 13.3 percent decline.
• Information literacy initiatives continued to grow slightly but had already become ingrained as a policy matter on many campuses.

NCES (Phan et al. 2011) updated figures in its Academic Libraries 2010 with equally troublesome indicators. For instance, the number of schools with information literacy programs in strategic plans stayed at roughly one-third, yet only 25 percent of those included the library in the implementations. Thirty-two percent of respondents reported having electronic reference services, but queries had undergone a massive two-digit decrease. Students were increasingly abandoning the library for research, and library turnstiles declined precipitously. The report also confirmed the fundamental shift from print ownership to electronic licensing: e-books dramatically increased from 32.8 million holdings in 2004 to 158.7 holdings in 2010, while spending on print dipped significantly; electronic journal subscriptions grew by 80 percent and surpassed costs for print versions, which in turn dipped by some 40 percent.

Drawing on ACRL accounts, the University Leadership Council (2011:27) included disquieting figures and increasingly "lonely reference librarians." A staple of library services is in rapid decline, including a 71 percent decrease for doctoral studies (see figure 4.1).

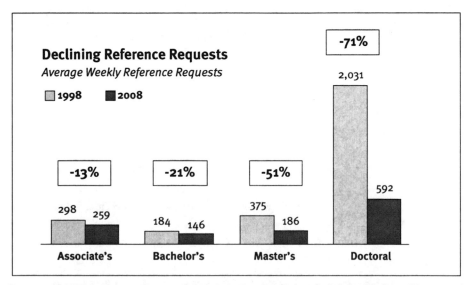

figure 4.1 Decline in library reference requests, 1998–2008 (University Leadership Council [20011;27], www.educationadvisoryboard.com/pdf/23634-EAB-Redefining-the-Academic-Library.pdf)

ISSUES AND CHALLENGES

The literature reflects a growing confluence of worries, including particular threats against research assumptions and practices—heretofore the academic library's main perceived mission. In the words of the New Media Consortium's *Horizon Report* (2012:6), the era brings unprecedented pressures on the dominant model:

> New modes of scholarship are presenting significant challenges for librar-
> ies and university collections, how scholarship is documented, and the
> business models to support these activities. While the university library
> has traditionally housed collections of scholarly resources, social networks
> and new publishing paradigms, such as open content, are challenging the
> library's role as curator. Students and educators are increasingly able to
> access important, historic research in web browsers on devices of their
> choosing. As such, libraries are under tremendous pressure to evolve new
> ways of supporting and curating scholarship.

› A Masstige Effect?

Even the best intentioned of efforts at the top can inadvertently bring challenges to those lower on the food chain. Will the "masstige"/prestige effects of the Library of Congress or a Harvard library destroy local brands? What about the Digital Public Library of America, European Union's Europeana, or World Public Library? Could utilitarian drives or library luxury labels draw away clients or help destroy lesser-known institutions? Prior professional work domains are increasingly automated into the cloud. What does this creeping outsourcing imply in terms of librarian obsolescence? Will the premise of *The Desk Set* be realized?

In "Working Together: Evolving Value for Academic Libraries," Claire Creaser and Valerie Spezi (2012) add unease from the web-era commercialization of information resources. *Inside Higher Ed*'s Steve Kolowich (2012) projects a slowly spiraling financial posture:

> The percentage of university funds allocated to academic libraries shrank
> for the 14th straight year in 2009, dipping below 2 percent for the first
> time, according to updated figures from the Association of Research Librar-
> ies. The latest decline . . . is part of a decades-long trend that has seen
> libraries get gradually smaller shares of funding as university budgets have
> increased overall.

Works like ITHAKA's (2010) *Faculty Study 2009: Key Strategic Insights for Libraries* and OCLC's (2010) *Perceptions of Libraries* enlarge on a troublesome picture. Michalko and colleagues' (2010) *Research Libraries, Risk and Systemic Change* points to dangers from large tenured staffs and the conservative nature of the field. Their study illustrates the presence of wariness over the dominance of the research mode. Directors also evince concerns over external commercial competition and difficulties in updating librarian skills. The report isolates ten "high-risk" concerns among establishment leaders:

1. Availability of online information resources (Google, etc.) weakens visibility & value of library
2. User base erodes because library value proposition is not effectively communicated
3. Recruitment & retention of resources is difficult due to reduction in pool of qualified candidates
4. Difficulty identifying candidates for evolving library management roles
5. Human resources are not allocated appropriately to manage change in the current environment
6. Current human resources lack skill set for future needs
7. Conservative nature of library inhibits timely adaptation to changed circumstances

> Consortia and For-Profits

As OCLC-sponsored research, the Milchako et al. (2010) report appropriately stresses consortial and cooperative enterprises as corrective agencies. Such collective approaches rose to prominence during the computer and web eras but do not necessarily translate to online for-profits. Although matters may be changing, the latter remain relative outliers and parvenus.

Internally, for-profit corporate mindsets and legal uncertainties over "restraint of trade accusations" may inveigle against membership. Externally, even regionally accredited for-profit universities find themselves lumped with trade schools. They can be subjected to differential pricing by vendors even though members of consortia like Lyrasis. OCLC makes sure to offer a special "For-Profit" tag for controlling ILL services. ALA and ACRL only vaguely awaken to the differences between this sector and prior distance education units in 2011 and 2012. Indeed, APUS had to petition for a number of years before becoming the first of the for-profits to subscribe to JSTOR in 2009 and positions to struggle for membership in the Council of Research Libraries in late 2012.

8. Library cannot adjust fast enough to keep up with rapidly changing technology & user needs
9. Increased inefficiencies and expenses due to lack of functionality of legacy systems & IT support
10. Due diligence & sustainability assessment of local or third party services is not completed, tracked or analyzed

ACCOUNTABILITY RISES

Extraordinary demands are appearing for articulating and enumerating the library's worth. The literature indicate the depth of concern and change at the highest rungs of the profession. Research library directors could not escape justifying their services as "value propositions." The Education Advisory Board (2011) brought together a high-powered assemblage of publishing leaders, library deans, provosts, academic vice presidents, and the like (but without a for-profit representative). They reflected on government- and economy-induced trends toward accountability in *Redefining the Academic Library: Managing the Migration to Digital Information Services*. The report reaffirms the decline of print and movement to the virtual. It argues for inevitable change from the "library's traditional role as a repository for physical books and periodicals." The study suggests themes that also resound within this text. Its list begins with six "transformations":

1. Collection size rapidly losing importance. Even the wealthiest academic libraries are abandoning the "collection arms race" as the value of physical resources declines. Increasingly, libraries must adapt to a world in which providing access to—rather than ownership of—scholarly resources is their primary role.
2. Traditional library metrics fail to capture value to academic mission. Libraries can no longer demonstrate their educational and scholarly impact via traditional input measures such as the number of volumes and serial titles held, expenditures on monographs and staff, gate count, and reference requests. New measures of success (still under development) will emphasize impact on student learning outcomes, retention and graduation rates, faculty research productivity, and teaching support.
3. Rising journal costs inspiring calls for alternative publishing models. Subscriptions to scholarly journals and electronic databases have steadily risen as a share of library budgets at what many believe is

an unsustainable rate. . . . many librarians and academic administrators feel that a transition to nonprofit, open-access journals would mean substantial savings and broader access for all.

4. Viable alternatives to the library now boast fastest growth and easiest access. With the rise of companies like Google and Amazon, as well as nonprofits like Wikipedia and HathiTrust, users now meet most of their information needs through sources outside of the library. The collections of articles, monographs, and ebooks made available through these organizations dwarf library collections.

5. Demand declining for traditional library services. Very few students and a decreasing number of faculty start research in the library building or via the library website, opting instead for search engines and discipline-specific research resources. Circulation and reference requests have been steadily declining for years.

6. New patron demands stretch budget and organizational culture. The modern library is caught between its historical role in managing print materials and new demand for digital resources and services, and it cannot afford to invest indefinitely in both. Today's users require a new set of services and accommodations from the academic library that necessitate a strategic paradigm shift: from building and maintaining a collection to engaging with students and faculty.

CRISIS DECADE

The academic library is under siege. University of California System vice-provost Daniel Greenstein laid out the stark realities in the 2009 keynote of ITHAKA's Sustainability Conference. He suggested devolution and radical redesign. Assumptions of support had wilted. The university library of the future would be lightly staffed and highly decentralized. Services would be electronically outsourced and physical operations increasingly shared among consortia. Facilities would shrink, to be composed primarily of special collections and study zones.

Greenstein's (2009) logic remains chilling and authoritative:

Accordingly . . . the budget trade-off decisions that involve the library are the most difficult for any university administrator to make. To put it crassly—sustain the library budget or pay the startup package for a new professor of chemistry, support the library or maintain a less commonly taught modern language. Such decisions are only complicated by the recent appearance of massive global digital libraries that seem poised, in the popular imagination at least, to replace the university library as the principal source of scholarly information. Why invest much at all in the university library when journals, reference works, and soon tens of millions of books and monographs, both in and out of print, will be available effortlessly and online?

To him, the 2010s would be pivotal. Unlike conditions in the print era, however, elements within the field were already in active response. The literature reflects a variety of tactical considerations for the information age, including remembrances from things past and willingness to challenge established tropes.

INFORMATION LITERACY

Alarm bells sounded in the 1980s. Despite pioneering roles in campus automation, academic libraries were being undervalued and shunted aside for the information age. New IT shops and business models caught administrative eyes for the microcomputer revolution and the university's automation future. In the mid-1980s, the Carnegie Foundation stepped forward with a call for correctives. Professional library associations sallied forth. Acting with the leadership of such enterprising librarians as Patricia Senn Breivik and Robert Wedgeworth, ALA and soon ACRL pushed a provocative counternarrative and valuable tool in the form of information literacy initiatives. As indicated in the report of the ALA Presidential Committee on Information Literacy (1989):

> Although libraries historically have provided a meaningful structure for relating information in ways that facilitate the development of knowledge, they have been all but ignored in the literature about the information society. Even national education reform reports, starting with A Nation at Risk in 1983, largely exclude libraries. No K-12 report has explored the potential role of libraries or the need for information literacy. . . . In fact, no reform report until "College," the 1986 Carnegie Foundation Report, gave substantive consideration to the role of libraries in addressing the challenges facing higher education.

The drive and terminology took effect. Information literacy was in place as part of the library's arsenal for the arrival of the Web. Academic libraries used the tool for leverage and visibility yet may have underplayed their hand. Libraries were often unable or unwilling to defend against competitive embrace by other academic units seeking a role in the web age. The field also may have underestimated ties to a fundamental shift. Instead of emphasis on the dynamics of the Web, formal response was homogenized. Consider ACRL's (2000) *Information Literacy Competency Standards for Higher Education:*

> Information literacy forms the basis for lifelong learning. It is common to all disciplines, to all learning environments, and to all levels of education. It enables learners to master content and extend their investigations, become more self-directed, and assume greater control over their own learning. An information literate individual is able to:
>
> * Determine the extent of information needed
> * Access the needed information effectively and efficiently
> * Evaluate information and its sources critically
> * Incorporate selected information into one's knowledge base
> * Use information effectively to accomplish a specific purpose
> * Understand the economic, legal, and social issues surrounding the use of information, and access and use information ethically and legally

DIGITAL PRESERVATION

Digital preservation has garnered center stage for library responses in the web era and takes two forms. The first systemic responses to the Web were appropriately conservative and strangely ironic. Archivists and special collections librarians, who had long been ignored in library automation drives for shared descriptions, took an early lead. The library world's main contributions and most distinguishing characteristics/draws on the Web returned to scribal functions.

> **› Is it Preservation?**
>
> By their nature, virtual academic libraries do not normally engage in digitization projects. They have nothing to scan and treat such products as merely another form of web publication. Indeed, one can readily argue that digitization in a web sense is an access question and not one of preservation. The output has no artifactual or original values; rather, it is a simple reflection that can take shape in a limitless and indistinguishable series of copies.

In keeping with discussions in chapter 2, librarianship joined its archival pre-decessors to extend concerns into born-digital records. The Research Libraries Group signaled this switch with the publication of Garrett and Waters's (1996) landmark *Preserving Digital Information.* The Library of Congress took up the cud-gel and in 2000 was able to secure $100 million in seed funds for a National Dig-ital Information Infrastructure and Preservation Program. As the Library of Con-gress (2011) indicated in *Preserving Our Digital Heritage,* such efforts extended to wide stakeholder involvement with a focus on the leading research libraries.

The Library of Congress played a singular role in pushing for global engage-ment. Nancy McGovern's (2012) *Aligning National Approaches to Digital Preserva-tion* suggests that such matters are reaching fruition. With its Europeana site, the European Union seems to confirm such directions. As seen in *The New Renais-sance* report, ambitions are high, with a call for a €100 billion investment. In the words of the Committee des Sages (2011:7):

> Can Europe afford to be inactive and wait, or leave it to one or more pri-vate players to digitize our common cultural heritage? Our answer is a resounding "no." Member States, Europe's cultural institutions, the Euro-pean Commission, and other stakeholders will all have to take up their responsibilities in order to ensure that Europe's citizens and economy fully benefit from the potential of bringing Europe's cultural heritage online.
>
> Our goal is to ensure that Europe experiences a digital Renaissance instead of entering into a digital Dark Age.

INFORMATION COMMONS

A more limited type of stop-loss response appeared toward the close of the 1990s. Librarians such as Donald Beagle (1999, 2006) lobbied for what would be variously called information, learning, or knowledge commons. Library space needed revision for web-engendered declines in usage. As evidenced in Stuart's (2008) *ARL Learning Space Pre-planning Tool Kit,* such reconfiguration implied alterations for enhanced student study and automation access. To Sinclair (2009) the Information Commons

> incorporates the freedom of wireless communication, flexible workspace clusters that promote interaction and collaboration, and comfortable fur-nishings, art, and design to make users feel relaxed, encourage creativity,

and support peer-learning. To this add self-help graphics services, color imaging, audio and video editing, and other production and presentation software and it becomes a one-stop collaboratory for out-of-class assignments, writing, research, and group projects.

The information commons offers a useful and what is proving valuable counter. Yet it remains intrinsically tied to the library as building and with unacknowledged roots to the undergraduate library movement of the 1960s. Although matters may be changing, with growing focus given to student learning encounters, the Web's seminal impact appears largely in the background.

EMBEDDED LIBRARIANS

The twenty-first century added "embedded librarian" to the reaction lexicon. Barbara Dewey coined the term as metaphor parallel to the intense interactions of journalists deployed in the second Iraq war. The phrase dramatized oversights of the library's potential in the new age. Hers was nothing less than a manifesto for involvement across the face of the university. As indicated by the abstract to Dewey's (2004) article:

> Librarians play a central role in advancing colleges' and universities' strategic priorities through constant collaboration. Embedding oneself at as many venues as possible will ensure that library staff, collections, and services are more fully integrated into all aspects of campus life. Participation by librarians helps the campus move forward because of their uniquely broad perspective and general point of view.

The literature reflects a subsequent narrowing of the concept. Cassandra Kvenild's and Kaijsa Calkins's (2011) *Embedded Librarians* compilation indicates innovative involvement stretching to student dorms and any other possible physical study spaces. Yet attention has turned primarily to the twin goals of building departmental liaisons and classroom involvement, including online courses and long-term relationships.

COST-CONTROL EFFORTS

Sustainability also involves cost containment. Web-era research libraries along with their consortia, professional associations, and allied nonprofits engage in price controls on a variety of fronts. Despite group buys and negotiation power, pricing in the marketplace remains unfortunately murky. Smaller facilities are in particularly vulnerable positions, with consortial ties required for any hope of balance.

ALA director Keith Michael Fiels (2011) reports on exploratory meetings with the Association of American Publishers (AAP). Fiels highlights a variety of library concerns and parallel reports from the ALA's Office of Information Technology Policy. His comments suggest an awakening across joint spectrums of interest but also lay out the library's case:

- **Licensing options.** Innovative licensing models need to be discussed and can provide publishers with improved marketing options.
- **Costs.** Given the billions of items purchased and role libraries play in developing readers, publishers have a concomitant interest in making e-books affordable for libraries to buy.
- **Availability.** Libraries are concerned about publishers, like Macmillan, that refuse to sell to them.
- **Archiving.** The library's responsibilities for preserving the cultural heritage and meeting researcher needs are also services of interest to publishers.
- **Privacy rights.** Publisher control of e-book access brings serious questions and legal challenges for the library community.
- **Accessibility.** Publishers and libraries share in the moral and often legal onus to enable reasonable access for all, including the handicapped.

PUBLISHING: THE OPEN-ACCESS MOVEMENT

Related answers bubble from the past. Although a portion was regained with university presses in the mass press era, academic libraries lost their "publisher" status to print centuries earlier. The Web proffers renewed opportunity. The medium and its Long Tail disturbingly remove limits from control of the means of production and distribution channels.

As discussed in chapter 3, universities turned opportunity into open access. Academic libraries have taken a major role in the movement against escalating prices from commercial intrusion into scholarly publishing. In 1998 the Association of Research Libraries' lent initial order by founding the Scholarly Publishing and Academic Resources Coalition.

Individual libraries also strive to enlighten their university presses to join the quest for digital liberation and free electronic access:

- California Digital Library (CDL) has opened a couple of thousand online titles for its constituents as well as hundreds more to all through an arrangement with Google.
- Florida's Orange Grove provides access to a range of textbooks and the outputs of the University Press of Florida.
- Indiana University Libraries promoted electronic access to IU Press imprints.
- University of Pittsburgh Library hosts its press's digital Prologue Book project, although with time embargos.

The push for action can also come from reaction against direct affronts to library engagement for students. In the wake of a copyright infringement suit against its electronic classroom reserves, for example, Georgia State University's library embarked on a campaign to warn new faculty to protect their copyright. As reported by Bryan Sinclair (2012), dean of libraries Nancy Seamans proclaimed:

> Scholarly communication models of the past are not sustainable from an economic standpoint . . . especially as the cost of library resources continues to rise and universities and libraries experience belt-tightening in almost every state. . . . the library hopes to increase awareness of scholarly communication alternatives and help faculty make their work accessible to the broader research community.

To James Mullins and his coauthors (2011) in the introduction to *Library Publishing Services: Strategies for Success Research Report Version 1.0,* rebirth has come with a rush:

> Over the past five years, libraries have begun to expand their role in the scholarly publishing value chain by offering a greater range of pre-publication and editorial support services. Given the rapid evolution of these services, there is a clear community need for practical guidance concerning the challenges and opportunities facing library-based publishing programs.

COURSE RESERVES/
CLASSROOM SERVICES

Movement into the classroom offers overlapping and equally intriguing reminders from the past, but with added incentives from the like of Common Core Standards and basic survivability. Academic libraries have a heritage of course reserves that stayed below the radar—a secondary consideration barely mentioned in schools of library and information science. Such oversight initially carried to electronic materials in the twenty-first century. Suzanne Thorne of Syracuse University's and I, for example, issued proactive calls for such involvement on the "Economic Innovations" panel that followed Greenstein's jeremiad in 2009—only to meet with a bit of audience incredulity.

Although suggesting receptiveness from academic librarians in Great Britain, Creaser and Spezi's (2012) *Working Together: Evolving Value of Academic Libraries* continued oversight. They detail the lack of "systemic" engagement by academic libraries for classrooms in Scandinavia, the United Kingdom, and the United States. Their efforts, however, may have missed a budding movement.

> ### › Oversights
> ### in Academia
>
> Personal experience attests to lack of consciousness on ominous display within the broader academic community. In 2010, IMS Global has to be goaded into consideration of library materials for Common Cartridge standards. A May 2012 session at WCET promises encompassing efforts in the battle against textbook inflation but needs genteel reminders of university investment in the largest and academically most important counterlocus. Blackboard's October 2012 Higher Education Executive Symposium was forced into uncomfortable admittance on the related lapses. Fortunately, the educational centrality of peer-reviewed literature and librarians is self-evident and readily propagandized. The problem is making sure these factors are stated and kept as part of the active conversation.

As one not surveyed, I can attest that Syracuse and APUS did not stand in complete isolation. Louis Shores had called for classroom involvement as far back as the 1930s. Greenstein's updated call also actively inserted libraries in California's efforts against textbook inflation. Hope exists that he will continue such directions in his new position as head of the Gates Foundation's higher education programs. Embedded librarians similarly helped alter the nature of the discourse. The Library of Congress and National Archives were actively leading a charge for classroom exercises from their primary source materials. The University of Michigan's library engaged course implementation standards in concert with IMS Global's new library materials committee. Springshare's Lib-Guides software facilitated related efforts. APUS quickly embraced the product to replace a less effective CMS. Duke University and hundreds of schools engage for subject pathfinders that stream into direct course support. In mid-2012, Georgia State University emerged with potentially game-changing news from a major copyright lawsuit over its electronic course reserves.

Accountability metrics. Movement toward classroom engagement is further substantiated by the ramping of evaluation indicators. Clark and Schonfeld (2011) issued a follow-up survey with *Insights from U.S. Academic Library Directors* for ITHAKA. "Teaching facilitator" appears as one of six functions for sustainability. In 2011, ACRL launched a multiyear Value of Academic Libraries Initiative. As collated in Brown and Malenfant's (2012) Connect, Collaborate, and Communicate, five main recommendations are headed by this one:

1. Increase librarians' understanding of library value and impact in relation to various dimensions of student learning and success.

ACRL's (2011) *Standards for Libraries in Higher Education* features two classroom-support "Principles" and the new trope of "student success" within its nine recommendations for the coming decade:

3. Educational role. Libraries partner in the educational mission of the institution to develop and support information-literate learners who can discover, access, and use information effectively for academic success, research, and lifelong learning.
   3.1 Library personnel collaborate with faculty and others regarding ways to incorporate library collections and services into effective education experiences for students.
   3.2 Library personnel collaborate with faculty to embed information literacy learning outcomes into curricula, courses, and assignments.
   3.3 Library personnel model best pedagogical practices for classroom teaching, online tutorial design, and other educational practices.
   3.4 Library personnel provide regular instruction in a variety of contexts and employ multiple learning platforms and pedagogies.

3.5 Library personnel collaborate with campus partners to provide opportunities for faculty professional development.

3.6 The library has the IT infrastructure to keep current with
advances in teaching and learning technologies.

⋮

5. Collections. Libraries provide access to collections sufficient in quality, depth, diversity, format, and currency to support the research
and teaching mission of the institution.

5.1 The library provides access to collections aligned with areas
of research, curricular foci, or institutional strengths.

VIRTUAL CAMPUS CRUCIBLE

Despite advances, response to the paradigm shift remains incomplete. Even with
the budding of electronic course reserves, a crucial element is overshadowed in
the discourse. Online education proffers the most important shift in higher education since the rise of the research university. By the early twenty-first century,
electronic classes, remote students, and LMSs had become expected and norma-

› More than Distance Education

Distance education offers a second bridge from the mainstream in addition to course
reserves. Yet foundations for both are weak, and the final span has not been laid. The
transformative nature of a virtual campus with telecommuting patrons and staff from across
campus or around the world continues underappreciated. Instead, the overriding blinders
of research services appear firmly in place. Despite the new realities, the academic library
stays preoccupied with the centrality of its physical domains and attracting visitors back to
the quadrangle.

As verified by ongoing engagement within ACRL and the fall 2013 edition of *Internet
Learning*, distance education remains on the fringe and too far removed from academic
leadership. Although sophisticated considerations are evident from the sector, operations appear relegated to rump status. Print and mail delivery roots continue to linger.
Distance education librarians seem oppressively few in comparison to the main library. In
Cinderella-like fashion, they may be forced to continue a "nine to five" routine and campus
presence. Services are hard pressed to reflect the richness of a distinctly developing form
of education with radical classroom differences. Although a start, distance education has
not been enabled for the fundamental change required for a virtual campus.

tive features across the face of higher education. As illustrated by the sudden rise of MOOCs in 2012, transformation can be dramatic and impactful. Colleges and universities of all stripes are committing and struggling with changing pedagogies and economies. Where is the academic library in this brave new world?

Virtual perspective. This book responds with a beacon from the furthest edge of online education—a fully functioning virtual campus in the disturbing realm of the for-profits—reflecting operations and experimentation that date to 2005 and the American Public University System (APUS). Instead of a subset, APUS distance education information services form the main library.

The new realm of the digital begets an altered vision. The pantheon of routines for physical books and journals or distance mailings does not appear. Views from the virtual inherently narrow to exclusively electronic solutions. Monumental buildings and large staffs are not considered. Smaller footprints and stripped-down operations are the expected. Location is barely mentioned. Rather than travel and parking, transportation is by a click within a "placeless" campus. The library natively engages new forms of scholarship and curation. Direct electronic access is not an option—it is the only way.

Implications are magnified in the for-profit space. Such facilities face the most direct financial tests. Insulating capital and drag from millions of dollars in materials and housing are absent. Prior sense of entitlement vanishes. Client-centric forces are at work. Demonstrations of value are preordained and may need to be blatant. Justification is demanded and turf defense expected. Why would an online university spend millions for "just-in-case" collections to lie fallow, overwhelmingly unused on virtual shelves?

CLASSROOM/RESEARCH INFORMATION SERVICES

This book steps forward with answers tuned to a web-based classroom/research information services (CRIS) model. Although developed independently, CRIS parallels embedded librarian concepts. Its evidenced-based call to action emerges through six interwoven drivers:

- **Curriculum/quality-centric.** Given origins within a teaching institution, classroom support is prioritized above research. Activities primarily map and are evaluated in keeping with the school's particular programmatic and classroom offerings.
- **Client community focus.** The library monitors and develops responses based on demonstrable usage patterns and technological capacities of two main client groups:

» *Departmental/program faculties.* The contours of the collection and its services are framed to meet academic needs and actuated through community building partnerships.

» *Students.* Delivery is tuned for students as the primary audience. Although subject to technological limitations, services are actuated in conscious regard for their success—as well as networking capacities, handicap adjustments, and pedagogical preferences.

- **Economic awareness.** Tactics demonstrate both the library as a value proposition and financial responsibilities to the students. Cost/benefit analysis and ROI are not fictive but built into the planning equation and reporting mechanisms. The model recommends entrepreneurial explorations and the creative expansion of the portfolio as vital elements for the sustainability of the academic library.
- **Institutionally sensitive.** CRIS situates the academic library politically within an organization in its own process of development. The model recommends institutional involvement beyond the academic environment.

› CRIS Origins

CRIS surfaced in partial reaction to nagging dogma. Academic librarians have long encountered a litany of tales of bewildered freshman looking in the library for their course materials only to be turned away and often to wry asides. Yet student logic is impeccable. Illogical barriers have been erected to the intellectual and financial detriment of the students. How can anyone intellectually justify separating textbooks and classroom materials from library resources, especially in an information age? How is it possible to teach advanced or graduate courses without reliance on peer-reviewed literature, which is uniquely curated through the library?

With CRIS, the intent is to decode the library as multilayered edifice. Meanings accreted over time are stripped away. Interpretation interpolates back to the origins—communally-based information services for students and faculty. Attributes are limited to physical space and artifacts vanish. Essence emerges as support for joint education and research mission. The idea of a library is singularly prepared for transposition to the virtual campus, a fungible and dynamic synthesis of the old and the new:

- **Sorbonne's creation.** In the thirteenth-century time of the book as limited and expensive treasure for the limited few, Robert Sorbonne authored the academic library as a university value proposition. This new communally-based service was designed to meet student and university informational needs affordably.
- **Berners-Lee's web.** In the early years of the information age, Tim Berners-Lee fostered the World Wide Web as an open scientific and scholarly forum, one that could also affordably facilitate student and university information needs.

It looks to tactics for penetrating bureaucratic silos and engaging other units for both promotional and defensive reasons. The library also seeks a place within the narrative for institutional identity building.

- **Librarian enabled.** CRIS drives to a seminal and applied inversion. Librarians, their services, and community-building skills replace collections as the library's centerpiece.
- **Web consciousness.** The library monitors and engages the Web as an independent dynamic. Rather than miles of internal storage, the Web acts as its Alexandria. CRIS moves beyond the Deep Web of published materials. It demands inclusion of open-web materials and constant awareness of new tools. Print-era atavisms are questioned and decision making reflects the realities of the new economy, including competing technologies.

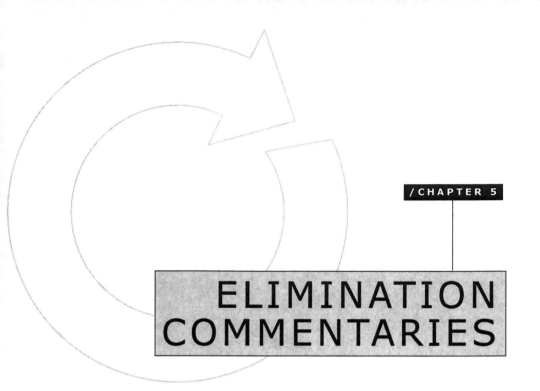

CHAPTER 5

ELIMINATION COMMENTARIES

WITH A PLAN FOR ACTION AND ANALYTICAL FRAME-
work in place, the reader is invited to change persona.
Assess the economic and technical realities of a new age
from a different platform. Augment research tropes with
instructional and entrepreneurial options. Engage from a
purely web perspective, one freed from physical distrac-
tions and engrained print practices. Explore for electronic information services
on a virtual campus. In sum, assume the mindset of a planner or manager engaging a virtual academic library.

We begin with deconstruction of established academic library practice in the
absence of physical storage and artifacts. Although Jacques Derrida's (1967) textual probing may be in evidence, "deconstruction" draws more from our form of
the "green" construction trades. Simplification is the first order of business. The
initial focus is on preserving the historical essence while peeling away superflu-
ous parts. The first phase of deconstruction for a virtual library thus begins with
studied subtractions.

Much of the day-to-day focus of library administration can be stripped away
to informational essence:

General context. The Web contributes elemental changes that involve both blended and virtual operations:

- **Onsite storage.** Direct storage is not a defining element for an online library. The bulk of virtual collections is handled on a rental basis. If "owned" or under permanent license, storage is still likely removed from the physical facility. Placement is virtual, with a vendor or perhaps a university server farm.
- **Processing.** With the cloud, central functions can be managed without the need for internal staff and facilities. Preparation, storage, and delivery of library materials can be effectively outsourced.

Virtual library setting. Thanks to the Web, the virtual academic library has the luxury of ignoring many time-consuming functions that were once central to a library identity:

- **Physical holdings.** Traditional procedures emanate from and are fully enmeshed with handling and maintenance of objects. Activities are differentiated by genre or type of publication—that is, books, journals, media. The printed book is the overriding trope. What does it mean when there is no material, only digital representations—when attention can be aimed at the information within rather than the container?
- **Physical housing.** Similarly, the "library" has previously been integrally intertwined with physical housing, including building, security, and stacks. What does it mean when such accommodations are replaced by electronic servers or live as rental/lease units, the essence contained within a digital cloud that is far removed from direct managerial oversight?

READERS' ADVISORY: DECODING ENTRY LAYOUT

Commentaries within this and the next two chapters are designed as nonlinear, immersive components. Readers can vary their views of such topics. For example, some may profit by skipping ahead to chapter 7 or the traditional narrative in chapter 8 before exploring specific entries.

Instead of precedence or fixed order of marching, entries in these three chapters array in alphabetical order. The approach is deliberately immersive, a potpourri of major and minor terms mixed together as one would encounter randomly in the field.

TAG LINE

Each term is distinctively tagged for virtual library (VL) orientation and paired with:

- **Functional category.** Basic operations are divided between
  - » *Service.* Information-oriented products and activities that are intended for client use
  - » *Tool.* Activities and supporting software that are used in support to shape the services

- **Status.** The nature of such functions is further refined as
  - » *Required* for expected activities within a broad CRIS orientation
  - » *Option* activities that may or not be adopted depending on the nature of the institution
  - » *Deprecated* to reflect categories that can be largely eliminated from consideration

BODY

Wiki-like "stub" articles provide the narrative framework. These vary widely in size from a couple of sentences to a couple of pages. Discussions reflect web thinking and virtual library analysis within a volatile situation. Entries are attitudinal and experiential, not definitional. Selections form more as "memo" devices—opinion pieces within a grounded theory exercise. Snapshots extrapolate from one set of experiences in time and place yet should be understood as open for discussion and a planned companion website. Indeed, the reader should expect as many questions as answers.

See also. Syndetic references recommend related commentaries. The hope is a hypertext-like alternative experience to enable the reader to follow a longer train of thought. Since entries are also intended to stand alone, expect overlaps and some redundancy.

ARCHIVES AND MANUSCRIPT COLLECTIONS

VL: *SERVICE, DEPRECATED*

Neither ink on paper nor primary documents in the classical sense exist in an online library. Though pursuit of a digital university archives is of interest, virtual libraries launch without and lack the mandate or facilities to deal with classical manuscript materials. The purely online-only facilities link to digital simulacra of manuscripts and archives. Such objects come without the artifactual and financial values of the original. Indeed, ideas of the original and rarity vanish in the virtual. Capture and presentation on the Web constitute a publication, which automatically disavows such factors.

Classroom involvement. Depending on the nature of their curriculum, virtual libraries engaged in classroom support have reason to pursue web renditions. In keeping with the best of scholarly traditions, such resources are likely freely available for discovery on the Open Web as well as out of copyright and fully available for manipulation. Products made available by vendors are more suspect. They may come with exceptional delivery platforms, but at added price for that which should be in the public domain. The library must also weight for curricular scope. What are the appropriate expenditures in money and time given enrollment and institutional political factors? That unfortunately does not bode well in for-profit universities, which tend to deemphasize humanistic fields for more lucrative business and technology engagement.

SEE ALSO: chap. 5: Preservation; chap. 6: Collection Development, Publishing, University Archives; chap. 7: Curation, Digital Preservation

BIBLIOGRAPHIC INSTRUCTION

VL: *TOOL, DEPRECATED*

Bibliographic instruction was largely replaced by information literacy programs before virtual libraries arrived on the scene, but it leaves a cautionary tale for web-age consideration. Modern librarianship emerged amid the nineteenth-century rise of the mass press and university press movements. The field partially defined itself as a profession through complex classification, cataloging, and storage systems. Sophistication also engendered patron confusion. Bibliographic instruction appeared as a logical response. Librarianship would remain psychologically and functionally committed to bibliographic descriptions. This continues to include subliminal embrace of complicated designs.

How do those trends translate for enhancing user responses in the web age, a time featuring transparency, the blending of delivery formats, and the full-text capacities of modern search engines?

SEE ALSO: *chap. 6: Cataloging, Information Literacy*

BINDERY OPERATIONS

VL: *TOOL, DEPRECATED*

There is nothing to bind or rebind, Library Bindery Institute standards to consider, or contracts to let when materials are in digital format. Concerns over book jackets devolve to availability for thumbnails in the virtual catalog.

SEE ALSO: *chap. 5: Preservation, Serials Management; chap. 6: Dissertations and Theses*

BROWSING

VL: *TOOL, DEPRECATED (LAMENTED)*

Lost is the powerful "serendipity" of researching by wandering among the carefully cataloged rows and surrounding oneself with bundles of likely resources. Scrolling through a computer screen is not the same thing. Although book jacket thumbnails may be included, one is bereft of valuable visual clues and random access adventures. Tradeoffs fortunately rise through the vastly faster ability to search automated library records, cross-item searching, and added features in the reading platform. Equally important, full-text retrieval alleviates much of the previously unacknowledged need for immediacy beyond that provided by bibliographic records.

SEE ALSO: *chap 5: Bindery Operations, Preservation, Stack Maintenance; chap. 7: Reading Platforms*

BUILDINGS AND GROUNDS

VL: *TOOL, DEPRECATED*

Instead of separate functional arenas (circulation desk, government documents, serials, audiovisuals, special collections), virtual operations funnel as one-stop shopping malls through computer screens. Heating, cooling, cleaning, bathrooms, sightlines, and their attendant costs are no more. On-site and off-site storage vanish. Collections are typically licensed and housed in the cloud by external vendors or on increasingly inexpensive institutional servers. Storage factors and attendant costs to ensure proper stewardship of the materials can largely be ignored. Managerial concerns are limited to select office space and telecommuting factors.

    SEE ALSO: chap. 5: Stack Maintenance; chap. 7: Digital Preservation

CARD CATALOG

VL: *TOOL, DEPRECATED*

Such artifacts were largely obsolescent before the appearance of the virtual library. The Web completed a trend begun at the onset of computerization. The awkward dumb terminals and software of the late 1970s and early 1980s would be replaced by microcomputer "smart" machines and transparent design. Web-based advances and economies made the next switch all but inevitable. Instead of rows of furniture with drawers of cards, the twenty-first-century virtual library emerged with an HTML version of the OPACs—a term itself already reverting to *catalog.*

    SEE ALSO: chap. 5: MARC; chap. 6: Cataloging; chap. 7: Federated Search, Reading Platforms

CIRCULATION DESK

VL: *TOOL, DEPRECATED*

Digital objects do not circulate as in checking out a book in the days of yore. Rather, an HTTP transfer takes a duplicate electronic stream and is dispatched for downloading or opened to access from the cloud. The tactile pleasures and side-economies of paper, book stamps, and the return slip vanish, as do the annoyances from mutilated pages, user underlining, and physical property theft. The checkout desk and clerks for processing are no longer needed. Returns and late notices are relegated to timing codes. Delivery becomes a transparent operation from the record, or even routing as predictive delivery through RSS feeds in reflection of a patron's profile.

SEE ALSO: chap. 5: Credentials/Check-In Station; chap. 6: Circulation, Collection Development

COPY CENTERS

VL: *TOOL, DEPRECATED*

Although the virtual library may have a digital copier for converting print materials, centralized copy centers are not needed. The facility lacks patron traffic. It delivers only digital materials. Assuming that the copy function has not been blocked by DRM, the responsibility for making print copies falls to users and their printers.

SEE ALSO: chap. 5: Microfilm Collections, Out-of-Print Market; chap. 7: Dark Archives

> ### › Digital Copiers
>
> Electrostatic photocopiers arrived on the scene in the 1960s. Their presence stimulated the 1976 Copyright Act. In the late 1990s that technology was supplanted. Copiers are now electronic and come with optical character recognition as well as electronic transmission and print-as-output functions.

CREDENTIALS/CHECK-IN STATION

VL: *TOOL, DEPRECATED*

Human identification checkers do not fit at the entrance of an academic virtual library. Users are greeted instead by automation with logon and authentication routines.

SEE ALSO: chap. 7: Authentication

GOVERNMENT DOCUMENT DEPOSITORY

VL: *SERVICE, DEPRECATED*

The virtual academic library has no place in the Federal Depository Library System and no need to house a separate government documents office. Although the materials within remain of unquestioned value, such genre-based departments are things of the past. As seen in figure 5.1, access is replaced by a simple link to the GPO's FDsys (Federal Digital System).

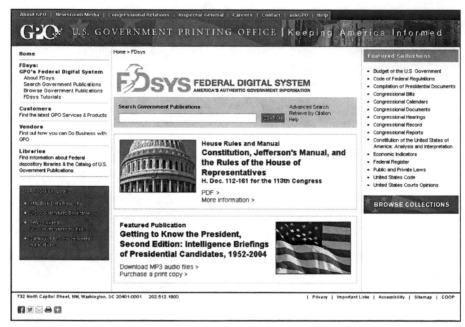

figure 5.1 FDsys portal (http://www.gpo.gov/fdsys)

Alternatively, the virtual library could choose to promote government documents. For instance, it could take a conventional approach by constructing a subject portal tailored to its university's particular needs. Yet the Web also opens for more entrepreneurial purposing. Sitting firmly within the public domain and with their own ADA 508 requirements, such resources are attractive for linking or downloading as part of the virtual library's "central collection." They feed open-web acquisition strategies and library empowerment. Rather than pay for vendors to repackage and serve up, the virtual library looks to cost-effective mining, especially for dedicated classroom purposes.

SEE ALSO: *chap. 5: Archives and Manuscript Collections, Map Collections; chap. 6: Collection Development, Departmental Libraries; chap. 7: ADA 508*

INTEGRATED LIBRARY SYSTEMS

VL: *TOOL, DEPRECATED*

A virtual library is a stripped-down operation. It has no practical need for the wide variety of integrated library system (ILS) modules. Operations can be captured in what amounts to a single ILL or catalog module.

Competition is also in the air. Open-source products are penetrating the established market and threatening the main ILS products. OCLC enters the scene with its cloud-based WorldShare and willingness to centralize all operations remotely. One can similarly predict that EBSCO or ProQuest, with its ebrary and Summon subsidiaries, will enter the zone. Such web-based alternatives may redirect much of library automation and perhaps eliminate ILSs for the mainstream as well.

SEE ALSO: chap. 5: Circulation Desk, Serials Management; chap. 6: Interlibrary Loan; chap. 7: Management Services—Cloud

MAP COLLECTIONS

VL: *SERVICE, DEPRECATED*

Map resources remain valuable, but web delivery both obviates print-era delivery approaches and adds new usage patterns. Like other special collections, separate map holdings thus blend within the general library or may be highlighted by constructing a "conventional" subject portal.

SEE ALSO: chap. 5: Archives and Manuscript Collections, Government Document Depository, Microfilm Collections; chap. 6: Departmental Libraries

> ### › GPS and Classroom Services

As with most web-affected arenas, maps and map librarianship also provided entrepreneurial opportunities. Satellite imagery and geographic positioning systems are making inroads in several academic disciplines. Sophisticated virtual libraries would tie to related Web 2.0 groups along with a subject specialist for information literacy outreach and supplemental classroom instruction.

MARC

VL: *TOOL, REQUIRED /DEPRECATED*

MARC (machine readable cataloging) stands in an anomalous position. Though it is still required, the web handwriting is on the wall. In May 2011 the Library of Congress's Deanna Marcum announced its coming demise. As reported in the *Library Journal* (Kelley 2011):

> "What is needed to transform our digital framework" in the light of technological changes and budgetary constraints. . . . "It's very important that we find a way to link library resources to the whole world of information resources not focusing exclusively on bibliographic information," she said. By rethinking MARC, . . . LOC hopes to determine whether the standard can "evolve to do all the things we'd like it to do, or do we need to replace it" with something more compatible with the Internet world.

While considering the ramifications of its loss, the virtual library planner will need to incorporate MARC for perhaps another decade. Note too that Marcum's analysis is driven by the replacement of AACR2 with RDA (Resource Description and Access), a switch that is not without its own problems.

    SEE ALSO: chap. 6: Cataloging; chap. 7: RDA

MICROFILM COLLECTIONS

VL: *SERVICE, DEPRECATED*

The mass storage advances of microfilming were supplanted by digitization during the 1990s. The older technology rose to revolutionary but unfulfilled promise in the first part of the twentieth century. It offered significant advantages in terms of compacted storage and preservation along with the handling of awkwardly sized maps and chemically unstable newspapers.

    Unlike digital copies, microfilm remains directly readable by humans without machine decoding. Though interesting, the format proved less than human friendly. More important, it is insufficient for the massive amounts of data in the web age. In addition, digital files come with automated searching and retrieval as well as enhanced reading experiences that extend to handicapped services.

    SEE ALSO: chap. 5: Map Collections, Preservation; chap. 7: ADA 508

OUT-OF-PRINT MARKET

VL: *TOOL, DEPRECATED*

The virtual library is concerned only with materials in electronic form, and copyright rears as the major determinant. Rather than relations with antique booksellers, acquisition looks to open-access sites like Project Gutenberg. Adventuresome virtual libraries consider making their own digital copies for works in the public domain. The main area of concern is the "doughnut hole" for "orphan" works. The United States faces multiyear challenges for dealing with items technically in copyright but as yet without clear payment options for electronic versions. The Google Books Project and, especially, efforts by HathiTrust command our attention.

    Recognize too that the marketplace is changing. Long Tail forces suggest that current books will likely remain electronically "in-print" during the life of their copyright. Court decisions continue to support licensing limits and deny an electronic resale market. The virtual library thus prepares for ongoing licensing demands from the publishers or by way of arrangements with JSTOR and similar bodies.

SEE ALSO: *chap. 6: Acquisitions, Collection Development, Publishing*

PHYSICAL SECURITY

VL: *TOOL, DEPRECATED*

Thanks to the absence of physical space, threats to persons and property from a fire, bomb, or other depredation are effectively absent. Patrolling for improper behavior in the stacks is impossible. Still, the virtual manager may need to remain watchful for untoward behavior in a different realm, such as through e-mails and in chat rooms.

SEE ALSO: *chap. 7: Security—Web*

PRESERVATION

VL: *TOOL, DEPRECATED*

The word preservation is bandied, but technically it is a misnomer in cyberspace. Concepts of the original and artifactual values are not present. In a world of bits and bytes, information objects can be infinitely reproduced without the ability to distinguish the original from copies. One deals with abstract information in an ever-changing variety of storage formats. No tangible objects exist to preserve in the traditional sense. Hence, bindery methods disappear. Restoration and repair facilities are not needed. Concerns for heat, humidity, deacidification, and lighting become things of the past. Unless the virtual library engages in electronic archives or digital publications, the death knell is sounded for physical stewardship.

SEE ALSO: *chap. 5: Archives and Manuscript Collections, Bindery Operations, Microfilm Collections; chap. 6: University Archives; chap. 7: Digital Preservation*

READY REFERENCE

VL: *SERVICE, DEPRECATED*

Ready reference is an area of immediate impact and questioning. An online repository has no need for separating such resources as a distinct type of material with its own separate space. Past restrictions on lending make little sense.

> **› Librarian-Access Subscriptions**
>
> If of overriding merit, the library may be able to engage a single as opposed to institutional subscription.

Costs enter the picture. The virtual library manager must be wary of ongoing publisher interest in the production of specialized and often overly expensive investments.

Most important, search engines and the ready availability of free resources dispatch the utility of much of what was once considered ready reference. Given such factors, the virtual library asks, "Why invest?"

SEE ALSO: chap. 6: Reference; chap. 7: Help/Reference

> Considering Wikipedia

Ongoing battles over the use of Wikipedia are quizzical. If one refers to the style manuals, there is no scholarly issue. General knowledge components are not normally cited in papers. The resource itself has steadily improved in quality and is now considered on the same level of reliability as *Britannica*. Though students may still be advised to avoid direct quotations, the crowd-sourced Wikipedia has developed into an interesting source of referrals in keeping with the established pattern of citation mining. Employing it calls for the caution and critical analysis applied to any type of resource—consider diaries and newspaper accounts. Above all, recognize the inevitable. Search-engine drivers and user demand mean that Wikipedia is unavoidable.

SERIALS MANAGEMENT

VL: *TOOL, DEPRECATED*

Serials management has been repurposed for the online world. Publishers and new database aggregators began exploring Internet delivery of article databases as early as the 1970s. Their efforts were transmitted with a vengeance to the Web in the late 1990s. Innovation in the marketplace melded with practical issues in the library and automation prospects. Institutions faced never-ending expansion of massive rows of shelving, normally uncirculating volumes, and annual bindery rituals. Librarians found measures to cope with preservation, storage, and expense issues for an ever-enlarging number of journals.

Changes came with understandable angst. Researchers lament the loss of immersive browsing—the delights of sitting in the stacks surrounded by volume on volume. In its place arise manifest financial, space, and technological tradeoffs. Automation alleviates bindery expenses, awkward processing waits, and nagging "claiming" problems for back issues. Cost differentials facilitate the addition of more titles, and the technology brings circulation and even automatic routing to user desktops.

SEE ALSO: chap. 5: Browsing, Microfilm Collections, Stack Maintenance; chap. 6: Acquisitions, Article/Research Databases, Collection Development

STACK MAINTENANCE

VL: *TOOL, DEPRECATED*

There are no stacks to be patrolled, food and trash to be policed, sightlines to be considered, or books to be reshelved. In the virtual world, the residue is queuing strategies in the case of limited access licensing.

SEE ALSO: chap. 5: Browsing, Circulation Desk, Physical Security, Serials Management; chap. 6: Collection Development

STUDY HALL AND SOCIAL SPHERE

VL: *TOOL, DEPRECATED*

Academic library buildings serve ancillary purposes. Undergraduate access to stacks and student-initiated use of the library as social sphere arose in tandem during the early twentieth century. The virtual library offers a weak draw for socializing. Thanks to Web 2.0, students and faculty have a wide range of applications for extending group and casual engagement. Current experience suggests diminution, or at least elimination of the virtual library as a dating service zone. Attempts in Second Life and other immersive environments are of interest but may be more profitable as prospects for meetings of remote librarians.

Dedicated applications of space for study heightened in response to the GI Bill's proliferation of commuters and adult students. Such activities vanish with the virtual university and library. One does not travel to campus or need a designated place for study and "holing-up" between classes. For the typical adult returning student, the Web is a medium for direct encounters with a task at hand—not for casual social interactions.

SEE ALSO: chap. 7: Social Networking/Web 2.0

TECHNICAL SERVICES

VL: *TOOL, DEPRECATED*

This once broad mainstay of library management disappears or has been significantly deprecated. In the virtual library, much of serials management can be effectively outsourced. The absence of tangible books and journals means the end of the shipping and preparation of materials as well as traditional circulation. There is no need to add spine labels, stiffen covers, or fill other tasks to make materials shelf ready. The lure of RFID tagging can be eliminated. There are no books or stacks to put them in.

SEE ALSO: chap. 5: Circulation Desk, Preservation, Serials Management, Stack Maintenance; chap. 6: Cataloging

CHAPTER 6

REDEFINITION COMMENTARIES

THE GREEN DECONSTRUCTION METAPHOR FROM THE building trades engages beyond the dismantling of obsolete structures. To Bradley Guy and Eleanor Gibeau (2003), the method features the "soft-stripping" or reordering of constituent parts for reuse. Phase two of these exercises follows with repurposing surviving activities for adaptive reuse. Every enduring function undergoes fundamental redefinition. The new realities of online classrooms, remote users, and entrepreneurial drivers actively intervene. The Web's user, technological, and economic realities lead to compromises, contradictions, and the "shoehorning" of legacy functions.

As suggested in previous chapters, the paradigm shift calls for coping strategies and willingness to question orthodoxy. Those dealing with a virtual campus must surface underlying suppositions from print and alter inquiry for the Web:

- **Automation/outsourcing balance.** The Long Tail is spawning specialized automation enhancements from the library niche market but also an intruding commercial marketplace. What were once exclusively human-powered practices that defined professional librarianship morph to the cloud. What is the appropriate cost/benefit balance of such employ for the future of librarianship and the identity of the university library?

- **Bibliographic vs. full text retrieval.** Library methods remain rooted in indexing and abstracting practices that came to fruition in the nineteenth and twentieth centuries. Librarianship remains wedded to this admirable line—albeit with enhancements like semantic networking and linked data. Yet search engines largely ignore the legacy, and users appear happier dealing directly with their full-text methods. How does one reconcile the dichotomy?

- **Curricular orientation.** Many of the academic library contributions on the Web (as opposed to vendor product lines) seem tipped toward history and the humanities. Though of undeniable merit, such orientation has a predictable endpoint. Moreover, it may not address the heart of the pedagogical challenges and financial realities. Growth and political factors point toward business, IT, and other applied fields. What is the appropriate disciplinary balance?

- **Print genre.** Modern librarianship remains rooted in print categorizations into books and articles. These blur on the Web with its rising tide of new media, formats, and retrieval concepts. How does the online library accommodate both avenues?

- **Stewardship.** Digitization efforts are commendable but legally confused when dealing with licensed materials. The virtual library sits on the sideline as potential consumer of such products. Does it have any professional responsibility, and what are the classroom implications?

- **Time/permanence.** The library presupposes "permanence"—the long-term maintenance of materials. An online education focus, rental basis, and nature of web materials alter that fundamental supposition. Usage becomes an active factor for retention. Rote default to long-term and passive storage is no longer justifiable. How does the library cope with the volatile versus archival nature of electronic materials in its institutional setting?

- **Unitary delivery.** The Web indistinguishably transports library bibliographic records along the same channels as the articles, books, and media being described. How does such confluence impact access and previous special collection distinctions such as government documents or maps?

- **Web as Alexandria.** The new medium obviates massive "just-in-case" collections. How do the Web's enlarged availability and "just-in-time" deliveries affect virtual library operations?

The examples that follow gloss the operational contours and different mindset generated for a virtual library but are not intended to be exhaustive. Selections also require a bit of vocabulary tweaking for the different nature of a virtual campus. Given the fluid nature between the library's computer and web stages, expect terminology overlaps with chapter 7.

ACQUISITIONS

VL: *TOOL, REQUIRED*

Acquisition is closely aligned with collection development and among the most dynamic arenas for consideration. The old of purchasing devolves to renting. As indicated by the number of ISBNs, web-era growth in books is explosive—moving from some 900,000 titles in 1990 to over 30 million by 2010. Acquisitions itself becomes at once the most financially accessible and inaccessible in modern history. Online applications are unsettled and unfolding:

- **Automation.** In the mid-1990s, Gobi introduces automated processing. Engagement through mail delivery and transfers to the stacks disappears. Visits to bookstores and out-of-print purchases are a thing of the past. Telecommuting options open.
- **In-boarding.** Print-era procedures evaporate. Virtual acquisition engages through electronic links to external sources. Research databases blend with those for journals. Scholarly communications, scientific social networking, and budding new web formats emerge.
- **Technology.** Acquisition adds consideration for a moving technological line. How does the institution deal with the overhead of navigation in a variety of web reading platforms? Does it address the burgeoning of e-readers—such as Kindles and Nooks—or tablets and mobiles? What about technical components to verify or authenticate the library's legitimate users—logins, IP recognition, proxy servers?

For the virtual library, the arena of operations is the Deep Web but opens for consideration and redefinition through embrace of the Open Web.

Deep Web. The nineteenth-century rise of the mass press and support of scholarly publications produced lasting motifs. Professional librarianship devolved from the structured purchasing of books and journals. The Deep Web continues along such lines, but with unprecedented variations and pitfalls. As indicated, purchasing has been largely replaced by licensing. The prior role as financial supporter of university presses is diminished. New decision skills are demanded for format and DRM along with copyright and handicapped user accessibility. The virtual library considers user options from automatic citations and bookshelves to downloading/printing and ability to make notations. The market opens to a variety of selection options:

- **Big Buy.** Uncertainties and the hunt for profit have combined with library financial interests in a craze for the large-scale bundling of journals and e-books. Such packaging comes with significant cost advantages. A startup virtual library can quickly grow to marketable size. Convenience also raises important professional issues:
  - » *Tailored packages.* Though some Big Buys are general, vendors and consortia tend toward coordinated subject packages. These offer a modicum of peer review, but at the loss of institutional discretion and only the weakest of professional involvement.
  - » *Paying for the free.* Analysis of vendor packages typically reveals a large amount of padding. Government documents, public domain, and otherwise free resources are inserted to inflate the size of the purchase.
  - » *Duplication and overlap analysis.* The manager must be aware of the inevitability of duplications and paying for multiple copies of the same resource, especially scholarly journals.
  - » *Selectivity.* Major intellectual questions arise from farming out decision making to consortia and external commercial forces. Librarians also become trained to a quantity-over-quality mindset. What does it mean to have five thousand journals for a field without being able to focus on the top five that really count?
- **Patron-driven demand (PDD).** With this set of options, faculty and students gain the option of selecting materials of interest along with many of the issues raised by the Big Buy. Fortunately, such transactions can be mediated. The institution sets a threshold figure for automatic purchase—anything above that calls for library approval. With its broadest approach, the PDD agent acts as the institution's book repository. The virtual library builds incrementally over time in response to patron requests.
- **Pay-per-view (PPV).** Pay-per-view models similarly vie for control. These are the publishers favored resort. Sage Press has already installed a successful system, and one expects others to follow in this line.

- **Rental programs.** The ability to rent an item temporarily for a patron provides a PDD and PPV variant that can also alleviate ILL services. Given joint institutional costs for an ILL transaction, this approach may prove quite cost-effective. Control and bottom-line issues remain, but rentals tend to come with interesting accumulation features; the library can set a baseline to turn the number of requests into an acquisition— for example, three rentals automatically converting into a purchase.

Open Web. The wealth of free resources on the Web offers countervailing and almost untapped potential. They awaken return to a different form of acquisitions for the virtual campus. Open access proffers a switch away from purchasing dependencies and toward entrepreneurial agilities:

- **Traditional research genre.** Although decoupling from publisher dependencies, articles and books remain the main objects for research consideration.
- **Expanding classroom options.** Curricular orientation invites expansion to media, blogs, and other emergent web tools. Although these will enter the academic research pantheon, expect such acceptance to be delayed beyond that of open-access journals.

Assuming the materials are appropriate to university purposes, how should the library address materials on the Open Web? To what extent and what should be cataloged? Copyright and Creative Commons licensing enter the picture along

> ## › Unfolding Purchasing Models
>
> How should web-age librarians weight acquisitions to ensure the most relevant results for classroom and research purposes? As the *Library Journal* reported in its annual "Periodicals Price Survey" (April 14, 2011), the library as institution must change:
>
> > We are going to evolve. As has been well documented, the library world was already suffering from funding and technological pressure before the recession officially began in December 2007. In the five years since, the pressure and pace of disruptive change have only accelerated. In order to survive the next five years, the library community will have to focus on the much more difficult task of finding new opportunities. Libraries, publishers, and vendors will all shed some legacy processes; information purchasing patterns will change, leading inevitably to new pricing models. Technology will continue its march forward. The library landscape of 2016 will be very different from today's.

with questions about in-house versus cloud-based storage. Does the library merely link or download to re-serve? What about fair use and dark archives?

SEE ALSO: chap. 5: Out-of-Print Market; chap. 6: Article/Research Databases, Cataloging, Collection Development, University Archives, Weeding; chap. 7: Dark Archives, E-books, Mobile Devices/Tablets, Reading Platforms, Scholarly Communications, Scientific Social Networking/Open-Science Movement

ALUMNI SERVICES

VL: *SERVICE, OPTION*

In a print past, alumni use of the campus library came with little downside. The Web complicates matters. On one hand, the virtual academic library retains the opportunity to participate in long-range strategies for building its university's identity. Alumni access contributes to lifelong learning and provides a conduit for alumni donations along with a lure to return for another program or coursework.

› Traditional vs. Electronic Donors

The availability of materials on the Open Web partially returns collection analysis to a time before acquisitions budgets, but with notable differences. Before the nineteenth century, donations provided the major mechanism for library growth. Donor relations and the associated processing of the gifts also continue as a point of interest for many mainstream libraries. Though largely out of scope for virtual libraries, a form of transfer is possible. Rather than the great book donations of the past, this type of conveyance is more archival in nature—for example, acquiring an individual's digital memoir or media creation. The donor, however, must own the copyright and be willing to transfer or license it for electronic usage.

On the other hand, alumni access for virtual materials raises economic and legal issues. The manager must balance financial costs and complex contractual nuance. Stress may be present with e-books, but article databases raise the highest flags. Though some vendors are comfortable, fears there are rife. Will the alumni "steal" access for their day jobs? What is a proper metric for calculating alumni use? Hence, some distributors will not grant licensure, others only through exorbitant surcharges. The virtual academic library may end up eliminating or controlling access for alumni with a separate interface and perhaps reduced content.

SEE ALSO: chap. 6: University Archives; chap. 7: Authentication, Security—Web

ARTICLE/RESEARCH DATABASES

VL: *SERVICE, REQUIRED*

With the Web, the art form of serials librarianship with its claiming and preservation binding vanishes. Vendor-based services and federated search engines handle most of the replacement niceties. Full-text journals and research databases dominate the scene. Appropriate technologies and database aggregators are present as formative elements to help birth virtual libraries. Though faculty allegiance to books may remain strong, the shorter length of articles and scholarly verification offered by citation analysis appear more congenial for LMS and virtual campus applications.

Despite relative maturity, these offerings boast challenges. As with books, the number of titles has exploded to previously unimaginable heights. Following the simplest of metrics, libraries are driven toward the convenience of quantitative growth. The selection hunt begins to engage an ever-expanding set of technical features. Mobile delivery, download/cloud access, automated citations, and ADA 508 compliance are soon firmly ensconced among selection criteria, soon to be joined by touch screen, voice recognition navigation, and as yet unpredictable advances.

> ### › Classroom Linking
>
> Although permanent DOI links and LTI (learning technology interface) standards offer solace, LMSs are currently underdeveloped for incorporating library materials. Instructors encounter problems with article placement. It is too easy to confuse the potentially varied results from a "Post" query with those of "Get," which deals with a fixed location.

The virtual library will encounter complaints and become cognizant of confusion among "Google-tuned" users. Information literacy and tutorial support step forward. Fixed help/training sites must be prepared along with prospects for personalized and classroom sessions. Quality and other issues arise, such as

- **Storage.** Freedom from physical storage concerns brings significant financial benefits, but also challenges. What are the implications and options for cloud-based outsourcing?
- **Open access.** As seen with the Directory of Open Access Journals, universities and libraries are at the forefront of a new wave of scholarly resources. How do these directions blend or balance with the established marketplace?
- **Pricing.** A selection of commercial producers and scholarly societies engage in seemingly exorbitant pricing. Journal publishers, vendors, and

library associations experiment with pricing models. Tiered and FTE-based subscriptions vie with pay-for-view opportunities. Are the days numbered for Big Buy bundling, inflationary pricing, and legions of unused electronic titles?

- **Embargoed editions.** Professors have theoretical rights under fair use to enable recently discovered materials for classroom use, especially for lectures. Could libraries already contracting for the holding journal make a digital copy available even if the issue is embargoed (not yet been made available)?

SEE ALSO: chap. 5: Serials Management; chap. 6: Acquisitions, Collection Development, Course Reserves, Information Literacy, Interlibrary Loan; chap. 7: E-books, Open-Access Journals, Training/Tutorial Services

AUDIO COLLECTIONS

VL: SERVICE, OPTION

Audio collections rose to prominence following Philips Electronic's commercial development of the cassette player in the 1960s. Music, audiobooks, and language tapes of the 1970s and 1980s morphed into CDs and DVDs in the 1990s. Transformation continued with the Web. Although complicated by a confusing variety of formatting, bandwidth, and streaming options, MP3 downloads expanded the soundscape. The library needs to be aware that sound and video holdings have special legal protections, including ADA 508 concerns. Facility raises Internet piracy concerns on campuses. Although of little practical effect for online universities, the Higher Education Opportunity Act requires campus awareness and warnings to ward off student piracy of such files.

Fortunately, delivery problems have smoothed and, with HTML5, are destined to become simpler. Indeed, virtual library treatment converges. Individual resources can be cataloged and directly accessed by the user with little to no differences from that for a book or article. Legal nuance aside, web delivery blends away from print distinctions.

The virtual library can also consider publishing or collecting audio files as collections along with publishing to YouTube, ITunes U, or other open-web sites. Classroom use offers prospects for injecting library oversight for ADA 508 and copyright compliance. Voice recognition applications expand opportunities for library/classroom cooperation, such as the language training programs Rosetta Stone and Mango.

SEE ALSO: chap. 6: Collection Development, Publishing, Video Collections; chap. 7: ADA 508

CATALOGING

VL: *TOOL, REQUIRED/DEPRECATED*

Cataloging proffers a particularly contentious and uncertain battleground. What is necessary for a web environment? The virtual library leans toward a minimalist perspective and simplicity wherever possible. With the possible exception of university archives, it has little to no need for original cataloging. Though some in-house expertise is required for communication with vendors, copy cataloging more than suffices—and that can be readily outsourced.

In keeping with utilitarian precepts, the virtual academic library continues to employ extant bibliographic records, but it also looks toward the present and future domination of search engines and full-text expectations. The Web adds a premium on user-based concerns for simplification and allied tools for study or research outputs. From such a perspective, the semantic web is interesting and external contributions gratefully accepted, but they are of questionable value given search engines and cost/benefit terms. Web-based success for students and faculty is not dependent on the bibliographic orientation of the past but on full-text retrieval.

Mixed sites and other dilemmas. The Web's flexibility creates significant problems for taxonomic practices that date to the nineteenth century. Scholarly communications and the open-science movement are but two examples of complex, mixed genre sites that defy library conventions. What are the most appropriate measures for extracting or excluding journal and article titles from the combined resources within Columbia University's CIAO or Praeger's Security International collection?

Similarly, where should the virtual library turn for current attempts to update cataloging for websites themselves? The pending loss of MARC makes sense, but what about what follows? What RDA guidelines? Will RDA or another metadata schema prevail, or could all of the library automation edifice fall to seemingly more user-friendly commercial approaches? Indeed, will W3C's devotion to semantic networks come to naught, or be significantly modified in response to the overwhelming amount of work in building ontologies?

The virtual library view must remain skeptical—"wait-and-see" with doses of paradigm-shift wariness and cost-consciousness in mind. What is the added value of the Dublin Core, library metadata, or other human-abstracted information versus hierarchical databases, Bayesian mathematics, and automated ingestion of full text—especially if the main search engines ignore the former categories? The repeated reality is that users are satisfied by commercial search engines and dissatisfied with library systems.

SEE ALSO: *chap. 5: Bibliographic Instruction, Card Catalog, MARC; chap. 6: Catalog Interface; chap. 7: Discovery Search, Metadata, RDA, Scholarly Communications, Scientific Social Networking/Open-Science Movement*

CATALOG INTERFACE

VL: *SERVICE, REQUIRED*

The hunt for the perfect entrance to the library's resources remains challenging in virtual space. The Web replaces the stolid consistency of catalog card furnishing with an ever-evolving round of interfaces. The web catalog resources rather than the stand-alone terminals became prominent fixtures on library landing pages. Technology in the 1990s extended Z39.50 drives for the book catalog to database coverage. ILS vendors followed in the next decade and took the competitive opportunity to push their designs.

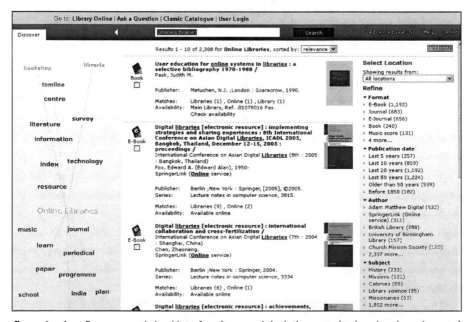

figure 6.1 AquaBrowser word cloud interface (www.serialsolutions.com/en/services/aquabrowser)

> Granularity Directions

A CRIS model leads toward boutique displays. The main library remains as the "laboratory" hub for research, but departmental libraries may be broken out for tailored curricular services. These directions lead deeper on the financial side and toward personalization. Library systems would benefit from additional granularity to deal with individual or group-level access. For example, one could negotiate pricing based on limited access for specialized classrooms. Related issues arise for the integration of a student's electronic textbook purchase into the library's holdings.

Thanks to the Web, users have come to expect the prominent placement of "all-in-one" Google-like search boxes. Library interfaces respond readily with prominent placement of federated and full-text discovery engines. At the moment, however, perfection awaits and prospects persist. Users are easily confused by federated concentration on bibliographic records. Not all products allow search-engine crawling and new prospects unfold. Semantic browsers and word clouds delve into computer and human interface options for more graphically oriented users (see figure 6.1). Such approaches should also prove of value for designing touch screen searching and exploring augmented reality prospects.

Monitoring and the flexibility for change are necessary. The virtual library's main allied drive is to maximize campus linkages back to the library. Even with discovery and federated search or word clouds, online librarians face repeated questioning about why web-era students should have to learn dated skills. APUS survey data confirm that online students are quizzical and unsatisfied by complex library catalogs and journal database engines. Moreover, the virtual library will need to prepare for the near horizon when touch screen and voice-recognition navigation kick off an inevitable round of confusion.

SEE ALSO: chap. 6: Article/Research Databases, Cataloging, Departmental Libraries; chap. 7: Digital Commons, Discovery Search, Federated Search, Help/ Reference, Website as Library

CIRCULATION

VL: *TOOL, DEPRECATED*

With the exception of physical interlibrary loans, nothing truly circulates in the online library world. Instead, identical digital copies are dispatched through

HTTP handshakes to the users' machines. The new means of distribution calls forth distinctly different and complex considerations, especially for e-books:

- Does delivery require downloading an application (app) to the computer?
- If so, are any of the potential users blocked by security or administrative rights controls?
- Is delivery restricted to or from certain types of hardware (e.g., Kindle, iPad, mobile device)?
- What are acceptable DRM limits in terms of time for loan or inactivity?
- How much printing will be allowed?
- If available, can multiuser licensing be financially justified?
- If only single licenses, how many?
- How many different types of readers should your readers be subjected to?

SEE ALSO: chap. 5: Circulation Desk; chap. 6: Collection Development, Copyright; chap. 7: Bookshelves—Electronic, DRM, Reading Platforms

COLLECTION ASSESSMENT

VL: *TOOL, OPTION*

The formal overview of departmental holdings offers a significant arrow for virtual library development. Collection assessments or analyses push to the fore. They are invaluable tools for reporting and affirming the library's value on a virtual campus. Prospects heighten during program reviews, specialized accreditation visits, and the mounting of new programs. The subject specialist liaison/embedded librarian should take the lead—or the library takes the opportunity to add such a position. Desirable tactics push toward structured involvement and a seat at review tables as early as possible in any scenario.

The makeup of such a document will vary, but it should be standardized across the curriculum. At what levels can the library currently support the individual program—general education, upper division, master's, doctorate? In keeping with the outline in figure 6.2, such exercises reveal strengths but also should expose weaknesses. The scan provides a proactive baseline for collection development and leverage for growing resources.

SEE ALSO: chap. 6: Acquisitions, Collection Development; chap. 7: Embedded Librarians

---

APUS Online Library Collection Analysis
Department/Program Name
School of...
Month, Year

Librarian Author

CollAnalysis 2008; Retention 3 years

Overview

- **Program Portal Traffic:**
- **Book Title #:**
- **Journal Title #:**
- **Dedicated Database Collections** (e.g., ProQuest, Ebsco)
  - ○
- **Course Guides #:**
- **Subject Specialist Librarians**
  - ○

Book Holdings

- LC Subject Headings
- LC Classification Ranges
- Key Titles/Reference Works
  - ○

Journals—Sample of Key Titles (check citation analysis)

- •

Media Resources

- •

CourseGuides (list courses, monthly traffic)

- •

Summary + Recommended Enhancements/Purchases

---

figure 6.2 APUS collection analysis template

COLLECTION DEVELOPMENT

VL: *TOOL, REQUIRED*

Acquisitions' intellectual compatriot faces a web remake. The medium, born-web, and classroom components proffer game changers. Prior assumption of long-term acquisition wanes. Consortial arrangements and rental packages come with time limits. Copyright concerns rise in prominence. Given search engines and the array of sites, the expenses for ready reference and large reference collections may be dismissed. Related concerns for "prepurchasing" scholarly monographs and massive "just-in-case" holdings lose out to practical economics as well as the ability to purchase or rent on demand.

Curricular perspectives. In one of the most difficult adjustments, collection development alters psychological commitments to research. A CRIS scenario places the university's curriculum and student concerns at the center. Tactics speak to program and course objectives. Methods look to rubrics and metrics, which are increasingly prominent for the virtual campus and accreditation. Evaluation builds systemically. Usage benchmarking is allied with content analysis from departmental portals, course guides, and collection assessments.

In this altered scenario, collection development rises in sophistication by highlighting a second track:

- **Research.** Research consideration remains in place, albeit simplified by electronic purchasing and rental options. In a CRIS setting, research materials are selected with an eye toward disciplinary methods courses. This approach ensures continuation of the established concept of visiting the library as "laboratory" for scholarly research but proactively injects familiarity and seeks to enhance usage.
- **Class readings.** Collection development extends to populating the classroom electronically and new realms of complexity. Course reserves may be put in place, but transparency must still be considered. Best practice for the online classroom advocates removing extra steps. Should the student have to travel to the library for regular in-class reading? Managerial concerns must map too in keeping with the typical three-year classroom development cycle. A range of related concerns come into play:
  - » *Tracking is required in general for limited multiyear contract "buys" through consortia.* It and the type/number of licenses are of particular importance when classroom materials are involved. The library has to consider proper licensing type as matched to potential and active user demand. Rather than preservation, consideration enters in preparation for possible withdrawals, such as a dark archives tactic.
  - » *Granularity by discipline will increasingly come into play.* Considerations for history and English are different from those for more volatile technical disciplines like engineering and computer science. Acquisition decisions for the latter trend away from book purchases toward the enhanced currency and cost benefits of websites.
  - » *Chunking and e-book considerations.* The Web and movement to mobile devices present significant challenges for e-books. In addition to currency, the book is difficult to read online. Electronic course materials thus trend toward "chunking" into chapters, articles, videos, or websites and respond to growing expectations for the extraction of subunits and the delivery of knowledge kernels.

Open-web resource mining. The medium reenables collection development beyond purchases. Librarians gain the ability to mine open-web resources to address collection "holes" dynamically. They may even commission specific titles. Although easily overlooked, many of the commercial article and research database products are also populated by large slices of government documents and public domain materials, which are otherwise available without copyright restrictions.

SEE ALSO: chap. 6: Acquisitions, Copyright, Course Reserves, Departmental Libraries, University Archives, Weeding; chap. 7: Course Guides, Resource Data Mining

COPYRIGHT

VL: *TOOL, REQUIRED/OPTION*

Copyright is a minefield but comes with opportunities. It requires knowledge of the law along with ongoing monitoring of court cases and interpretations from the Librarian of Congress on the Digital Millennium Copyright Act (DMCA) as well as policies and procedures. There are applications for two states of engagement:

Required. Academic libraries must consider copyright for their own site operations. Fortunately, the bulk of engagement is transformed into a by-product of contract negotiations for resource acquisitions. Vendor licenses supersede copyright for the establishment of authorization protocols, DRM, and usage limits. Copyright issues per se occur more with downloading of web materials into the library's collections or support pages. Assuming the originating site does not prohibit and is not visibly violating someone else's copyright (e.g., reposting a first-run movie or new song release), recommended practice calls for embedding links. Avoid the temptation to download and re-serve content, except as narrowly allowed under fair use exemptions.

> ### › DMCA Letters
>
> The value of clearly defined policies and procedures rises to the fore with receipt of "cease and desist" claims under the DMCA. University libraries may encounter "slam" operations, which cruise the Web in the hunt for financial opportunities but may also find themselves in unwitting violation. Response procedures include a posted copyright policy and relations with the university's legal offices. Both cases also call for documentation and studied action to determine the validity of the violation. For suspected slamming, the recommendation is to avoid immediate reply. For a violation, act in good faith to remove the offense.

File To Upload		Browse...	
Display Name			Hide details
Description			
Copyright Status	Fair Use or Public Domain Assumption		▼
Copyright Alert	Fair Use or Public Domain Assumption		
	Instructor owns Copyright		
	Library/University License		
	Student Owned		
	Temporary Work Product: Not intended for publication		
	Unsure--contact requested		

figure 6.3 Detail of APUS copyright declaration

Other problems may arise from the posting of dissertations or theses and commissioned publications. Such cases recommend active library review and declarations of compliance from the authors.

Optional: classroom services. Copyright expertise can extend to auditing opportunities for the classroom. The library lobbies to lend its authority to decision making/declarations as well as providing guidance and easing the burden on faculty. The Sakai LMS implementation schema illustrated in figure 6.3, for example, directs instructors through a simple set of queries when downloading materials into their classroom. These include textbook-related "Student Owned" and open-access "Instructor owns Copyright." "Library/University License" is deliberately leading and joins "Unsure—contact requested" in triggering a staff review and appropriate interventions.

SEE ALSO: *chap. 6: Acquisitions, Collection Development, Dissertations and Theses; chap. 7: ADA 508, Authentication*

COURSE RESERVES

VL: *SERVICE, REQUIRED/OPTION*

The basic idea of course reserves remains, but it can accelerate for the virtual campus. Academic libraries began as small collections for the collective needs of students. Research libraries continued that trend with dedicated course reserves.

Books are pulled and isolated from the main collection and articles photocopied or issues made available. Such materials are then relegated for separate check-out privileges under a specific course and professor. The virtual library offers a roughly equivalent approach. Instead of limiting access to the students in said class, current technology leads to a "work-around": electronic copies technically remain open for the campus but can also be highlighted in separate course reserves or perhaps as a designated tab within a course guide.

Classroom embedding. The separate course reserves site is best considered as supplemental. In classrooms, transparency and reducing user overhead are highly desirable. Library materials should be embedded for direct access in the syllabus or LMS's course assignment module. Although ADA 508 and copyright considerations remain, open-web mounting is straightforward. Library involvement rises with deep-web holdings, such as these:

- E-books are enabled by copying and pasting links from the catalog record (MARC 856 field) or linking to the external site, but there are complications. Unless it has multiple user licensing or owns copyright, the library needs to monitor for queuing, including the potential for adding licenses based on demand and possible removals.
- E-articles are typically available for multiuser access. Confusion may arise with linking tactics. The instructor assumes that a link from a search is the same as a DOI or fixed location.

SEE ALSO: chap. 6: Article/Research Data-bases, Collection Development, Copyright, Pathfinders; chap. 7: Authentication, Dark Archives, E-books, Reading Platforms

> **› Georgia State Reserves and Copyright**
>
> Course reserves remain fraught with unsettled issues on copyright compliance and extension of fair use. Judge Orinda Evans's decision in *Cambridge University Press, Oxford University Press, Sage Publications v. Georgia State University* (2012) may help encourage extensions of electronic course reserves. In a generally favorable ruling, Evans provided tacit approval for reasonable employ (e.g., roughly 10 percent of a book) under fair use of digital library holdings in university classrooms. One must also note, however, that Sage Publications prevailed in the only sustained complaints. It had put in place a readily usable payment system, which may become a model for the rest of the academic publishers and game changer for U.S. university libraries.

CURRICULUM LABORATORIES

VL: *SERVICE, OPTION*

The creation and maintenance of curricular libraries offer intriguing prospects. If the university includes an education department, such facility can take on a dual role as training laboratory. Like government documents and map collections, electronic materials fold into the general holdings—

> ### ❯ History Note
>
> According to Rita Kohrman (2012), the use of "laboratories" for dedicated libraries of curricular materials dates to 1932 and was based on pioneering 1929 services at Western Michigan University.

yet, they also bring opportunities for marshaling together in a departmental or subject guide.

Given its origins, a virtual academic library has a native affinity to monitor developments, which can stretch into partnership opportunities. Information on the development of web-based pedagogies offers prospects for proactively informing the faculty and other support units. Facebook or other Web 2.0 groups make additional tactical sense. Indeed, such directions offer generalizable fodder for cross-institutional cooperation.

SEE ALSO: *chap. 5: Government Document Depository, Map Collections; chap. 6: Departmental Libraries; chap. 7: Social Networking/Web 2.0*

DEPARTMENTAL LIBRARIES

VL: *SERVICE, REQUIRED*

As suggested for government document depositories and map collections, usage statistics and new knowledge realities raise questions. How much attention should be given to library-determined genre- and subject-based taxonomies? Thus, subject-based pathfinders decline in priority to course guides, but attention also turns to dedicated portals for the university's various departments and programs.

Debates over the general library versus disciplinary collections emerged as early as the fourteenth century, but one thing remains a political constant: academic departments look favorably on their own library. That proclivity creates openings for library reinvention and sustainability. Web technology facilitates efficient multipurposing from a centralized base. It offers tactical advantages for partnership/community development. In keeping with a CRIS model, departmental portals work in concert with course guides as part of a new library-centric dynamic to enhance university quality and currency.

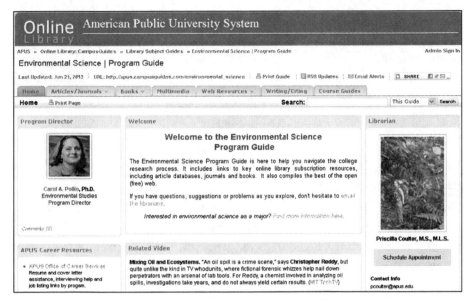

figure 6.4 APUS program portal

Librarians or a team of librarians engage their faculties to build boutique domains (as in figure 6.4). The site as designed is a work in progress. It offers information literacy and a research launching pad. Results roughly equate to a methods course for the field with extension toward broader involvement of the knowledge community.

SEE ALSO: *chap. 5: Government Document Depository, Map Collections; chap. 6: Curriculum Laboratories, Dissertations and Theses, Pathfinders; chap. 7: Course Guides*

DISSERTATIONS AND THESES

VL: *SERVICE, OPTION*

Bindery demands may have passed, but virtual university libraries should consider continuing that traditional role as web publisher of record for student theses and doctoral dissertations. Copyright and ADA 508 can help open the door for this sort of library involvement. End products are marketed as part and parcel of scholarly reputation building; they proffer vital evidence of the university's scholarly credentials along with furthering partnerships with academic departments.

Deposit can overlap too with the development of university archives and digital commons, which proffer future involvement in institutional research.

Accumulation of student products over time enables the future study of academic trends and departmental evaluations—as well as an element for accreditation reviews.

SEE ALSO: *chap. 5: Bindery Operations; chap. 6: Copyright, Departmental Libraries, Publishing, University Archives; chap. 7: ADA 508, Digital Commons, Metrics, Portfolios*

INFORMATION LITERACY

VL: *SERVICE, REQUIRED*

The virtual library reconstitutes information literacy into web information literacy—its main outreach tool. The approach tailors beyond general skills to the peculiar methods of the university's departments. Focus is given to the proper employ of the holdings in the library.

Information literacy training should be viewed as part of an integrated process. The site as well as the librarians should be prepared with appropriate tutorial resources. Support pages, online writing labs, and program portals all have roles to play, but engagement with academic departments and support units is crucial to success.

Online librarians should be expert in such matters and appropriately credentialed for the academic disciplines in questions. They must be ready to handle related reference questions but proactive in proselytizing information literacy for the university. The desired path routes their support materials and also embeds librarians in the classrooms; moreover, we look to add the resulting skills as differentiating elements in the evaluation of online universities.

SEE ALSO: *chap. 5: Bibliographic Instruction; chap. 6: Departmental Libraries, Reference, Tutorial Services; chap. 7: Course Guides, Embedded Librarians, Metrics, Online Writing Laboratories*

INTERLIBRARY LOAN

VL: *SERVICE, REQUIRED/DEPRECATED*

Without creative footwork, consortial participation, or outsourcing, the fully virtual library is limited in terms of participation. Journal prospects are dependent on licensing agreements. E-books could be totally out of the picture. The fully virtual library is without the property to share, hence, technically ineligible for participation.

⟩ Supplemental/ Transitional Subscriptions

The cost-conscious virtual library manager may entertain alternate tactics for certain journal loans. ILL monitoring, for example, surfaces journal requests that threaten to exceed recommended practice limits or where access is temporarily thwarted by embargo. In such instances, a full library subscription may not be financially merited, available, or suited for request. Instead, the library may consider a single supplemental or transitional subscription.

Despite such issues, ILL remains a fundamental interest. It also reflects a most intriguing and highly conflicted arena. At this moment in time, for instance, ramifications of the *Authors Guild v. HathiTrust decision* (Oct. 10, 2012) remain to be seen. Will academic libraries be able to create an electronic ILL book exchange forum? Will the post-1923 "doughnut hole" for orphan works close?

The future of ILL remains in doubt. In theory, paper-based ILL becomes a thing of the past. Trucking, mail, and packaging demands are technologically outmoded and often too slow for a virtual university. Operations are an expensive burden on both cooperating libraries. The virtual library thus considers scanning/publishing alternatives for works in the public domain. Cost/ benefit analysis recommends purchasing consideration, patron-initiated actions, or rental procedures.

Vendor options. Attention turns to the library economy for burgeoning opportunities. On May 3, 2011, for example, ebrary sent out an advertisement on e-book services that replace the ILL clerk:

> **ebrary Launches the Industry's First Usage-Triggered Model for Short-Term Loans**
>
> Our new Short-Term Loans can be your standalone cost-saving service, or used in conjunction with our Patron Driven Acquisition (PDA) program to offer an additional layer of mediation before titles are triggered for purchase. As YBP's preferred e-book vendor, ebrary also makes Short-Term Loans available through YBP's Demand Driven Acquisition service.
>
> ebrary's Short-Term Loans are available for one or seven day periods. When the loan is triggered, libraries receive a notification and are given a number of flexible options including purchasing the title, making it available for purchase through PDA, or offering another Short-Term Loan. Libraries may offer up to three loans per title.

Additional features and benefits:

- Ability to offer as a standalone service or in conjunction with PDA.
- Triggering system ensures titles receive real usage.
- Growing selection of eligible e-books from such renowned publishers as Cambridge University Press, Elsevier, The McGraw Hill Companies, Wiley, and many others.
- Robust, do-it-yourself title selection and real-time management of collection profiles, fund codes, and alerts.
- Seamless integration with other ebrary products including Academic Complete™ with DASH!™, recently added to the CHOICE OAT List.
- Available any time through any web-enabled device including the iPad.
- ebrary InfoTools™, which turns every word into a portal to additional information on the Web.
- Notes and highlights that are automatically stored on a personal book-shelf.
- Ability to copy/paste and print text with automatic citations and URL hyperlinks back to the source.

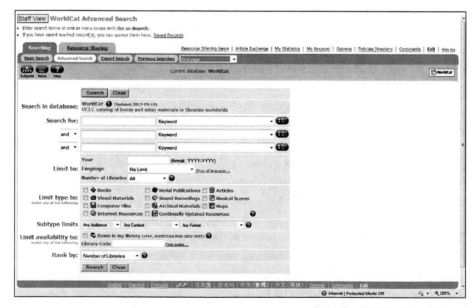

figure 6.5 OCLC WorldCat ILL form

- Personal bookshelves with moveable folders that can be shared with others.
- Multiple options for searching, navigating, and browsing.
- ADA 508c compliant content, text-to-speech, and other accessibility features.
- Free on-demand MARC records.
- Granular COUNTER-compliant usage reports.

Processing. There is no doubt of the Web's effects on processing. Electronic copies and scanning eliminate the need for fleets of trucks and mailing services. As illustrated by the staff view of OCLC's WorldCat in figure 6.5, the medium has also enabled the automation and transformation of the work.

SEE ALSO: chap. 6: Acquisitions, Article/Research Databases, Collection Development; chap. 7: E-books

PATHFINDERS

VL: *SERVICE, OPTION*

From a virtual library perspective, pathfinders (subject or research guides) offer 1980s era transitional frameworks. They moved gracefully from typewritten to electronic formats as among the earliest library contributions on the Open Web. The concept, however, requires tweaking. Search engines alter computer-age assumptions. The volatility of the Web complicates maintenance and readily leads to obsolescence. Usage statistics and university politics recommend different priorities. Library-oriented research guides give way to departmental portals, subject guides to course guides.

SEE ALSO: chap. 5: Bibliographic Instruction; chap. 6: Departmental Libraries, Information Literacy; chap. 7: Course Guides, Search Engines

PLAGIARISM CONTROLS

VL: *SERVICE/TOOL, OPTION*

Plagiarism has been around for centuries but has surfaced as an increasing point of rub on virtual campuses. Rather than policing and punishment, such oversights should start with educational responses and are a natural offshoot for online writing lab services. The library may take the lead or share expertise with a center for teaching and learning or curriculum laboratory in the production of related training materials for students and faculty. Related opportunities arise for the management of an automatic detection system, such as TurnItIn.

SEE ALSO: *chap. 6: Copyright, Curriculum Laboratories; chap. 7: Online Writing Laboratories, Training/Tutorial Services*

PUBLISHING

VL: *SERVICE/TOOL, REQUIRED/OPTION*

Anything mounted on the Web can be considered published. The library website and its ancillary pages are automatically a form of publication. Course guides, department portals, and the like may be regarded as new variants in a line with printed bibliographic indexes. These new genres form valuable resources for sharing, comparison, and scholarly purposes.

The library should also consider promoting its publisher persona for other university units. For example, it should play a role with dissertations and theses along with highlighting the like of "great student papers." This extends to archival functions and reputation management applications. The virtual library has similar potential for engaging internal and staff newsletters.

By supplanting controls on the means of publication and distribution, the Web even facilitates entry as a scholarly publisher. The virtual library gains the ability to showcase through oversight of peer-reviewed scholarly journals and monographic contributions. Such activities should lead to studied consideration of open-access participation and ties with university presses.

SEE ALSO: *chap. 6: Departmental Libraries, Dissertations and Theses, University Archives; chap. 7: Course Guides, Open-Access Journals, Social Networking/Web 2.0, Website as Library*

REFERENCE

VL: *SERVICE, REQUIRED*

The Web's impact on reference is among the most intricate. On one hand, search engines have transformed user practice and expectations. Instead of having to go "there," the library becomes a second stage after Googling. Ready reference effectively disappears under the weight of Wikipedia. Virtual library managers adjust for decreased demand and operational styles. High-priced collections call for a careful approach. How can one justify investment in expensive reference products of limited classroom and citation value, especially if comparable resources may be found on the Open Web? Do they have countervailing and overriding research value?

On the other hand, reference services are an expected feature and major element in sustainability. In some virtual institutions, the reference librarian effectively defines the library's presence. Despite reduced demand, library doors do not close on a virtual campus. Management needs to consider staffing requirements along with reasonable response times and mechanisms for the new environment. The Web impacts other internal practices and decision making as well. Does the library rely on e-mail, chat, or widgets (like a Meebo) or employ other web applications? Scheduling, passoffs, and monitoring mechanisms must be orchestrated for extended hours and remote workers. Reactive reference desk models with on-duty librarians are revamped with such construction features as these:

- **Web 2.0.** In addition to reacting to inquiries on the library's external Facebook, Google +, LinkedIn, Second Life, or similar pages, online reference librarians patrol their university's Web 2.0 sites to intercept queries proactively.
- **Site design.** Somewhat akin to preparing signage for navigating a traditional facility, expect web-era patrons to hunt for answers on their own. The virtual library site must thus be built with self-reference in mind. In addition to prominent "About the Library" and "Getting Started" links, librarians include background pointers and construct subsidiary help pages. In APUS, such sensibilities have led to morphing reference traffic under a prominently placed "Help" button. Tactically placed as the far right-hand button on the top navigation banner, this simple switch has dramatically raised queries and enhanced user satisfaction.
- **Outsourcing options.** For-profits in particular are likely to investigate outsourcing to a web service. Issues are many. A portion rests with cost/benefit analysis. Given declining demand, what is the breakeven point between reduced staffing and contracting tactics? External providers should be able to brand for the university and handle simple queries. How will they integrate responses with the library's specific holdings and the university's curriculum? Questions arise too on the loss of high-touch treatment of faculty and students. The online library also loses internal marketing advantages and may forgo opportunities for building institutional identity/reputation management.

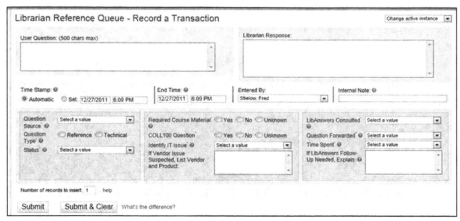

figure 6.6 Control screen for automated reference service (APUS library screen capture from Springshare LibAnswers)

- **"Clouding" of FAQs.** Automated reference management products are emerging on the market. They are valuable in bringing managerial order to the new demands of 24/7 and telecommuting services for a new era in reference. Software tools can give librarians the ability to observe and control the user's operations remotely. Another set can automate FAQ methods from the early days of the Internet (figure 6.6). Artificial intelligence and semantic analysis enable the prepositioning of instantaneous Google-like responses; one need not wait for the librarian. Mechanized procedures handle the bulk of routine questions and allow additional time for more in-depth services. Reference is reformulated in the process.

> **> Chat or Not to Chat?**
>
> Chat and related telephonic services for instantaneous communications are vexatious. The concept of direct contact with the reference desk is ingrained in librarianship. Web-based facilities may make use of the Meebo widget or other applications to indicate that an online librarian is on duty.
>
> Yet instantaneous human responses are rife with problems. Immediacy leads to quickened responses. It thwarts the ability to take extra time for studied responses. The 24/7 nature of the virtual library also complicates staffing. It requires queuing strategies for passoffs among shifts and methods for dealing with "clashing" communications. Open chat sessions and Second Life–type conversations unfold linearly with the prospects of added confusion from multiple players. Rather than "threaded" lines of discussion, the Q&A process can be broken and conversation disjointed. And, in addition to sloppy grammar, the informal nature of chatting may occasionally encourage patrons into confrontational stances.

SEE ALSO: *chap. 5: Ready Reference; chap. 7: Discovery Search, Help/Reference, Online Writing Laboratories*

SYSTEMS LIBRARIANS/DEPARTMENTS

VL: *TOOL, OPTION*

Systems librarians and departments are a product of automation in the computer stage of this history. Given their pioneering adventures, academic libraries were frequently left to their own devices with separate IT sections. The ILS thus ended up well ensconced or proved too alien for absorption into campus ERP (enterprise resource planning software).

The virtual library must still ensure good communication channels and timely support services, but conditions are changing with the Web. Elements of the systems librarian may remain, but support operations and staffing demands are shifted. The rise of the cloud and vendor options eliminate much of the need for full-time positions. Operations are increasingly outsourced or, as native to an online library, incorporated within the broader web domain of campus IT (which experience reveals can be problematic).

SEE ALSO: *chap. 5: Technical Services; chap. 6: Cataloging; chap. 7: Authentication, Proxy Servers*

TUTORIAL SERVICES

VL: *SERVICE, OPTION*

The library may be able to parlay information literacy into related tutorial operations. Online librarians have responsibilities for training on databases and e-books as well as the construction/linkages to fixed help resources. Online writing labs offer a natural progression. The library should consider companion approaches for mathematics or reach out across the curriculum in support of student success.

Depending on opportunities, such directions may extend to the control of other services—plagiarism or contracted tutorial services (Smarthinking, Net-Tutor, Tutor.Com), for example. If employed in this fashion, the library should anticipate immersion in contract negotiations and comparison shopping. Alternatively, the library may engage in coordination with related campus centers for learning, curriculum laboratories, or in-house tutors.

SEE ALSO: *chap. 5: Bibliographic Instruction; chap. 6: Curriculum Laboratories, Information Literacy, Plagiarism Controls; chap. 7: Help/Reference, Online Writing Laboratories*

> ## › Defining Archives
>
> The Web has expanded the meaning of *archives*. Uniqueness and intrinsic/economic value vanish in the modern equation. Rather than artifacts, web repositories deal with "digital archives"— scanned arrays of historical texts and images. In addition, paper-based ties to record keeping have morphed into electronic backup procedures.

UNIVERSITY ARCHIVES

VL: *SERVICE/TOOL, OPTION*

Since they typically rent and own nothing, virtual academic libraries could be destined to sit on the archival sidelines. That would be a shame. My wish list remains optimistic. A virtual university archives program offers exceptional possibilities for validating information services and building university reputation/identity. Such a presence directs a portion of the virtual library's thinking back to the historical narrative and long-term planning for the creation of supplemental services on the virtual campus.

As new and business-oriented institutions, online universities have been slow to appreciate the importance of tradition building. Market forces and the importance of differentiating products are, however, hard to deny for the long term. Without intervention, the university loses out in the drive for staff and alumni identification. Much of the potential is lost for building academic reputation over the long haul.

A university archives can claim added potential. Marketing departments can use the help in preserving their products for reuse over time. Such prospects are similarly appealing in preparation for an anniversary of the founding—as well as personally to board members and retiring senior executives. Oral/video histories and commemorative websites emerge to prominence.

Online universities also can be reminded of their institutional documentary heritage. Such materials originate and are best handled in the computer but offer curation and developmental prospects as well. Without proactive involvement, historically valuable records are easily dispersed across the hands of IT, the registrar, lawyers, and other bureaucratic functionaries. A professionally maintained university archives even offers legal and developmental benefits.

As indicated elsewhere in these commentaries, a university archives speaks to the traditional capture and storage of theses and dissertations. Archival practices come to the fore too with considerations of dark archives. Related support should be considered for student portfolios and integrated with publication initiatives. Such directions and the idea of permanence are appropriate turf for the entrepreneurial virtual library. They also suggest staffing tactics. The manager should consider taking the opportunity to build a case for hiring an archive specialist.

SEE ALSO: *chap. 5: Archives and Manuscript Collections; chap. 6: Alumni Services, Dissertations and Theses; chap. 7: Dark Archives, Portfolios*

› EAD: Atavism

In the early 1990s, the archival field rushed to meet the onslaught of the Web. Beginning as an SGML DTD project, EAD (encoded archival description) morphed into the guise of a web solution. The approach was adopted as a descriptive standard for archival finding aides—professional booklets that provide background information on the origins of the collection and its contours. This methodology drew directly from the library world. AACR2-based elements helped standardize idiosyncratic archival practice.

EAD faces multiple challenges. It effectively eschewed the key archival concept of "series." Instead of those functional knowledge categories, this catalog card variant deals with storage location. Inclusion of electronic records is taxing. The amount of construction labor is considerable, with little prospect for automated help. Descriptions themselves will need to be updated from AACR2/MARC to RDA, which is itself suspect. Considerations are thus similar to those given to the library catalog and semantic web. Finding aides are likely to fade from the scene. Users prefer to mine the full-text material directly.

VIDEO COLLECTIONS

VL: *SERVICE, OPTION*

Film and videotape holdings have a long and problematic history in academic and public libraries. In a forerunner to publisher objections to e-books, media producers frequently retreated to licensing versus sales. ILL and mass showings could be banned.

The Web's built-in facility and lowered capital expenses alter a portion of this picture. Video is no longer an exotic prospect. Based on APUS survey data, student demand for such resources is on the rise and highly desirable for virtual classroom use. Early complications from multiple formats and bandwidth issues with dial-up modems have been largely alleviated. Storage issues have lessened. Delivery has eased with higher-speed connections, streaming, and the onset of HTML5's added capacities.

Although commercial restrictions still abound and lawsuits threaten, Alexander Street, Annenberg, and others offer increasingly affordable commercial access. The construction of "playlists" emerges as a scholarly skill set. Applications may be further enabled with "derivative" rights and editing tools. The presence of YouTube, iTunes U, and other sites creates a new open-access zone. Lecture capture programs and student/faculty-produced videos populate the virtual classroom.

As mentioned under "Audio Collections," media come with collection-building opportunities—but also added legal burdens. ADA 508 compliance and Higher Education Opportunity Act piracy notifications enter the discussion.

SEE ALSO: chap. 6: Audio Collections, Collection Development, Interlibrary Loan, Publishing; chap. 7: ADA 508

WEEDING

VL: *TOOL, REQUIRED*

Weeding takes on a wholly different character for a virtual library. No longer does one periodically pull from the shelves and dispose of texts. Procedures engage by disrupting the link or deleting the electronic record from the online catalog and subsidiary locations. In the virtual environment, discarding triggers from physical damage are gone along with concerns for overflowing shelves. What amounts to weeding may also be somewhat out of the library's control, instead automatically generated from failure to pay a bill, the end of contracts, or whim of the vendor.

The need for reconsideration and discussion across the field is significant. Time factors are distinctly different. Intellectual considerations turn in part to the shorter time span for classroom purposes. Implications of renter status and server storage options await full investigation.

SEE ALSO: chap. 5: Preservation; chap. 6: Acquisitions, Collection Development; chap. 7: Course Guides, Dark Archives

CHAPTER 7

CONSTRUCTION COMMENTARIES

The limits of my language mean the limits of my world.
—*Ludwig Wittgenstein*

THE NEXT EXERCISES TURN FROM GREEN TO NEW CONstruction. Immersion extends beyond retrofitting. The reader is invited to engage in a potpourri of web-induced elements. As illustrated in chapter 2, technology has actively intervened to redefine the academic library. This chapter probes further into specific additions on the virtual campus. Form natively follows function. Print-era distinctions between services and the tools to produce increasingly blur. Results take shape as a distinct web variant, one in a constant state of construction with a growing array of potential services and multiplicity of unanswered questions.

The examples run a gamut of major and minor topics but again are far from exhaustive or definitive. The information highway accelerates language dilemmas with a rush of acronyms and neologisms. Virtual academic libraries struggle with their very newness and rarity. Their terminology remains dependent on mainstream library usage and the commercial marketplace.

Uncertainties thus rule. Expect overlap within a rapidly unfolding but uncertain vocabulary. Tools and services tend to merge. Strange borrowings like *discovery* enter the lexicon. Definitions alter for even long-established concepts, like *curation* and *preservation*. Librarians encounter a growing host of phrases and spelling dilemmas in the ongoing redefinition of their professional jargon for new virtual operations. As McLuhan suggests, the issues can be remarkably basic. Should it be "Web" or "web"? Will proprietary names web pathfinders or e-bibliographies become common nouns or, even, turned into verbs—like *google*—under a product line like LibGuides?

ADA 508

VL: *SERVICE/TOOL, REQUIRED/OPTION*

Like copyright, Aid to Disabled Americans Section 508 compliance brings responsibilities and opportunities. Web-era potential is preconditioned under the 1996 Chafee amendment to the ADA Act. Thanks to the *Authors Guild v. HathiTrust* decision (2012), the academic library can be recognized as an "authorized entity" with a duty to provide handicapped information services. In the court's view, 1998's Section 508 amendment for electronic accessibility pushes those responsibilities firmly onto the virtual campus.

Given the legal onus/opportunity, the online library steps forward. It could consider marketing its expertise as a university service and seek insertion within what is a growing arena of campus politics. Diligence is heightened with classroom services—for example, monitoring home-grown presentations and oral history projects for scripts along with posting alerts about lingering problems from older PDF or Flash-based products.

Requirements. Whatever the added campus role, the library must take "reasonable" steps to ensure access. Be aware that this test differs between the stringent accommodations for land-based offerings and the added flexibility that comes from a virtual setting. Ethical responsibilities are clear, however, and legal actions a strong possibility for failure to act. External activity centers on contract negotiations and validation. Vendors are assigned the bulk of the responsibility, and HTML5 appears to be a coming saving grace. Familiarity with international

> ## › Positioning
> ## *Digital, Electronic, Online, Virtual*
>
> Such adjectives are convenient during the current transit of operations. Yet they are redundant in a virtual context. The virtual library needs to be analyzed as library unto itself. Electronic resources are its only resources. The following commentaries thus reorder this type of prefix into a suffix: e.g., Electronic Bookshelves becomes Bookshelves—Electronic. The exception is *digital*; that word is reserved for internal electronic publications and archival purposes that do not necessarily require Internet access.

Daisy Consortium (audiobooks) standards and WC3's universal access principles should be expected.

Site compliance is also rather straightforward. Alt tags for images, scripts for videos, and avoidance of color schemes for navigation may be all that is necessary. Section 508 articulates specific legal minimums under "Electronic and Information Technology Accessibility Standards" (Dec. 21, 2000):

> **§ 1194.22 Web-based intranet and internet information and applications.**
>
> (a) A text equivalent for every non-text element shall be provided (*e.g.*, via "*alt*", "*longdesc*", or in element content).
>
> (b) Equivalent alternatives for any multimedia presentation shall be synchronized with the presentation.
>
> (c) Web pages shall be designed so that all information conveyed with color is also available without color, for example from context or markup.
>
> (d) Documents shall be organized so they are readable without requiring an associated style sheet.
>
> (e) Redundant text links shall be provided for each active region of a server-side image map.
>
> (f) Client-side image maps shall be provided instead of server-side image maps except where the regions cannot be defined with an available geometric shape.
>
> (g) Row and column headers shall be identified for data tables.
>
> (h) Markup shall be used to associate data cells and header cells for data tables that have two or more logical levels of row or column headers.
>
> (i) Frames shall be titled with text that facilitates frame identification and navigation.
>
> (j) Pages shall be designed to avoid causing the screen to flicker with a frequency greater than 2 Hz and lower than 55 Hz.
>
> (k) A text-only page, with equivalent information or functionality, shall be provided to make a web site comply with the provisions of this part, when compliance cannot be accomplished in any other way. The content of the text-only page shall be updated whenever the primary page changes.
>
> (l) When pages utilize scripting languages to display content, or to create interface elements, the information provided by the script shall be identified with functional text that can be read by assistive technology.
>
> (m) When a web page requires that an applet, plug-in or other application be present on the client system to interpret page content, the page must provide a link to a plug-in or applet that complies with §1194.21(a) through (l).

(n) When electronic forms are designed to be completed on-line, the form shall allow people using assistive technology to access the information, field elements, and functionality required for completion and submission of the form, including all directions and cues.

(o) A method shall be provided that permits users to skip repetitive navigation links.

(p) When a timed response is required, the user shall be alerted and given sufficient time to indicate more time is required.

SEE ALSO: *chap. 6: Acquisitions, Copyright, Interlibrary Loan; chap. 7: Reading Platforms*

> ## › *Authors Guild v. HathiTrust* (2012)
>
> This landmark decision confirmed the academic library's responsibilities under ADA Section 508 for electronic course reserves and ILL. The judge drew on the Chafee amendment to declare the library responsible as an authorized entity. His decision reflected ADA requirements that declared it incurs "a primary mission to provide specialized services relating to training, education, or adaptive reading or information access needs of blind or other persons with disabilities." Accordingly, the library has the duty "to reproduce or distribute copies . . . of a previously published, non-dramatic literary work . . . in specialized formats exclusively for use by the blind or other persons with disabilities." (17 U.S.C.§ 121)

AUTHENTICATION

VL: *TOOL, REQUIRED*

Web-based services replace human credential checkers. Some form of intellectual (user ID plus password) or physiological (facial, thumbprint, eyeball, keystroke recognition) begins the process. That sets off a series of secure HTTP handshakes between the library and vendor through a web application (e.g., EZproxy, Shibboleth, or related software). If one is entering through a library site on the Open Web, authentication controls engage on entrance or through automatic intercepts on encountering secure objects. For-profit university libraries are often sequestered behind a campus firewall. In such cases, expect library entrance through the campus ERP or LMS.

Once recognized, the ideal is transparent transactions. Library reauthentication should occur automatically in the background of patron requests to external providers.

Vendors will handle most of the technical issues in this arena, but the library should preposition help information. The virtual library may also be required to differentiate among faculty and student—and especially alumni—privileges.

SEE ALSO: chap. 5: Credentials/Check-In Station; chap. 6: Alumni Services; chap. 7: Bookshelves—Electronic, Help/Reference, Proxy Servers, Reading Platforms, Security—Web

BOOKSHELVES—ELECTRONIC

VL: *SERVICE, OPTION*

Publishers, vendors, and ILS products offer an increasing span of add-ons for e-readers, including note taking, bookmarking, highlighting, and automated citations. A dedicated user bookshelf is among the most important of these. A significant and highly recommended step on the road to personalized learning environments, such applications typically call for a separate logon. Unfortunately, implementation remains limited by publisher walls for textbooks and difficulties in merging resources among different vendors.

SEE ALSO: chap. 6: Circulation; chap. 7: Authentication, Reading Platforms

> ### > Limited Accounts
>
> In addition to general institutional access, librarians may want their own access to dedicated services. Individual journal subscriptions, for example, offer a cost-effective, interim solution for ILL purposes—but they call for the maintenance of user ID/password logs. With CRIS, access controls may also require identification for course or individualized delivery. Librarians could engage "token" distribution—rotating licensing by semester as students enter and finish particular courses.

BOOKSTORE—ELECTRONIC

VL: *SERVICE, OPTION*

University bookstore operations typically divide between course materials and "spirit," or logoed, materials. Both are high-return and well-established university facilities, but they may be less so or barely existent in the virtual world. The library could enter this picture, especially for course materials. For example, it gains the option of enabling "click-through" associates' memberships to an Amazon, Barnes and Noble, or Follett-like vendor. These include finder's or percentage fees. In exchange for unlimited access to library editions, a publisher such as Springer-Verlag could ask for help with student purchases of a print copy. Links can be set in place to external print-on-demand services, or even to machines housed in a headquarters facility. Does the library advertise or cooperate in such ventures? Should it expand to spirit store operations? Are branding rights a prospect?

Publishers and vendor interest in title discovery for sales similarly suggests a bargaining chip in the licensing/ownership battles. OverDrive has loosed trial balloons for public library cooperation. Established bookstore competition and tax servicing/status may need to be considered. For-profit university libraries will need to consider possible advertising complications and join their nonprofit brethren in ethical address.

SEE ALSO: *chap. 6: Collection Development, Course Reserves, Publishing; chap. 7: Open-Access Journals, Scholarly Communications*

BROWSERS

VL: *TOOL, REQUIRED*

Web browsers sit in the background as the virtual library's gateways for user engagement. These software agents regulate traffic and interpret the site for presentation. Although these are largely stable operations and beyond the library's control, monitoring is required for compatibility issues with product line upgrades—for example, Internet Explorer 7 and earlier versions run into problems with full HTML5 implementation. Determining the browser type and version is also useful for remote troubleshooting; online librarians should consider having a variety on hand for testing new products.

SEE ALSO: *chap. 7: Mobile Devices/Tablets, Reading Platforms, Search Engines*

> Considering External Advertising

Commercialization and advertising have been ethically suspect but worthy of exploration in trying economic times. Taking a stand based on precopyright and open-access principles is laudable and may be regulated for state institutions. Yet one also notes that the purity threshold was crossed long ago. Private universities—Duke, Johns Hopkins, Stanford, and hundreds of others—are already branded with the names of capitalistic founders and donors. State universities join in the similar branding for libraries, stadiums, and other buildings. Municipal public libraries notably celebrate the largesse of Andrew Carnegie, one of the greatest of the robber barons.

Should the library consider publisher or other ads? What about percentage-making links to Amazon Associates? For-profits will have fewer qualms but need to be watchful of accidentally infiltrating their space with material from their competitors. In any such case, decision making should involve marketing departments and will likely be made by authorities outside the library.

CAREER LIBRARIES/JOB-HUNTING SERVICES

VL: *SERVICE, OPTION*

Such services are often the domain of students, alumni, or specially designated campus career centers. Given rising federal demands for accountability on post-graduation or "gainful" employment, interest will continue to grow. Expect students to come naturally to the library for this type of information. By the nature of its disciplinary support, the library already holds valuable professional material in preparation for applications and job interviews. These can be linked to independently contracted career libraries along with supplemental resume-writing and job-hunting tutorials. Hence, the online library has the opportunity to partner or, in the absence of established competition, to take a lead role.

SEE ALSO: chap. 6: Alumni Services; chap. 7: Curriculum Materials Centers

CONTENT MANAGEMENT SYSTEMS

VL: *TOOL, OPTION/REQUIRED*

A variety of options exist for building the library site. ISPs, ILSs, and related library software vendors offer such facilities. Some libraries may create through DreamWeaver or other downloadable and cloud-based construction software. Expect many to employ a groupware content management system (CMS). CON-TENTdm, Drupal, or Springshare's CourseGuides figure prominently for libraries, but those operating on a virtual campus should expect to accommodate their institution's designated product. Such products enable multiple contributors along with editorial privileges and style conformity controls.

Although one expects selective staff expertise, all online librarians will need operational skills. Given extended hours and the nature of the job, the remote staff must be enabled to build resources and mount alerts.

SEE ALSO: chap. 6: Departmental Libraries; chap. 7: Course Guides, Website as Library

COURSE GUIDES

VL: *SERVICE, REQUIRED*

Course guides (e.g., e-bibliographies, LibGuides) form bedrock for the sustainability of academic libraries. Building from their pathfinder forerunners, librarians produce tailored electronic bibliographies in support of individual classes. Although construction can be managed through a variety of web applications, Springshare's LibGuides has captured much of the market. Software selection is not enough in and of itself. The library will need to campaign and build communities to ensure success. Entrepreneurial, subject-specialist librarians reach out to show their wares and build partnerships with faculty and departments. Faculty engagement is their main action item.

As featured in figure 7.1, course guides cut across genre to address specific information needs and learning objectives. Traditional peer-reviewed journals and monographs may be featured, but they do not stand alone. The web environment extends to librarian-vetted open websites, media selections, RSS feeds, and Web 2.0 communities. Such combinations offer the university invaluable quality and currency controls for enhanced curricular development. At APUS, the approach is building in two stages:

1. **Research launching pad.** Initial concentration follows from the academic library's research bent. The guide acts in support of the course's training methods by way of a launching pad, which has been culled to select the most appropriate vehicles and key resources.

2. **Classroom material support.** When feasible, a guide can be built out in cooperation with the faculty. It is fleshed out as an extension of

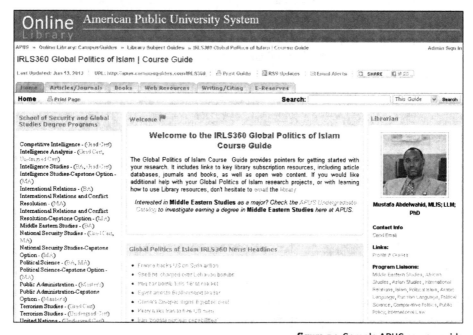

figure 7.1 Sample APUS course guide

the syllabus with resource suggestions and course reserves in support of weekly assignments and learning objectives—even extending to measurable rubrics.

At its broadest and most promising for library sustainability, the approach extends to systematic address for the university's entire curriculum. Like medieval copyists, courses are visited within a reasonable schedule—albeit based on staffing limits. Recommended updating comports to the typical three-year class development cycle, but accelerated for more volatile arenas such as technology and courses based on current affairs.

SEE ALSO: *chap. 6: Course Reserves, Information Literacy, Pathfinders; chap. 7: Content Management Systems*

CURATION

VL: *TOOL, OPTION*

Reflecting an old word with new meanings, digital curation extends archival approaches into the control and application of electronic information assets on the Web. For virtual libraries, the term focuses through a university archival component. Implications go beyond long-term storage to active applications. Materials and their processing are actively employed to foster institutional identity and reputation management. The phrase readily extends into care and handling of university publications and research materials.

SEE ALSO: *chap. 6: University Archives; chap. 7: Dark Archives, Digital Commons, Digital Preservation*

CURRICULUM MATERIALS CENTERS

VL: *SERVICE, OPTION*

Libraries, especially those with ties to schools of education, have long organized curricular support collections. Such a presence helps make a logical bridge for the information age. The Web and rise of online universities accelerate and broaden interests in new types of teaching methods, including the employ of emerging technologies. Online education demands specialized training and opportunities. It should include or be infiltrated with library options and information literacy components. Centers for teaching and learning emerge as possible partners or in competition for this space.

SEE ALSO: *chap. 6: Curriculum Laboratories; chap. 7: R&D, Syllabus Archives, Training/Tutorial Services*

DARK ARCHIVES

VL: *TOOL/SERVICE, OPTION*

Those engaging in classroom operations have added responsibility for ensuring the presence of electronic materials. Such items can disappear or be pulled with alacrity. Results wreak havoc with a class and break faith with the library. Backup procedures are thus required and a new task added to the library's portfolio. Part of the answer lies with purchasing from other sources when available. Consider too enabling exemptions in Section 508 of the 1976 Copyright Act, Digital Millennium Copyright Act, and Copyright Term Extension Act—as well as ADA Section 508. What are the library's rights and duties and those of professorial fair use? Should the virtual library digitize from a print version or otherwise duplicate and store materials in isolation to be prepared for classroom emergencies? Answers point to a type of course reserves or restricted collection tactic—a dark archive.

An understanding of licensing agreements remains crucial, but implementation is straightforward. Electronic storage itself is inexpensive. If an issue occurs, the instructor is informed and may act as the transfer agent. Material can be sent as e-mail attachments but may need to be chunked to no more than 3 megabytes to ensure delivery. The hard part is mechanisms/communication channels to remain aware of what is in the classroom. The library will also have to limit carefully the amount of time that the substitute is available. In addition, watermarking and DRM controls should be considered along with a clear message to this effect: "Not to be shared or forwarded to others. The attached information is being provided on an emergency basis in keeping with fair use exemptions. The recipient is free to use only for the purposes of this course."

SEE ALSO: *chap. 6: Acquisitions, Course Reserves, University Archives; chap. 7: Curation, Digital Commons*

DASHBOARDS

VL: *TOOL, OPTION*

A virtual library encounters more than its share of remote staffing, scheduling, and measurement issues. Internet-based dashboards project as significant tools for this environment (figure 7.2). They provide management and telecommuting

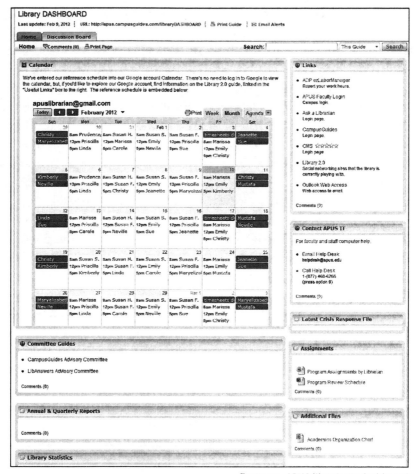

figure 7.2 APUS librarian's dashboard

librarians with one-stop coordination and communication zones that are pre-
dicted to rise in importance.

> **SEE ALSO:** *chap. 7: Metrics, Resource Data Mining*

DELIVERY OPTIONS

VL: *TOOL, REQUIRED*

Information literacy and tutorial responsibilities extend to basic points of confusion with the Web. Despite claims of transparency, the multiplicity of reading
platform adds complexity and learning curves. At this stage of the Web, the

virtual library expects differences between students and faculty, with user confusion based on two modes of delivery:

Download. Users, especially those in the military with limited access time, want texts delivered directly to their machines. Although positive steps are in the offing with EPUB 3/HTML5 capacities, publishers resist this option. If made available, the material typically arrives with DRM in place—including timeouts (e.g., two weeks before shut-down), printing capacity, and ability to use on more than one machine. More opportunity arrives through the Open Web. For the moment, the library prepares as best it can for Adobe PDF format. This legacy is somewhat outmoded. It may arrive with two-column formatting, non-OCR copy, awkward delivery for mobile devices, and ADA 508 complications.

Equally important, those engaged in classroom support must be on alert for well-meaning faculty. Though cautions are in order for overreaching and a "police" mentality, outreach and monitoring are added to the agenda. Rather than extending links to copyrighted materials, expect attempts to download and resend the resources directly to the students. Confusion can also arise for ADA 508 compliance and ensuring the "reasonable" response required under law.

Cloud delivery. The cloud and its control delivery dominate deep-web options. Users engage material and applications on demand through externally housed web repositories. This method brings powerful enticements beyond downloading and for acquisition considerations. Faculty will likely make mistakes in importing electronic articles. It is far too easy to paste the results from a search string as opposed to linking to the actual location (document object identifier [DOI] or permanent URL). What should the library expect in the form of automated footnoting, bookmarking, cross-text searching, and note taking? Are there downloading, security, or other implementation issues? What happens with a lost password for a student's bookshelf? And how does the library promote and support the toolsets? The library may also have to consider queuing questions. If multiuser options are not available, how many licenses should be secured? What is the appropriate idle time to close a session?

SEE ALSO: *chap. 6: Acquisitions, Copyright; chap. 7: ADA 508, Bookshelves—Electronic, DRM, E-books, Mobile Devices/Tablets, Reading Platforms*

DIGITAL COMMONS
VL: *SERVICE/TOOL, OPTION*

The term *digital commons* arrived early in the new century, largely courtesy of a product line from Berkeley Electronic Press (a.k.a. bepress). It describes a mass

storage solution for a university or consortium's publications and archival treasures. Bepress has been joined by campus servers along with cloud-based options
from DSpace, DuraSpace, and Fedora Commons.

Bepress's product name has broadened into a generic noun. Virtual libraries
exploring beyond rentals should consider engagement. A digital commons can
take space as a new resource cluster alongside article/research databases, course
guides, and e-books. The tool showcases outputs, student and school newsletters,
theses, and university archives as well as open-access commitments through the
deposit of e-press and faculty contributions. The approach is particularly appropriate for managing reputation, building institutional identity, and cooperating
with institutional research.

SEE ALSO: *chap. 6: University Archives; chap. 7: Curation, Dark Archives, Digital
Preservation*

DIGITAL PRESERVATION

VL: *TOOL, DEPRECATED/OPTION*

Given its rental nature, virtual library involvement in digital preservation should
be tangential. There the concept is somewhat alien and better recast under
access issues. Involvement comes as a by-product to collection development for
classroom access and ILL operations. Professional participation is effectively limited to indirect financial support—purchasing or memberships in the Center for
Research Libraries, HathiTrust, JSTOR, Project MUSE, and the like.

On the optional side, those engaged in university archives and publishing
should consider involvement. At one extreme, libraries can become embroiled
with massive data streams as well as the unstable interplay between content and
enabling software. Methods can encompass emulation, migration, refreshing,
and replication tactics along with metadata and significant standard considerations. Fortunately, virtual library engagement can be minimized. Internal alternatives revolve around regularized copying cycles as part of scheduled maintenance or the employ of patrolling and refreshing software such as LOCKSS (Lots
of Copies Keep Stuff Safe) shareware from Stanford. The LOCKSS program also
works in conjunction with publisher agreements. The goals can also be accom-
plished through outsourcing to external storage vendors.

For those interested, Cornell University Library's (2000–2003) "Moving Theory into Practice: Digital Imaging Tutorial" remains an excellent introduction.
OCLC, library consortia, and the Library of Congress's National Digital Information Infrastructure and Preservation Program with its recent National Digital

Stewardship Alliance (NDSA) offer appropriate institutional starting points.

SEE ALSO: *chap. 5: Archives and Manuscript Collections, Preservation; chap. 6: University Archives; chap. 7: Curation, Dark Archives, Digital Commons*

> **Internet Archive**
> In 1996, Brewster Kahle began an ambitious effort to archive the Web. His efforts have branched out to offer public access to a variety of other media and other materials, including some three million books.

DISCOVERY SEARCH

VL: *SERVICE/TOOL, REQUIRED/OPTION*

The twenty-first century witnessed the ascendancy of "discovery." On one hand, user attention was captured by full-text searching and relevancy rankings exemplified by web search engines. The virtual library must account for external use of a Google by the bulk of users. Adjustments are made to reference services. The site needs to be equipped properly with identifiers for those who avoid formal navigation and wander in blindly from search results. Since JSTOR is crawled by that product, the library may be driven toward its selection. Google Scholar rises as a logical and affordable choice on the discovery path.

On the other hand, the library must confront user realities. Continued reliance on bibliographic indexes is increasingly perceived as insufficient and overly complex. Federated and discovery searching have thus ascended from the library niche market—albeit with dogged deference to bibliographic elements. Discovery is emerging to prominence in the critical second decade of the twenty-first century. Serial Solutions' Summon is joined by EBSCO Discovery Services, Ex Libris's Primo, and OCLC's WorldCat Local. LMSs begin to roll out their versions. Ex Libris pushes the dialog on centralized indexing toward a related open-discovery initiative in collaboration with NISO. Overlap with semantic web endeavors is not visible in the literature but somewhat obvious for the future.

Virtual library analysis at the time of this writing suggests caution but strong impetus toward embrace. Current enhancements raise user satisfaction beyond that of federated searching. Yet discovery suffers from many of the same limitations and at significantly higher costs. Not every resource is willing to be covered, and the depth of those covered may be uncertain. Impact measurement is insufficient; controls for relevancy factors are awaiting exploration.

SEE ALSO: *chap. 6: Catalog Interface, Reference; chap. 7: Federated Search, Semantic Web, Website as Library*

DRM

VL: *TOOL, REQUIRED/DEPRECATED*

Publishers and vendors of e-books in particular tend to DRM (digital rights management) controls as part of the library's acquisitions process and licensing agreements. Techniques involve encryption and other software controls to limit checkout time, copying, printing, sharing of e-books, and time available. The major approaches:

- **Adept DRM** is a popular Adobe product that can be applied to PDFs and is used by several third-party e-book readers.
- **Fairplay DRM** comes from Apple for use on its hardware.
- **Marlin DRM** was developed by the international Marlin Developer Community, which was founded by Intertrust, Panasonic, Philips, Samsung, and Sony.
- **Mobipocket Encryption** is used by Amazon to control its Kindle products.

The virtual library, however, sits on the Sorbonne side of the fence. It should reflect primary allegiance to the needs of its faculty and student users. The drive is to maximize and simplify into the most transparent and contractually allowable experience. Online librarians should thus raise DRM to bargaining status and seek the most open and cost-effective compromises for their clients.

SEE ALSO: chap. 6: Acquisitions, Publishing; chap. 7: Authentication, Delivery Options, E-books, Metadata

> **Watermarks**

Digital watermarks appear as part of a systematic DRM effort or a way to indicate origins of internal publications, including audio and video files. Like any metadata, they may be quite useful but are also easily bypassed.

E-BOOKS

VL: *SERVICE, REQUIRED*

Electronic books technically date to 1971 with University of Illinois student Michael Hart and Project Gutenberg—or even earlier to 1948 and Roberto Busa's concordance of Thomas Aquinas. Still, active e-book presence in academic libraries properly belongs to the web age. A seed change is in process. By the 2010s, e-books had become a prominent presence in mainstream reports and a bedrock expectation for a virtual library. Accrediting agencies, students, and faculty now expect direct access to a reasonable and growing selection of titles.

> ## > Online Instructional Issues
>
> Though invaluable to an online library's identity, e-books may be destined to become secondary to journal/research databases for the virtual campus. The web classroom lends itself to "chunking"—smaller units of information fit Internet instruction.

Classroom considerations. Those engaged with classroom materials must be aware that e-books can be pulled with short notice. Monitoring is necessary to avoid major disruptions for anything used within a course. The ideal is a dashboard setting that regularly pulls an automated listing or issues flags. Lacking this, the library and allied course materials staff must rely on a less reliable, informal accounting or watch list. When a pull is noticed, the faculty must be quickly informed, then librarians immediately start a hunt for alternative sources.

If purchasing fails, the institution faces an interesting situation. The item must disappear from the catalog and general use; but does the library act in keeping with fair use assumptions when populating the classroom temporarily? Planning for short-term emergency access suggests a dark archives approach: resources are prepositioned and then electronically enabled for e-mail distribution to the students. Such distribution may come with embedded time limits, but at least they clearly indicate the emergency intent and an admonition against sharing.

Open Web. In keeping with Project Gutenberg, the Open Web and prospects for internally published books set up different sets of questions. Does the library catalog? For material in the public domain or available through Creative Commons license, does the library link or seek to house and even reedit a duplicate copy?

Deep Web. E-book purchasing raises significant questions for the online library. The for-profit university retains little interest in underwriting scholarly presses. The purchase of intellectually justifiable volumes must be weighed against actual classroom or research employ. Business complications and confusion are particularly trying. Rental versus purchase remains the pivotal and unresolved issue.

As seen later in figure 7.5, the virtual library recognizes that not all licenses are the same. Vendor policies vary widely. They need to be charted for comparison purposes and should be considered for negotiation. Consideration must be given to DRM issues such as printing and downloading. Multiuser licensing may be favored. Single-user and consortial purchases call for calculations. Cost/benefit analysis may call for limiting to a single "courtesy" copy. Does one construct an optimum ratio based on user patterns, such as one for every four enrolled? If it is not preset in the contact, the library considers rule sets for length of individual use and timing out from inactivity. If used for classroom purposes, is a dark archive approach appropriate?

Online libraries also wrestle with a variety of reading platforms and enhancements that may be limited by vendor. The wall between textbooks remains an unconscionable annoyance. Expect too that the number of "books" will be considerably smaller than their land-based counterparts. E-book availability is largely limited to twenty-first-century titles.

SEE ALSO: *chap. 6: Acquisitions, Article/Research Databases, Circulation, Collection Development, Course Reserves, Publishing; chap. 7: Dark Archives, Delivery Options, DRM, Open-Access Journals, Reading Platforms, Webliography*

> Emerging Book Formats

The Web has begun to affect and even redefine the underlying nature of the book. Jenna Wortham (2011), for example, notes a rise of shorter pieces in response to e-reader experiences, such as those in the *Atavist*, which is described as a leader in the development of new, blended literary genres: "among the growing number of organizations that are cultivating a certain niche of writing—stories and articles that are longer than the typical magazine article but shorter than a novel—. . . [to] find a comfortable home on the glassy screens of evermore prevalent mobile devices."

New formats are appearing with interactive time lines, character biographies, and other tools for a different type of reading experience. Vook, APUS ePress, and others offer hybrid e-books with embedded videos. Amazon launched Kindle Singles to also populate this unfolding arena.

EMBEDDED LIBRARIANS

VL: *SERVICE, REQUIRED/OPTION*

Embedding is a subtly different option for online librarians. It joins on a virtual campus with telecommuting faculty and 24/7 asynchronous classrooms. The term has taken on two complementary meanings:

Liaisons. The required portion involves "informationists"—liaisons assigned to each department and school. They seek to engage in faculty meetings as well as provide supporting presence in related social networks. The librarian also seeks to engage instructional developers and other support staff with similar assignments.

Classroom involvement. This option depends on the library's staffing and program receptiveness. If suitable, embedding begins with a prelude. Librarians need to take specialized training to understand the nuances of online teaching and the peculiarities of the LMS.

The highest form of classroom embedding takes place through the provision of faculty instruction in that same required LMS introduction. In addition, librarians can build relations as an outgrowth of attending the course as students. The student classroom component looks in particular to the university's mandatory introduction and methods classes.

Whether for faculty or student instruction, the virtual library gives stress to web information literacy. Web 2.0 involvement is encouraged. Training is tailored to the library's deep-web holdings and open-web vetting. Course guides and program portals take major support roles, but the library should be prepared to add training tools. By-products include the construction of lasting client bases and collection development assistance.

SEE ALSO: chap. 6: Collection Development, Departmental Libraries, Information Literacy; chap. 7: Course Guides, Social Networking/Web 2.0

FEDERATED SEARCH

VL: *TOOL/SERVICE, OPTION*

The Web has stimulated a multiplicity of article/research databases with their own search engines. Federated search (a.k.a metasearch) reflects attempts to address that potential Tower of Babel. A single interface rides over the disparate product lines and engages library-based bibliographic searching. Such directions are highly recommended in theory. They are a step toward desirable one-stop Google-like shopping. Yet the reality has lagged behind the promise. Individual product engines continue to produce far superior results. And, like discovery, federated search suffers from contractual inabilities. Not every product will grant access to such services. The library must thus be careful in how it presents such products.

SEE ALSO: chap. 6: Reference; chap. 7: Discovery Search, Search Engines

HELP/REFERENCE

VL: *VSERVICE/TOOL, REQUIRED*

This discussion overlaps with entrance of automated services indicated in chapter 6's Reference entry. Web design and user expectations call for "help" links.

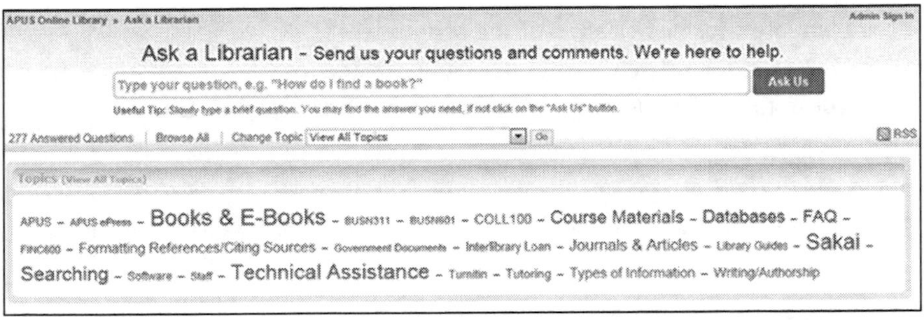

figure 7.3 APUS help resource

These are most frequently displayed as buttons at the top left or, especially, top right of the page. The web convention suggests analysis and possible "mashups" for the virtual library. Help as a function directly overlaps with the library concept of reference. Given the decline in reference activity and user preferences, should the library consider a switch or blending of terminology—such as that illustrated in figure 7.3?

The help/reference nexus takes distinct shape for online higher education. Users, for example, expect automatic contextual support and training options for database applications. Responsibility properly falls to the application or data services vendor. The library's role is ensuring the presence and access to such resources. Librarians should similarly be awake to opportunities for information literacy and tutorial support. LMS and electronic course guide versions could be wired by course with options to dedicated library or other tutorials. An introductory writing class could be linked to an online writing lab, math to a math lab, methods courses to information literacy resources, and so on.

The virtual campus remains open to exploration on the nature of help resources and their integration as mechanisms for student success. In a CRIS model, for example, the user could be looking for assistance from any of the following:

- Classroom support, for technical or academic aid with an assignment or LMS feature
- Information technology support, for a web or computer issue

> **APUS Example**

APUS provides a practical example of the utility of switching from reference to a help motif. With the switch to a help button and addition of the LibAnswers search engine, reference use exploded. Reference activity grew from some 5,000 reference queries to librarians in 2011 to over 120,000 help inquiries in 2012 and continues to rise.

- Instructor, for clarification of the assignment
- Librarian, for reference or bibliographic guidance
- Tutor, for added, personal guidance on method or presentation

SEE ALSO: *chap. 5: Ready Reference; chap. 6: Information Literacy, Reference; chap. 7: Online Writing Laboratories, Search Engines, Training/Tutorial Services*

INFORMATION COMMONS

`VL:` *SERVICE, DEPRECATED*

As presently used in the library community, *information commons* refers to redefined physical space with automation resources for student study and social engagement. Though applauded for the mainstream library, the concept does not fit the virtual library.

SEE ALSO: *chap. 6: Information Literacy; chap. 7: Digital Commons, Embedded Librarians*

LINKED DATA

`VL:` *TOOL, OPTION*

Berners-Lee (2006) coined the term "linked data community" to illustrate the basic rule set and involvement needed for an operative semantic web. The idea borrows from the use of controlled catalog headings, inferences from scholarly citations, and expert crowd sourcing. Communities of interest and machine harvesting combine for a constantly growing data commons of RDF datasets. The concept is increasingly gaining traction in research libraries. Like the semantic web and RDA, virtual libraries must monitor and engage such advancements as they become useful—but active engagement in development is less likely for financial reasons.

SEE ALSO: *chap. 7: Metadata, Semantic Web*

MANAGEMENT SERVICES—CLOUD

`VL:` *TOOL, OPTION*

In further indication of a pivotal period, library vendors have announced the arrival of encompassing cloud-based, SaaS (software as a service) management services. OCLC led the way in late 2011. Its innovative WorldShare offers to take over acquisitions, cataloging, circulation, discovery, licensing, and web development for individual or cooperative library operations. As indicated on the WorldShare platform site:

> The *OCLC WorldShare Platform* is a global, interconnected Web architecture . . . provides flexible, open access to library data through APIs and other Web services. Libraries, developers and partners can use this data to innovate together to build and share apps that streamline and enhance their local library workflows. The OCLC WorldShare Platform facilitates collaboration and app-sharing across the library community, so that libraries can combine OCLC-built applications, library-built applications and partner-built applications.

For the virtual library manager, this type of product seems the almost inevitable outgrowth of the cloud and OCLC's drive toward commoditization. The approach also signals existential disturbances. ExLibris acted quickly to enter the scene, and one expects response from elsewhere in the ILS community as well as competition from EBSCO and ProQuest. The hope is that additional entrants will drive down pricing levels. The danger to library sovereignty is implicit. Without a countervailing narrative and ROI, such resort implicitly challenges much of the rationale and argument for an individually branded university library.

SEE ALSO: chap. 5: Integrated Library Systems; chap. 6: Circulation

MEDIA LITERACY

VL: *SERVICE, OPTION*

Digital media literacy is an expected flourish or extension of the information literacy agenda. Although textually oriented, the Web is inherently a multimedia environment; moreover, student preferences and the absence of the lecture's entertainment value are driving classroom experimentation in online education. Courses, training, and library opportunities are likely in the offing.

SEE ALSO: chap. 6: Information Literacy; chap. 7: Training/Tutorial Services

METADATA

VL: *TOOL, REQUIRED*

Metadata is information about information, in our context information abstracted about a resource and its contents that the computer can analyze. For web-era libraries, the term typically reflects cataloging information, MARC, and the

Dublin Core. Web metadata, however, must also be understood as aimed at computer manipulations, not visible catalog entries. It speaks to declarations on the nature of the document and its structures. These lie hidden from view in the HTML and XML code but under the purview of the exchanging machines and search engines.

The virtual library engages metadata as part of the background to the construction of its site and tuning for search engine discovery. These activities should be addressed carefully but relatively pro forma. Emphasis is given the language for the title tag, adding structural headings, and ensuring ADA 508 compliance. Expect added emphasis with the onset of HTML5 with its new abilities for touch screen, voice, and 3D navigational features. Second, the virtual library deals with vendor-supplied resources. The utilitarian nature of a virtual library mitigates against heavy involvement and seeks automated mechanisms in such regard. If transparent and available as a byproduct of automated exchanges, fine. If added labor is required, why—especially given the power of search engines? In addition, the library may become involved in preserving patron privacy rights and FERPA enforcement through its metrics.

SEE ALSO: *chap. 6: Cataloging; chap. 7: ADA 508, Linked Data, Metrics, RDA, Search Engines, Semantic Web*

METRICS

VL: *TOOL, REQUIRED*

The term *metrics* came to prominence in the web age. It is indicative of rising administrative imperatives and drives toward quantifiable accountability. The virtual library must engage such reporting mechanisms but encounters a presently weak state of affairs. Expect externally dictated government and institutional mechanisms that can lead to underinformed "window dressing." Academic librarianship remains conceptually weak in codifying appropriate standards for virtual campus operations. For the moment, the virtual library remains somewhat on its own in seeking and developing definitions to guide management and improvement.

Basic setting. In 1966, NCES's Integrated Postsecondary Education Data System (IPEDS) kicked off the systematic collection of the nation's educational activity. Higher education is a featured category, including recommended reporting standards that may apply to online libraries. As seen in the NCES IPEDS summary (Phan et al. 2011), these devolve to relatively simplistic quantitative tables with a scattering of percentages:

- Number of academic libraries, by public service hours per typical week, control, level, size, and Carnegie classification of institution
- Gate count, reference transactions per typical week in academic libraries, and total information service to groups, by control, level, size, and Carnegie classification
- Number of academic libraries, by volumes held at end of fiscal year, control, level, size, and Carnegie classification
- Number of volumes, units, and subscriptions held at the end of the fiscal year at academic libraries, by control, level, size, and Carnegie classification
- Number of volumes, units, and subscriptions added during the fiscal year at academic libraries, by control, level, size, and Carnegie classification
- Number and percentage distribution of different types of FTE staff at academic libraries across institutional characteristics, and number and percentage distribution of FTE across staff types within institutional characteristics, by control, level, size, and Carnegie classification
- Number of academic libraries, by total academic library expenditures, control, level, size, and Carnegie classification
- Expenditures on different functions at academic libraries and salaries and wages as a percentage of total expenditures, by control, level, size, and Carnegie classification
- Expenditures for different types of information resources at academic libraries, by control, level, size, and Carnegie classification
- Operating expenditures for equipment and other selected expenditures at academic libraries, by control, level, size, and Carnegie classification
- Percentage of academic libraries with selected electronic services, by control, level, size, and Carnegie classification
- Percentage of academic libraries reporting information literacy activities, by control, level, size, and Carnegie classification
- Number and percentage of responding academic libraries, by level, control of institution, and item
- Number and percentage of nonresponding academic libraries, by level, control of institution, and state
- Total number of academic libraries, by level, control of institution, and state

Opportunities. The nature of the Web makes it far easier to track transactions and time on task as well as project ROI. Online universities are given to satisfaction surveys and focus group analysis. Deep-web products supply extensive usage data. Web traffic applications add detail on internals, such as load patterns by time and location. Given the politics and amount of data at an online university, the virtual library must consider proactive engagement on several levels:

- **Reporting/marketing.** Material should be orchestrated for at least quarterly and annual reports. The results should be put together as institutional and accreditation "sales" documents; bullets and graphics are preferred over dense narrative.
- **Staff management.** The data are also vital to managing remote staff. Dashboards and other mechanisms provide needed accountability for reporting to higher administration and helping librarians self-inform/compete.
- **Future prospects.** Other intriguing and potentially powerful opportunities await fulfillment. What standards should be set in place for virtual campus integration? What are the prospects for big data dives? How does

> ## › Mainstream and Metrics
>
> In recent years, the mainstream has begun to explore complicated and informative metrics. The Education Advisory Board, for instance, issued *Redefining the Academic Library* (2011). It summarized the weakness of the current model and a basic quandary under the first two of its six:
>
> 1. **Collection size rapidly losing importance.** Even the wealthiest academic libraries are abandoning the "collection arms race" as the value of physical resources declines. Increasingly, libraries must adapt to a world in which providing access to—rather than ownership of—scholarly resources is their primary role.
>
> 2. **Traditional library metrics fail to capture value to academic mission.** Libraries can no longer demonstrate their educational and scholarly impact via traditional input measures such as the number of volumes and serial titles held, expenditures on monographs and staff, gate count, and reference requests. New measures of success (still under development) will emphasize impact on student learning outcomes, retention and graduation rates, faculty research productivity, and teaching support.
>
> ACRL's 2009 creation of the Committee on the Value of Academic Libraries demonstrates its intent to address the insufficiencies in point 2. Unfortunately, Megan Oakleaf's (2010) follow-up *Value of Academic Libraries* and the subsequent *Standards for Libraries in Higher Education* (ACRL 2011) produce mere wish lists. They are of limited value for virtual library operations.

one actually determine the effect of the library on student recruitment or retention? Indeed, does one define library impact factors for classroom, alumni, or research services?

SEE ALSO: chap. 7: Dashboards, Metadata, Resource Data Mining, Webliography

MOBILE DEVICES/TABLETS

VL: *TOOL, OPTION*

The virtual library must consider delivery on multiple devices. The movement beyond personal computers to handheld, multipurpose telephonic implements is undeniable. Demands are greatest for those entertaining international operations.

Although LMSs and classroom delivery models struggle, the virtual library is relatively well positioned for rendering from HTML to mobiles. As Lisa Carlucci Thomas (2012) found, library accommodations quickly and fortuitously arrived on the scene:

> Nearly two years after the 2010 LJ Mobile Libraries Survey mobile devices, such as smartphones, ereaders, and tablets have become mainstream, and the mobile library landscape has broadened significantly. . . . Suddenly everyone (and no one) knows best how to meet the ever-changing mobile demand for information. From marketing, packaging, and licensing, to delivery, participation, and integration with existing services and practices, we're all experts in training.

Vendors and publishers in the commercial marketplace assume the bulk of the burden. Compositions through an internal CMS will likely be adaptable—as are newer product lines like Springshare's LibGuides. The ultimate hope rests with HTML5, which promises near-term address of device delivery through built-in standards.

SEE ALSO: chap. 6: Acquisitions; chap. 7: ADA 508

> ### › PDF Legacies
>
> Although Adobe has active solutions for enabling newer PDF on mobile devices, expect lagging problems with noncloud delivery and earlier formatted resources. Storage and delivery of pages with multiple column displays remain a particular issue, especially for ADA 508 compliance and mobile delivery. Reading may be complicated by insufficient resolution, which leads to fuzzy and occasionally impossible rendering.

ONLINE WRITING LABORATORIES

VL: *SERVICE, OPTION*

Purdue University (though not its library) innovated the OWL (online writing lab) in the early days of the Web. The approach inspired enterprising libraries to join the path. Opportunities depend on the campus political situation and competing presences. Library approaches take into account the interests of English and writing departments as well as extant campus tutoring or writing labs. Virtual library offerings concentrate on the construction of fixed training resources or management of outsourced services. Extension into live reference service adds further caution. Depending on staffing levels and active duty hours, the latter may be a problematic stretch.

   SEE ALSO: *chap. 6: Information Literacy; chap. 7: Help/Reference, Training/ Tutorial Services*

OPEN-ACCESS JOURNALS

VL: *SERVICE—OPTION*

In addition to the Big Buy and individual journal subscriptions, universities and their libraries have individual and collectivist interests in "Gold" open-access journals, which are institutionally based and peer-reviewed. Similar support is appropriate for high-quality output from government agencies such as the National Library of Medicine. Such contributions offer bedrock for cost controls and a redefined Creative Commons for educational purposes.

   Resource mining for such materials is added as part of the online librarian's professional portfolio. Virtual libraries include overlap analysis to uncover the

> ## › Mainstream Movement

By late 2010, the Directory of Open Access Journals could report more than 5,500 open access journals. Major universities were signing up in a Compact for Open Access Publishing Equity:

> Each of the undersigned universities commits to the timely establishment of durable mechanisms for underwriting reasonable publication charges for articles written by its faculty and published in fee-based open-access journals and for which other institutions would not be expected to provide funds. We encourage other universities and research funding agencies to join us in this commitment, to provide a sufficient and sustainable funding basis for open-access publication of the scholarly literature.

amount of such materials within Big Buy packages for enhanced bargaining positions.

SEE ALSO: *chap. 6: Acquisitions, Article/Research Databases, Collection Development; chap. 7: E-books, Resource Data Mining*

PERSONALIZED LEARNING ENVIRONMENTS

VL: *TOOL/SERVICE—OPTION*

Personalized learning environments (PLEs) are destined to loom large on the higher education scene. The term can refer to independent learners and self-study efforts but also to an institutional form of web-based instruction and information delivery. The learner engages in a highly personalized electronic environment, which is not unlike Vannevar Bush's memex concept (1945). Educational materials arrive at the student's electronic desktop, which is also populated by related Web 2.0 connections, applications, and research resources. Strategic provision and ensuring a role with that last element are of vital concern for the future of the academic virtual library.

SEE ALSO: *chap. 7: Social Networking/Web 2.0*

PORTFOLIOS

VL: *SERVICE, OPTION*

Web-based portfolios are a recent fact of life in higher education. They offer students a dynamic method for displaying academic progress. Such services may be controlled through the LMS or an external vendor. The library or university archives gains an opportunity parallel to the collection of dissertations and theses. It should consider reaching out to engage and capture at the point of graduation. These materials could become a major pointer and research object in the evolution of online education.

SEE ALSO: *chap. 6: Dissertations and Theses, University Archives*

PROXY SERVERS

VL: *TOOL, OPTION*

Although Shibboleth and other methods exist, libraries tend to rely on web proxy servers/software. Replacing the original hardware solution, Chris Zagar simplified matters and set the stage for the massive growth in access to remote

```
Name ezproxy.university.edu
Option DisableSSL40bit
LoginPortSSL 443
LoginPort 80
DNS
Option ProxyByHostname

HAName ezproxy.university.edu
HAPeer http://ezproxy1.university.edu

MaxSessions ####
MaxVirtualHosts ###
MaxConcurrentTransfers ###

MinProxy #### pocheck:remotely

## Databases begin

Group

############## Database #######################

Title     Database
AllowVars u
EncryptVar u astringyoupick
EBLSecret code-string
Title Database
URL http://university.database.com
DJ     eblib.com

###########################################
# All other database definitions from here on down go into the
Default group
###########################################

Group Default

############### Database ######################

Title Database
URL http://university.database.com
Host database.com/
```

figure 7.4 Sample EZproxy script (Courtesy of author)

> Reverse Proxy

The proxy technique can be reversed for those seeking controlled access for archival materials or publications. Instead of the Open Web, the library becomes part of the Dark Web and can restrict access to its faculty, students, or others authenticated on its extranet.

databases with his EZproxy software solution in the late 1990s. Now owned by OCLC, his approach has been opened to the cloud and outsourcing. The middleware acts as a centralized entryway to simplify access to externally licensed resources on the Deep Web. Such mechanisms allow the geographically dispersed users on a virtual campus access as though they were on a campus library computer. The system employs simple scripting and runs in the background (figure 7.4). The library and its vendors exchange IP ranges. Working with the authentication methods of the campus ERP/LMS or ILS, the proxy service passes through validated users and may dynamically distribute load. Remote staff should have IP data and vendor contact information at the ready in case of technical problems. Once set up, however, engagement should be minimal with the exception of IP changes along with the addition/deletion of databases.

SEE ALSO: *chap. 7: Authentication*

R&D

VL: *TOOL, REQUIRED*

Libraries helped introduce automation and the Web on college campuses. Other units may have pushed aside, ignored, or partnered with their academic library. Whatever the case, online librarians must remain active in ferreting out and trialing useful applications for themselves and others on the electronic campus. Failure to engage such a role could prove fatal.

SEE ALSO: *chap. 6: University Archives; chap. 7: Curation, Scholarly Communications*

RDA

VL: *TOOL, OPTION/DEPRECATED*

Though the virtual library is willing to adopt benefits, overly active engagement with RDA (Resource Description and Access) is open to questioning at this time. Given the success of Google and user demands for full-text retrieval, it is hard to understand the added overhead for expanded indexing and library taxonomic systems. What does a cost/benefit analysis recommend before investing in ALA's support packaging and training?

From the perspectives of a virtual academic library, RDA appears atavistic. Why actively engage rather than promote publishers' metadata solutions that are more likely to be employed by search engines? In the *Report and Recommendations of the U.S. RDA Test Coordinating Committee on the Implementation of RDA—Resource Description and Access* (U.S. RDA Test Coordinating Committee 2011), the main national libraries agreed to lead the field with RDA activation within two years. Yet they admitted to failing in their basic charge. Their investigations failed to build a reasonable business case:

> The test revealed that there is little discernible immediate benefit in implementing RDA alone. The adoption of RDA will not result in significant cost savings in metadata creation. There will be inevitable and significant costs in training. Immediate economic benefit, however, cannot be the sole determining factor in the RDA business case. It must be determined if there are

› Mainstream Criticism

The virtual library perspective on RDA is not the only criticism. Karen Coyle and Diane Hillman (2007) launched a devastating attack in *DLib* online magazine. They argued that library systems had been surpassed and lost their place as the head of information providers. RDA seemed atavistic and tinged by almost religious adherence:

> Modifications to the rules, such as those proposed by the Resource Description and Access (RDA) development effort, can only keep us rooted firmly in the 20th, if not the 19th century. A more radical change is required that will contribute to the library of the future, re-imagined and integrated with the chosen workflow of its users . . .

> Since the development of the first OPACs, libraries have been trying to move forward while dragging behind them the ball of a century of legacy data and the chain of an antiquated view of the bibliographic universe. The defense of this legacy universe has all of the elements of a religious argument rather than a systematic analysis of the actual requirements for a 21st century library. The prospect of change challenges libraries' investment in their current catalogs as well as their desire to feel competent to do the business of running the library. But institutional change today cannot be gradual. . . . if libraries do not step up to the challenge of change they will become increasingly marginalized in the information age to come.

significant future enhancements to the metadata environment made possible by RDA and if those benefits, long term, outweigh implementation costs.

SEE ALSO: *chap. 5: MARC; chap. 6: Cataloging, Catalog Interface; chap. 7: Metadata*

READING PLATFORMS

VL: *TOOL, REQUIRED*

The virtual library is on alert and in the hunt for unifying solutions. Its users can encounter a variety of retrieval mechanisms and reading platforms with attendant learning curves and prospects for confusion. Variations from individual publishers are compounded by a multiplicity of article/database, catalog, and e-book vendors (figure 7.5). Although database aggregators simplify some of the problems, search and retrieval are different among the overlapping collections of an EBSCO and a ProQuest. Issues are likely to increase with the arrival of touch screens and voice recognition systems.

Vendor	Cloud-based, print/download	Licensing	Features/notes
ebrary	Chapter printing (60-page limit); Adobe Editions 7–14 day download	Single and multiuser	Bookshelf, notes highlighting
NetLibrary	Printing one page at a time	Single, three-user, multiuser	Multiusers lock-out possible
EBL	Check-outs too at one or three days; print roughly 20 percent of the content	Multiuser, 325-day annual license	Rolling licenses as time runs out
Books24/7	Printing one page at a time	Multiuser	
MyiLibrary	Printing one page at a time	Multiuser	Multiusers lock-out possible
ABC-CLIO	Printing one page at a time	Multiuser	
Safari	Printing one page at a time	Multiuser	Ten simultaneous user limit
CRCnetBASE	Chapter-level printing and downloads	Multiuser	

figure 7.5 2012 e-book vendor comparison

Matters are accentuated with e-books. Individual student purchase cannot be readily integrated with the library's holdings. Download and print options vary. Standards have not taken hold. Bookshelves and other advanced features are not compatible and often require separate logons—in other words, password problems.

SEE ALSO: *chap. 6: Catalog Interface, Collection Development; chap. 7: Book-shelves—Electronic, Delivery Options, E-books*

RESOURCE DATA MINING

VL: *TOOL, OPTION*

Data mining in resources reflects a concept in need of clarification and more precise terminology. The term *data mining* has taken on a life of its own. In a general sense, this subset of computer science plumbs large datasets for hard-to-discern relationships and the design of operative applications from those findings. Such approaches are stretching into librarianship and analysis of resource content/usage. As the corpus of knowledge is digitized, automated engines go beyond computation to engage textual analysis through artificial intelligence and Bayesian algorithms in runs through massive datasets and a burgeoning new arena of scholarship. Several broad and inchoate categories are on the immediate horizon and in need of defining terminology:

Altmetrics. The computerization of information and its electronic delivery on the Web create the opportunity for new types of quantitative scholarship. Google's digitization projects enable powerful frequency studies across time. Others are conducting studies on the nature of HTML composition and search engine retrieval. The term *altmetrics* has begun to surface for impact measures with extensions beyond citation analysis. As indicated in the Altmetric Manifesto,

› Outsourcing Options

A new supporting industry has begun mining for data points that search engines and business can exploit. Gnip, DataSift, and other specialized miners focus on harvesting social networking results for "crowdwise" computations. Microsoft offers the general Azure Marketplace with trillions of data points. Factual, under Gilad Elbaz, whose Applied Semantics' content parser helped ratchet Google's searching successes, has collected zettabytes in a drive to hold all possible facts on the Web. On the as yet noncommercial side, Google has fostered diachronic analysis of words across its Books database. It is being joined by linguistic research tools and emergent scholarship. Bookworm, for example, offers "probabilistic topic modeling" to explore arXiv's article database for language shifts to uncover paradigm shifts.

scholars are increasingly transferring their work to the Web and engaging new methods of communication:

> These new forms reflect and transmit scholarly impact: that dog-eared (but uncited) article that used to live on a shelf now lives in Mendeley, CiteU-Like, or Zotero—where we can see and count it. That hallway conversation about a recent finding has moved to blogs and social networks—now, we can listen in. The local genomics dataset has moved to an online repository—now, we can track it. This diverse group of activities forms a composite trace of impact far richer than any available before. We call the elements of this trace altmetrics.

Nonconsumptive research and **culturenomics** are related neologisms surfacing in response to the massive digitization of Google and Amazon. One also notes the appearance of "article-level metrics" (ALM) terminology.

New scholarly forms. As seen with e-books, the Web is beginning to generate new types of scholarly publications. The open-science movement leads to opportunities beyond open-access journals. Multifaceted "scholarly communication" knowledge sites, annotated play lists/media editing options, blogs, and the like are rearing their heads. Some of these will engender their own fields of study.

Online librarians must monitor such developments. They need to be in the vanguard of the metadiscipline—reporting, tuning their collections, and advising the university on developments.

SEE ALSO: chap. 6: Acquisitions, Collection Development, Publishing; chap, 7: Linked Data, Metrics, Semantic Web, Webliography

RSS FEEDS

VL: *SERVICE, OPTION*

RSS (Really Simple Syndication) is a way to update information by pushing "web feeds." Coming on the scene in the early twenty-first century by way of Netscape, the approach syndicates and automates publication from a point of origin to multiple subscribers. Technically an XML channel operation, RSS is a de facto standard with implementation through simple plug-ins. Employ works well for a CRIS environment and is encouraged for course guides and program portals. Feeds help keep a site up-to-date and a draw for returning visitors. They can also be linked to prepositioned questions/query strings as refresher devices for FAQ-type operations. Yet, like other applications, the virtual library planner must be aware that RSS is likely a transitory application.

SEE ALSO: *chap. 6: Departmental Libraries; chap. 7: Course Guides*

SCHOLARLY COMMUNICATIONS

VL: *SERVICE/TOOL, OPTION*

Although the term has been around since the 1970s, *scholarly communications* stepped to the fore in the early twenty-first century. The phrase encapsulates the life cycle of knowledge creation, distribution, and preservation on the Web. Some use it as shorthand for reactions against attempts to control/commoditize the academic exchange of information.

In libraries, the term may also be a collective noun for emerging, multicomponent sites (e.g., scientific social networking sites). The focus seems to remain on research, but the concept can theoretically broaden to the classroom and is congenial to a virtual academic library's course guides program.

> **ARL Interests**
>
> Befitting the current critical era, the Association of Research Libraries recently took institutional notice of scholarly communication sites. They are featured in "Strategies for Opening Up Content" (ARL 2010), a special issue of *Research Library Issues.* More important, ARL's "Strategic Plan, 2010–2012" (2009) embraced a strategic goal for "reshaping scholarly communications" and proclaimed, "ARL will be a leader in the development of effective, extensible, sustainable, and economically viable models of scholarly communication that provide barrier-free access to quality information in support of the mission of research institutions."

SEE ALSO: *chap. 6: Departmental Libraries; chap. 7: Course Guides, Scientific Social Networking/Open-Science Movement, Webliography*

SCIENTIFIC SOCIAL NETWORKING/OPEN-SCIENCE MOVEMENT

VL: *SERVICE/TOOL, OPTION*

This web-based development helps demonstrate the burgeoning complexity of scholarly communication and current linguistic mélange. Academic journals have long codified research results through a peer-review siphon. To the chagrin of traditionalists and such commercial appendages as Elsevier, the Web enables disruption of that pattern. A selection of open-access scientific journals is attempting to speed up the system in the face of publisher attempts to embargo or otherwise restrict availability. The new model allows for criticism on the fly. Interactive exchanges and group consensus replace and streamline the blind referee process.

Dynamic publication zones are also joining a new variety of dedicated, scientific social networking sites. These creations can combine articles in progress, archives, cooperation zones, current affair, job listings, meeting announcement, and so forth by disciplinary cluster. Results could be a harbinger of a postuniversity future for knowledge incubation, but they are certainly of interest and challenging as a multiple resource zone for academic libraries.

At the moment, ResearchGate is the most prominent exponent and indicates a trifold mission for its participants:

- **Engage and interact with fellow researchers.** ResearchGate allows you to network with the largest global community dedicated to science and research: we help you to expand your contacts, share knowledge and find potential research partners.
- **Build an online presence for you and your work.** ResearchGate profiles let others know what you're working on: listing your education and experience, your research interests and sharing publications will make your work visible to your research colleagues throughout the world.
- **Know what's happening in science.** ResearchGate makes keeping up with your field simple: from conferences, jobs, and the latest publications, to the topics your peers are discussing, we enable you to stay informed and up-to-date.

SEE ALSO: *chap. 7: Open-Access Journals, Scholarly Communications*

SEARCH ENGINES

VL: *TOOL, REQUIRED*

As emphasized by the twenty-first-century arrival of Google, search engines represent the Web's single most disturbing element for librarianship. On one hand, they pull away potential clients and threaten the existence of the institution. On the other hand, the search engine becomes a persistent and pervasive presence that helps to define a virtual library. The software acts as part of the staff, but its presence is much more than that:

- **Audience.** The virtual library must consider consumer search engines for most aspects of its construction. These applications drive users around fixed navigation paths. Consideration includes ensuring proper address information on arrival. HTML heading structures enter the picture to improve machine ability to determine relevance and enhance retrievability.

- **Site elements.** The library site may be populated by several types of search engines:

  » *Catalog/database engines.* The core of virtual library functionality remains access to a deep-web catalog and journal/article databases as enabled through search engines. The software comes as basically plug-and-play devices tuned by their vendors.

  » *Federated/discovery search.* Although problems remain, virtual libraries are driven to all-in-one search engines, often as the first and most visible functional element on their sites. Such tools primarily ride over their deep-web resources but may be tunable to open-web selections.

  » *Site search.* The library may wish to include an engine for its internal site but should be aware that such facilities may confuse patrons.

- **Training/tutorial component.** Search engines are the objects for tutorial modules and information literacy classes.

- **Work.** Online librarians also rely on search engines for the bulk of their professional labor, from collection development and reference to training purposes.

The centrality of search engines strongly urges more library engagement. The virtual library, for example, seeks methods to tune search engines to its setting. APUS is campaigning for control of relevance factors by type of discipline, including the ability to weigh for the top journals and key texts in any given field of study.

SEE ALSO: chap. 6: Reference; chap. 7: Discovery Search, Federated Search, Help/Reference

SECURITY—WEB

VL: *TOOL, REQUIRED*

The movement of services outside the building eliminates the bulk of traditional security concerns but raises others. Although publishers and aggregators take most of the burden for their products, the manager gains concerns for the safety of the home-grown parts of the virtual library. Up-to-date virus protection, regular backups, and restoration plans are part of the cost of doing business.

> **> Active X Experience**
>
> The formerly popular DOM-related application Active X is used to enable remote program engagement in Microsoft web environments. It also introduces significant security risks. Those serving students or faculty in the military or other high-security settings will likely find its implementation blocked.

Remote staff adds a layer of complication. Be prepared for periodic infestations and the need to cleanse machines from afar or by shipment back to the maker or school's IT help. In addition, those with military or other high-security clients can expect to make accommodations. And expect FERPA intrusions in terms of protecting the privacy rights of students.

> *SEE ALSO: chap. 5: Preservation, Stack Maintenance; chap. 7: Metadata*

SEMANTIC WEB

VL: *TOOL, OPTION/DEPRECATED*

As proposed by W3C, the semantic web attempts to extend structure to documents for computer discernibility. Resources on the medium are linked into a "web of data"—an accumulation that could be facilitated, mined, and manipulated by machine intelligence. The approach relies on W3C's Resource Description Framework (RDF) and interlaced ties to explanatory ontologies. With it, machines should be able to comprehend and respond as "intelligent agents."

The ultimate utility of such mechanisms remains to be seen, but their use in higher education and amount of labor required raise questions. For the virtual library, cost/benefit analysis presently leans instead toward reliance on full-text implementations and search engine heuristics. Although major research libraries and national libraries are exploring "linked data" prospects, the utilitarian view remains more "wait and see." For the moment, one monitors, evaluates, and is ready to embrace when appropriate.

> *SEE ALSO: chap. 6: Cataloging, Catalog Interface; chap. 7: Discovery Search, Federated Search, Linked Data, Metadata, RDA, Search Engines*

SOCIAL NETWORKING/WEB 2.0

VL: *SERVICE/TOOL, REQUIRED*

Community-building is vital for the sustainability and growth of the online library. Web 2.0 involvement can extend the library's footprint beyond the virtual campus into a new realm of cross-university knowledge communities.

Immediate tactics, however, need to focus internally. Opportunities arise for blending the traditional, interpersonal skills of librarians within the atomized atmosphere of the Web. Social networking applications form the online librarian's main tool for personal engagement of faculty and students but call for nuance. The library can benefit from:

- **Early adoptions.** Online librarians look to establish their institutional presence as soon as possible where students and faculty are likely to gather; even better if they are there to greet on arrival.
- **Lurking presence.** The virtual library extends its presence by placing a flag (contact information) in sites where students and faculty gather. Engagement should be measured. Online librarians lurk to monitor for directions and forward resource information, including RSS feeds if possible.
- **Library sites.** Expect social engagement in the library's own sites to be minimal, but necessary. Facebook, LinkedIn, and Twitter accounts are

figure 7.6 Library on AMU Island, Second Life

now anticipated. Experience suggests that immersive educational ventures into Second Life and the like may be less productive, especially with nontraditional students (figure 7.6).

SEE ALSO: chap. 5: Study Hall and Social Sphere; chap. 6: Departmental Libraries; chap. 7: Course Guides, R&D, Website as Library

SYLLABUS ARCHIVES

VL: *SERVICE, OPTION*

Although syllabus archives have appeared sporadically in the past, MIT kicked off a sharing fad in the web age. For-profit schools prove hesitant in such matters, competitive and proprietary instincts often overriding university traditions for sharing. Yet student demands and the growing horde of published syllabuses on the Web suggest inevitability. Such resources may emanate from IT, a registrar, or other office, but regardless of origins they are well placed as a library service. Their presence enables comparative analysis in the future as well as providing a collective tool for building the university's historical identity. Housing can readily overlap digital commons and university archives.

SEE ALSO: chap. 6: Dissertations and Theses, University Archives; chap. 7: Curation, Digital Commons, Metrics

TRAINING/TUTORIAL SERVICES

VL: *SERVICE, OPTION*

The virtual library can cluster database training, information literacy, online writing laboratory, and other student support services/training modules into a tutorial center. Related entrepreneurial prospects arise with automated plagiarism checkers and remote tutoring services. Personalized writing and math help, for example, is important for an open university yet extremely difficult to implement for remote 24/7 operations. The library may thus have the opportunity to insert itself in the contract negotiations, management, and access to such outsourced products.

Clustering can also work in concert with student advisors, centers for teaching and learning, and the like. The joint drive is for student success. The library, however, need not be the featured locus. It should nevertheless not shirk from marketing the benefit of high traffic and librarians as symbolic features as well as experts in such matters as copyright and plagiarism.

SEE ALSO: *chap. 6: Copyright, Information Literacy, Plagiarism Controls; chap. 7: Career Libraries/Job-Hunting Services, Curriculum Materials Centers, Online Writing Laboratories, Syllabus Archives*

WEBLIOGRAPHY

VL: *TOOL, OPTION*

The word *webliography* (or *webography*) appeared in the mid-1990s. It holds echoes to the development of print scholarship. Results harken to analytical, descriptive, and enumerative bibliographic studies but also to newer scholarship in resource data mining. Library and information science should consider marking its turf but will certainly need to share this area of scholarship with other disciplines.

SEE ALSO: *chap. 6: Curriculum Laboratories; chap. 7: E-books, Open-Access Journals, Metrics, Resource Data Mining, Scholarly Communications, Scientific Social Networking/Open-Science Movement*

WEBSITE AS LIBRARY

VL: *SERVICE/TOOL, REQUIRED*

Massive structures on the quadrangle with checkpoints at the entrance are absent from the virtual campus. The online library as website is tautological. Concrete presences of the past give way to an unfolding mélange under a leaky facade with multiple access points and remote outposts. Librarians replace construction engineers in the ongoing building of responsive information services.

In terms of design, the perfect academic library interface has yet to emerge and appears impossible in the near term. Best practices build from an understanding and tuning to the audience(s). Yet online libraries recognize that they are partially constrained by continuity with academic traditions and terminology. Despite student cries for Google-like simplicity and full text, libraries remain invested in bibliographic methods and the compensating services of information literacy.

At the moment, the state of the art appears to stress professional compromises and functional capacities. The trend is to simplify. Still imperfect all-in-one search boxes are augmented by groupings for electronic databases, e-books, journals, and media—accumulations that are rendered complicated for the user by their sheer size. To the traditional core, the library adds its entrepreneurial concentrations—course support, publishing, tutorial operations, university archives, and the like. Mainstream requirements for hours and street addresses are vitiated, but the user should also expect similar background about the library, contact information, current affairs, and help tabs. In a CRIS model, the library also seeks granularity through boutique departmental sites and invests in maximizing Web 2.0 contacts.

In this description, the virtual library remains a work in process. It needs to monitor and remain flexible. Current web technology is destined to alter present construction habits. Mobile devices are already leaving an impact. Tablets and the touch screen facility of new computers will inevitably effect navigation and retrieval—perhaps eliminating the mouse in the process. Although slow as input media, voice recognition is similarly destined. It, eyeball-, and even thought-initiated approaches are backed up by ADA 508 spurs. Google Glass with augmented reality and the prospects of ubiquitous computing has arrived. As indicated in the Epilogue, the academic virtual library must also consider transit to personalized library environments—memex redux.

SEE ALSO: All, but especially chap. 6: Catalog Interface; chap. 7: ADA 508, Reading Platforms, Search Engines, Social Networking/Web 2.0

CHAPTER 8

REWIRING ONLINE LIBRARIANS

THIS NEXT EXERCISE EMBRACES A DIFFERENT TYPE OF construction. The virtual library demands a new supporting craft. A reoriented band of professionals is required to meet the challenges of a burgeoning communications revolution and global economic forces. Online librarians need to retain high-touch traditions and their narrative strengths but add web-based substance. They must engage the student, professor, and staff on a continuum as fellow telecommuters in the alien environs of a virtual campus. Practitioners proactively and entrepreneurially construct the library as a living value proposition, one positioned on the cutting edge of emerging knowledge communities.

Professional emergence is, however, complicated by timing. Online academic librarianship remains an art form in process within a transitional era. Current specialists are still born to print and inured to the ideals of the research library. Few in this generation can come fully prepared for altered modes of address, let alone the financial factors and entrepreneurial demands of a for-profit university. They remain bereft of precedents within an uncertain economy and fight for survival.

How does the librarian think with the born-web, within the context of a virtual university, and without the reassuring physical structures of the past?

Formal library education is not yet honed for the purely virtual. Those with little experience proclaim expertise. Vendors purloin and siphon training toward their products. At the moment, practitioners remain relegated to on-the-job, experiential learning and by way of "virtual water cooler" chatter.

This chapter looks to background tuning and indoctrination for virtual practitioners. It surfaces rewiring requirements and coping tactics for a new type of professional by entwining among:

- **Institutional portfolio.** Positions are retailored away from past professional library concentrations and toward those that mirror their university's curricular and research programs. The online librarian works within a dual portfolio. One portion is the general, or shared, collective expertise. The other calls for point-of-contact liaisons as departmental or program specialists.
- **Long Tail/competitive awareness.** The Web thrusts the library into competition and the ongoing need to demonstrate value. Online librarians must be willing to engage, including offering economically driven responses in a for-profit university.
- **Web thinking.** The immersive and pervasive nature of the medium fosters singular and somewhat alien patterns of thought and problem-solving approaches.

INSTITUTIONAL PORTFOLIO

The university and its programs form the librarian's laboratory. Online librarians respond with Janus faces. Their personas partake of a collective blend of web information skills and subject specializations.

COLLECTIVE EXPRESSIONS

Library holdings and applications extend as shopping services for classroom and allied research needs. The facility is seen as fungible; activities can no longer be wholly contained within fixed walls. Instead, they build seamlessly across the web divide:

- **Deep Web.** The library's licensed holdings are the launch zone for professional involvement. Citation analysis and other quality/use measures add to the professional equation. Point-of-contact designations should be expected for the article databases and e-book platforms as well as a growing array of media outlets, combined knowledge centers, and simulations. The online librarian's portfolio extends to monitoring for interface changes, possible withdrawal of products, and the onset of alternative products or even new modes of delivery. Specializations are significant for training purposes, to enhance student usage, and for outreach to engage faculty adoptions.

- **Open Web.** The online library extends beyond its licensed zones. It acts as an open system with evaluative insights for the rest of the Web. Disciplinary specializations continue to hold forth. The librarians' professional vetting and monitoring skills work in concert with active Web 2.0 communal partnerships among faculty and students.

> ### › Web Construction and Networking
>
> Survival tactics feature the library near or at the head of the university's web pack. In addition to assembling resources, the virtual library's professional construction crew systematically contributes fixed resources. Online librarians proactively contribute course guides, portals, tutorials, and other support pages. Tactics are also interpersonal. Librarians utilize their communication/networking skills within the institution and through Web 2.0 venues. What related internal services are linked from the site, what are missing, what is new, and where else should the library be linking?

DATABASE/ DEPARTMENT SPECIALIST

Another side of the professional coin arises with subject and database expertise. The day of the pure generalist may be past. Engagement calls for specialization in terms of web skills and subject knowledge as well as their marketing for campus visibility:

- **Database points of contact—internal demonstrations.** The virtual academic library exists as a flattened organization (see chap. 9). Heretofore dedicated library "departmental" positions—cataloger, government documents librarian, systems librarian—blend together within a team concept. The Web counters with demands for information literacy and a rash of specialized research tools. Online librarians expect assignment as points of contact for the latter. Tasks include particulars for enhancing user skills, advanced information literacy training, and construction of training devises. Librarians may be called on to maintain relations with the supplier and its technical support, or even to engage in pricing negotiations.

- **Departmental liaisons—campus demonstrations.** The overriding demand is mapping and infiltrating subject specialist librarians to degree programs. Advanced degrees or related experience become crucial for building credibility. Tactics focus on community building—establishing professional relationships with the faculty member and students. Involvement goals feature:

> **> Artificial Intelligence Conundrum**
>
> One of the ironies of the new age is that highly specialized skills are the most susceptible to artificial intelligence applications. Many of the knowledge areas described are destined for automated augmentation. These could eventually obviate a portion of the proposed librarian roles but would still leave the portal for focused delivery community involvement as an anchor.

> » *Departmental portals.* Building program-specific library subsets and electronic course bibliographies emerges as a basic and *measurable step, one that stresses faculty involvement as stakeholders.*
> » *Embedding.* Participation extends from involvement with the faculty and academic administration. The online librarian creates canned tutorials and seeks entry as a teaching assistant, especially in college introductory and discipline-specific methods courses.
> » *Social networking.* The online librarian steps beyond even virtual library "walls" to provide a supporting presence and information updates within a department's Web 2.0 community.

ENTREPRENEURIAL ARENAS

The new professionals and their library's sustainability extend into other arenas. Individual abilities are merged within a team concept for coverage, in areas such as these:

E-publishing/Information Centers

Online librarians keep apace and involved in the electronic information marketplace. The library moves away from passive receipt and permanent acquisition of research materials. Dynamic and contextual operations call forth a cluster of professional responsibilities:

- **Ethics/public good.** As members of the library profession, academic virtual librarians incur ethical responsibilities for public or at least university research and student community access to pertinent information.
- **Publishing/authors.** Like anything appearing on the Web, virtual libraries need to be understood as types of publications. Online librarians go further. In addition to being information miners and presenters, they embrace roles as multifaceted editors and publishers:
  - » *Dissertations/theses.* The Web turns traditional housing roles into a publication forum.
  - » *Internal construction.* Librarians author supplemental tools and pages in support of their university. Course guides and tutorial products should be regarded and evaluated as new forms of scholarly publication.
  - » *Publishing options.* The library can consider extending its classroom and research functions into the realms of peer-reviewed scholarship as well as use its financial entrée to assist faculty with commercial and university presses.
- **Scholarly monitors.** Online librarians need also be vigilant and share findings on developments in the web arena, including new teaching applications and genres.

Online Education/Training Specialists

Emphasis on classroom materials extends into the "meta" of online instruction. Teaching remains mired in twentieth-century paradigms. Web-based pedagogical methods are only beginning to appear. Appropriate approaches for born-web students, granularity by way of differentiating methods for individual disciplines, and the integration of interactive applications all await development. Online librarians are advised to insert themselves and their resources into this process. As discussed in chapter 9, they do not stand alone or at the top of these directions but as part of a team with faculty, instructional developers, and centers for teaching and learning.

> **> Trainers**
>
> One of the best ways to ensure participation is infiltrating librarians or library exercises into required faculty training for online instruction and the basic introductory courses for students. This approach is strengthened if contact with the librarian is involved.

> **Open Access/Intellectual Freedom**

In keeping with their heritage and the public good, academic librarians are joining their public library compatriots at the forefront of free access and moving toward defense of intellectual freedom on the Web. Those in the for-profit sector may have to be somewhat circumscribed, but they can join the campaigns by demonstrating win-win situations. Open access with its economic savings, ROI, and student-centric orientation enables marketable prospects for the entrepreneurial library. Support for academic integrity, fair use, new educational copyright standards, and the open exchange of information can similarly prove valuable and add promotional distinctions for enhancing a university's reputation.

Quality Control/Audit Specialists

The Web heightens the importance of regulatory compliance. This can open the door to extend related skills for campus-wide application and partnerships in keeping with a CRIS model. Several topics may occupy online librarians' attention:

- **ADA 508.** Although complexities will arise with newer interactive genres, digital library materials are now among the most readily adaptable for handicapped access. Online librarians remain cognizant of the importance of and applications for principles of universal access in regard to the library but also can extend their abilities to the evaluation of classroom materials.
- **Copyright.** Online librarians must be aware of copyright law and fair-use implications for electronic material. There is a collective responsibility to monitor and shared information/decision making in regard to the Digital Millennium Copyright Act and court decisions. Online librarians walk a tightrope to both guard against attacks and project their university's rights under fair-use principles.
- **Education regulations.** These will come increasingly on the radar as states and the federal government extend jurisdiction into higher education.

Web Generalists

Familiarity, a modicum of expertise, and ongoing monitoring of web operations are sine qua non—the defining characteristics of the online librarian. Fortunately, the need for advanced technical expertise is declining. Programming skills may be useful, but the cloud and easy-to-use software have lifted much of the burden. Current expectations include a basic understanding of:

- **HTML/CMS.** For the moment, some familiarity with HTML/XHTML through a standard software package (e.g., DreamWeaver) remains useful, as does the willingness to engage new cloud-based applications. HTML5 is certainly commanding attention. Most work, however, is likely to flow through a content management system (CMS). Expect the need for training. A duty librarian, for example, needs to be enabled to put up notices of an outage or other problems. Moreover, online librarians must be able to contribute and edit within their designated subject and application zones.
- **Site design/construction.** Related skill sets and a dash of flexibility appear for site-level considerations. All sites are works in progress that call for team efforts. The perfect model for an online library has yet to evolve, new tools are constantly appearing, and audience demands are changing.

› Hunting for Online Professionals

Not every professor can teach well online, and not every librarian can become a successful online librarian. Today's applicant pool varies widely. There are great variations in the ability to grasp the revolutionary scope of online services or respond to the mundane demands for metric-driven results, economic strictures, and proactive marketing as highlighted in a for-profit university.

Even with web facility, recent print-era MLS graduates seem challenged by the special requirements of the new environment. Library school programs logically remain driven by established market forces. These do not necessarily map against unfolding virtual academic library directions. The generalist MLS may, however, become a thing of the past. The one-size-fits-all reference librarian model and newer information science are not well suited to service pragmatics and bottom-line orientation. Those without additional advanced degrees or specialized experience will find matters difficult. Such credentials matter in developing partnerships with faculty and managing the library's reputation.

Although far from a scientific sample, APUS job searches over the past half-dozen years reveal a sizeable pool of professionals interested in the online, for-profit space. Applicants tend to be drawn by the flexible schedule and ability to telecommute. Our winnowing process looks to the tenor of e-mail messaging and facility with producing electronic course guides. Age variations have not proved to be great barriers. Those who have worked in special or scientific libraries seem among the most adept at the transition. They are prepositioned for the added demands of engaging faculty in a concise and directed fashion.

The most difficult recruiting remains at the managerial level. The pool of middle managers tuned to remote management peculiarities, reduced bureaucratic hierarchies, and entrepreneurial demands of a for-profit enterprise remains sparse—the rewiring perhaps more difficult.

- **Search engines.** All eyes must also train on interactions and use of this newest audience and dominant method of location for online services.

LONG TAIL/ECONOMIC AWARENESS

A second major rewiring strand for the new librarian engages accountability as a value proposition—directions that take stronger shape within a for-profit unit. As with profit-motivated publishers, it is easy to speak past each other. Though educational quality remains an overriding mantra, the online librarian has to come to grips with the management drives for ROI. Online librarians need to factor themselves into marketing and branding concepts. They must engage as frontline troops and embrace a defensive and offensive economically driven ethos. Rehoning into capitalistic embrace may extend to such attributes as:

- **Entrepreneur.** Resting on past laurels and assumed values may prove disastrous. Librarians, especially those in the for-profits, realize that they are in a competitive and dynamic environment. Opportunities abound, but not for the passive. As discussed in the next chapter, success demands awareness and the hunt for options. It also involves the protection of established areas of library engagement and awareness of new information avenues, places where the librarians' skill sets can come to bear. In the sixteenth-century words of Niccolo Machiavelli at a similar stage of development within the print revolution, *Entrepreneurs are simply those who understand that there is little difference between obstacle and opportunity and are able to turn both to their advantage.*
- **Metrics master.** In similarly uncomfortable accommodation, web-era management tends to metrics. Such employ is particularly relevant to remote operations. Rather than "bankers' hours" of convenience, service and staffing levels are driven to reflect actual demand. Reliance on citation analysis or other evaluative methods becomes assumed practice. Librarians are hired and assigned in keeping with program size and institutional prestige. Production requirements are set in place and monitored for electronic bibliographies, training sessions, and other products. Data form the basis for funding and staffing requests.

- **Marketing agent.** The library requires nuanced but ongoing marketing to ensure that its contributions are not overlooked or taken for granted. Librarians have to sell proactively to faculty, students, and their institution.
- **Negotiation specialist.** Although solid professional relations with vendors and copyright holders are appropriate, online librarians understand that they come with primary fiduciary responsibilities to their universities—and reawakened duties as advocates for students. Be aware too of turmoil in the marketplace. With CRIS operations, carefully documented intent and proactive defense of educational mission are in order. Expect increasing reliance on the collective power of the library purse and consortia for rational pricing and copyright matters. Pricing remains a proverbial crapshoot. Those in the for-profit arena are particularly at risk. They are occasionally excluded from group pricing and come with an added capitalistic onus to demonstrate competitive success. Hence, willingness to engage in bargaining—or at least the reputation for negotiation—should be regarded as a plus.

WEB THINKING—TRANSITION STAGE

The third strand in the rewiring requires subtle and not so subtle mind shifts for the new medium. The French Annalistes speak of *mentalités*—a communal set of imbued directions, ways of behaving, and belief structures. Though something is clearly happening, the web mindset presently defies clear definition. Google and search engines, for example, have made a difference. Those who learned to ingest information by reading a printed page need to think differently to engage the clicking and scrolling forces of onrushing web natives.

PERSONALITY TRAITS
Although far from firm and with terminology not fully formed, one begins to tease an overlapping set of positive traits for engagement on the Web:

- **Community builder/supporter.** Community involvement is the single most important tactic in the online library arsenal. Such skills are on display with a library's Facebook, Google+, LinkedIn, Twitter, or other Web 2.0

identity-building venture. Yet expect internal traffic to be light. Web 2.0 tactics are more successful as by-products of participation in the university's communities. The idea is not to dominate but to infiltrate quietly and help ensure that the library is not overlooked. The side-benefits extend to collection development and new product offerings in response to the community's interchanges.

- **Electronic communicator.** The new breed of librarian comes with high-touch dexterity. The best of the online librarians conquer the new forms of communication. They prosper based on inestimable ability to communicate remotely. Tactics are twofold:
  - » *Giving good e-mail.* The main activity focuses on effective communication in interactive forums such as e-mail and chat.
  - » *Building response mechanisms.* The secondary but significant advancement is capture and reuse as fixed resources in response or anticipation of repeated queries.
- **Excitement/engagement.** Functionaries doing their jobs are not the most desirable candidates for launching an online library. Prime candidates demonstrate a high level of commitment and individual initiative. The joys of the book are transferred to the experiences of the Web. Trips to campus and desk chatter are replaced with the satisfaction from a high number of "hits" with one's course guides. The ideal online librarian demonstrates fascination and inherent delight with the revolutionary challenges as well as eagerness to explore new directions.

PROBLEM APPROACHES

The Web is an associational labyrinth. Instead of one route, librarians look for multiple corridors, new unfolding pathways, and multiple ways of associating. Dealing in this fashion calls for the conscious and unconscious embrace of:

- **Link sharing.** In the web world, the more links the better. Online librarians look to proselytize and publicize through active referral building and link exchanges.
- **Multipurposing.** One of the key stages of awareness is automatic embrace of multipurposing. The single-use "one off" is discouraged as inefficient. The web mindset is modularly oriented.

- **Quality over quantity.** Ascendancy of quality factors proves difficult. Librarians have bought into the Big Buy mentality. They remain notorious among faculty and university administrators for not knowing when to stop. The visceral satisfaction of multiple hits must be controlled. Search engines do that nicely. Users appreciate selectivity and abstracting services. The online library returns to the conservative times before the wealth of riches with the Web. At the same time as they point to the panoply, online librarians need to concentrate on their specialized skills and new measurement tools to vet for the most significant resources. Fixed resources and reference outputs require consistent quality-driven limits—for example, a discipline that questions undifferentiated lists of more than ten items.

SILO AVOIDANCE/PARTNERSHIP CONSCIOUSNESS

The bureaucratic tendencies to silo and control information are as real now as when Max Weber (1922) posited them in the early twentieth century: "Bureaucratic administration fundamentally means domination through knowledge." Although such practices do not necessary fit a networked web world, expect turf battles. By politely confronting such tendencies, online librarians may gain added opportunity to foster partnerships and an institutional communication niche.

- **Internal.** Librarians need to share their specialties and general knowledge areas as members of a corps and professional community through remote engagement.
- **Academia.** Librarians concentrate on involvement with the faculty and establishing liaison ties with departments as well as enhanced services for the students.
- **Institution.** On one hand, look to share and cooperate with other units. The library offers excellent neutral and symbolic territory for cooperative ventures. On the other hand, be alert to "poaching" and lack of awareness of what the library has to offer. The library may have pioneered topics, like information literacy, which others with the best of all intentions rediscover and attempt to silo as their own.

TRANSPARENCY

In a still demanding transformation, the days of responding with increasing complexity and countering with bibliographic instruction responses are numbered. Google has triumphed. The online librarian subscribes to the mantra of making access as simple as possible. The library is framed with introductory assistance for newcomers but designed with transparency in mind for returnees. In keeping with CRIS mode, activities channel between dual missions:

- **Research.** The platform remains designed for research but as also linked to methods instruction. Hence, the library should be readily available from the web classroom along with links to supplemental faculty and student portals. Once there, the research experience is framed as part of the collegiate/disciplinary experience. The librarian's position continues within the research library mode, albeit with new-found emphasis on validating the burgeoning wealth on the Web.
- **Classroom mode.** Regularly assigned library materials should be instantly available within the online classroom. There is no reason to put the student user through extra hoops; moreover, every effort should be given to facilitate the faculty's selection and automatic ingestion into the classroom shell. For students, the librarian's role is mitigated as a simple provider and help resource in the case of lost materials. For faculty, the librarian seeks to engage as a partner in populating the classroom.

> **› Communal Crucible**
>
> No clear pattern has emerged for rewiring online librarians in this transition period. Training is presently inadequate or lacking. Understanding runs against the grain of established professional mores and print dominance. The logical tendency is continuity—belief that prior training and experience are adequate preparation. Matters are accentuated within a for-profit setting and its added economic consciousness.
>
> At the moment, conversion proceeds primarily as a by-product of work engagement and community building. Not everyone proceeds at the same pace, and some may be permanently challenged. In some magical fashion, however, exchanges framed by increasing familiarity within the immersive enterprise reach a tipping point. Staff begins to move forward organically to engage collective and individual leadership.

CAPTURING THE MOMENT

Understanding revolutionary change can readily bedevil even the best of historians, let alone those immersed and struggling on the scene. The juxtaposition in figure 8.1 attempts to address this challenge with a quick snapshot: word cloud images from an AquaBrowser search offer visual counterpoint between *librarian* and *online librarian* in the critical 2010s.

Although online librarianship is only beginning to form, such indicators are already telling. "Teacher" seems the only overlapping phrase—and a pleasant

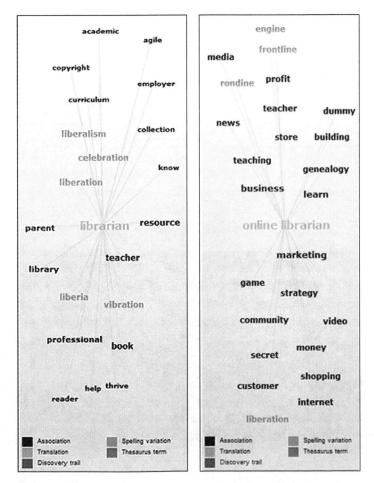

figure 8.1 *Librarian* (left) vs. *online librarian* (right), AquaBrowser word cloud

addition. Librarian returns solid building blocks for a narrative composed of "book," "professional," "copyright," and "academic" as well as such positive indicators as "agile" and "help." In keeping with the directions of this text, the online librarian garners a surprisingly larger set of associations. These include such potentially significant concepts as "community," "marketing," "strategy," and "profit" along with the signing of "internet," "media," "game," and "video." Strangely, however, the term "library" is conspicuously absent, and "academic" has been replaced by "business."

> ## The Philosophical Challenge

Though arguably simplistic on its surface, developing a web mindset can be framed within the most basic dichotomy in philosophy. Modern librarianship reflects Platonic precision and nineteenth-century scientific taxonomies. When faced with an information asset, action tends toward the archetype—to focus on the "correct" location and the "proper" term. Even with subject-added terms and modern data linking, the library trope remains that of classified objects with designated slots on the shelf. Such exactitude may be alien to the Aristotelian nature of the Web. As seen with archival traditions, an alternative is the relativistic exposing of the range of phrases. Rather than worry about where to place the resources, energies turn toward ensuring access points where users can reasonably expect to find them.

CHAPTER 9

MANAGERIAL STRATEGIES

The general who loses a battle makes but few calculations before-
hand. Thus do many calculations lead to victory and few calculations
to defeat: how much more if no calculation at all! It is by attention to
this point that I can foresee who is likely to win or lose.
—*Sun Tzu*, The Art of War (300 BCE?)

SUN TZU'S APHORISM RESONATES FOR THOSE ENGAGING
on a virtual campus. This chapter is based on one set of relatively successful experiences in that venue. As argued, vigi-
lance is vital. The battleground lies in largely uncharted territory with few defenses. Despite unquestioned potential and
tradition, online libraries are in a struggle for existence. Pas-
sivity and assumed academic privileges or past glories are recipes for disaster.

In keeping with Sun Tzu, strategic calculations are required. These project
from the strengths and narrative of the field but do not stand alone. The fight
is for visibility—to avoid being overlooked. Entrepreneurial engagement and
Machiavellian political awareness are requisite. Communication skills, marketing, and community development afford the best supplemental tactics. And,
though conflict avoidance is preferred, considered combat may be necessary.

COMMUNICATION ZONE

Calculations must account for the disturbing potentials of the Web in pragmatic concert with internal bureaucratic structures. Initial tactics deconstruct to engage the various players and opportunities on the virtual campus.

HIGHER ADMINISTRATION: BECOMING A MARKET DIFFERENTIATOR

Calculations in the for-profit space can even extend to the boardroom. Communication remains the central tactic but must be nuanced for a nonacademic audience. Engagement is with "MBAs" and "CPAs"—the business mindsets at the head of decision making. The challenges are complex. What to librarians may appear irrational slights can be quite cogent to business-trained eyes and for the new realities of the Web. Commercial modes and financial strictures lead to shortcuts, the questioning of prior practice, and belief in technological fixes over pedagogical ones.

> ### > Outsourcing Options
>
> Outstanding, cost-effective opportunities are offered by such places as Johns Hopkins, Indiana University, and the University of South Alabama as well as through commercial reference services and other supplements. Such services may be necessary for ILL purposes. Indeed, this type of approach could be a transitional tactic toward the goal of a branded library for each university.

Often launching on a shoestring, those in this new sector may not inherit a library. Such capital investment is all too readily minimized, lacking, or belated. Beguiled by business acumen and occasionally lacking academic inoculations, the business-minded can easily ignore complexities, underlying importance, and ethical underpinnings developed over a millennium. Educational imperatives give way to bottom-line expediency. Why not rely on local public libraries, rest on the Open Web, or outsource?

Survival within such an environment demands a persuasive counternarrative. It builds on the shared residue of the library as inherent to the idea of the university and, as discussed shortly, drives for regional accreditation. But the library must also be prepared to make a solid business case. Online library directors need to understand and "speak" web business. Awareness extends to the corporate context of underwriters, drives to take a university as company "public," and the interests of investors. Can the library become a point of interest for the board of directors, or even a positive element within "stock calls"?

> ## > Taxation Tactics
>
> The absence of tax-free status places for-profit university libraries in an anomalous position. Some twenty-four states have laws that could be read as applying sales tax to library databases. Institutions with multiple locations may thus wish to consider billing addresses carefully.

Accreditation

Fortunately, successful for-profit universities appear to mature with some form of branded library. Library existence remains contingent on a single main factor. Regional accreditation, the sine qua non for the American university, remains the key driver and baseline tactic. Future success demands the library surface itself in such endeavors. Though visiting teams normally set their own agenda, for example, the library should not shy from seeking a place on its schedule. Given the tendency of for-profits to grow by adding programs, the library should similarly consider laying groundwork for specialized accreditations.

Opportunities surface too from U.S. Department of Education scrutiny. The library offers the bulwark of tradition and sign of academic commitment. The online variety has related values for the university's planning apparatus. Sustainability is enhanced by its potential as agent of curricular quality and currency. As mentioned in chapter 6, tactics can engage through collection analyses. Departments and their learning objectives are profitably mapped to the types of holdings and librarian support. Critical analysis allows for targeting to promote areas of desired growth. Course guides are used for granular proof of educational quality and currency. At the least, such resources provide great fodder for the appendixes and help to bolster the formalities of successful submissions.

5 Rs: Talking Points

Even with accreditation, virtual library success suggests a broadened portfolio. The library is advised to surface values through financial, auditing/legal, and information literacy initiatives. Refrains to research may help but need to be tempered. Nonprofits and, indeed, most schools are not primarily research institutions. They are instructional venues. Attention is garnered by matching that "business" model. Communication advances through conscious refrain to "5 Rs"—with particular emphasis on the first two items:

1. **Recruitment.** Methods for attracting students are of overriding concern and a major budgetary issue. Onlines compete as national institutions. Recruitment is central to their survival but complicated by

the absence of geographic identification, compelling reputations, and an established alumni base. The industry norm is reportedly 25–30 percent of net for marketing. How can libraries enter this picture? Are there ways to make the library and its services part of the draw for potential students?

2. **Retention.** Retaining students through graduation runs second in emphasis. It involves financial, regulatory, and ethical issues. The industry's drive is to simplify student "on-boarding," monitor progress, remove points of rub, and add support for student success. Like junior colleges, however, onlines frequently feature low or open admissions policies. Attrition rates will be high, especially during the first courses. Lifelong learning and multiple degrees enter the calculations. Recruiting pays extra dividends if students remain to transit from associate, to undergraduate, to graduate or other programs. Is there a role for library services and librarians in this vein? Can they ease student transitions, assist with the mantra of student success, and help make for a "stickier" situation? How does one quantify such remediation?

3. **Regulations.** The federal government and states are in the picture with a growing number of reporting requirements. Online universities have justifiably come under scrutiny. Can librarians and the legitimating nature of a library insert themselves in this process? What is the potential and need for librarians to monitor the regulatory arena?

4. **Reputation management.** Reputation management strategies have begun to take their place. Online universities struggle to differentiate themselves, including a push for positive academic identities. Quality, job placement rates, and institutional reputation/ranking are being added to web click-throughs and media recruiting campaigns. What do the library and, especially, its online librarians need to do to ensure that the library is not overlooked in the process? Aside from faculty, what other campus support body has even close to the abilities to actualize and elevate a virtual university into

> **❯ Trademarking and Branding**
>
> If traction proves difficult, branding and "trademarking" potentials may prove more understandable for the decision makers.

greater respectability? Such directions are also significant for building student, faculty, and staff identification with the institution. They enter into retention considerations as well as long-term positioning for alumni relations and endowment prospects.

5. **ROI.** The bottom line is the bottom line. Online universities compete and do so without tax breaks or state subsidies. Library acceptance starts as part of the necessary superstructure and overhead expense. What can be done to alter that status, to give the library the image of a contributor? Could or should library publishing outputs become a profit center? Could parts of the CRIS model serve as inducements for those universities that do not subsidize course materials? Can librarians, especially those embedded in the classroom, be factored as a recoverable educational expense within the university's cost-recovery formula? Could cost savings through consortial purchases or bargaining skills be thrown into the tote sheets?

> **> National Interest**
>
> Retention and student success are of growing interest to all universities and part of a national crisis. In the first decade of the twenty-first century, the United States dropped from a worldwide first place into the teens in terms of the number of college graduates per capita.

BUREAUCRATIC STRATEGIES

Virtual campuses are newly forming. Calculations require engagement across the face of a different type of university, albeit with an eye to bureaucratic sensibilities and drives. Communication and community building again become the order of the day. Experience suggests a modicum of political and economic awareness. Successful engagement calls for working in concert with other units but may entail defensive positioning and "polite" competition.

Academic Support Zone

Where the library was once almost alone, the academic support field has gotten crowded. Online education engenders a coterie of specialists. Such entrants often boast technologically attractive pedigrees. As with any bureaucracy, expect competitive drives and tendencies to silo. New players may wittingly or unwittingly seek empowerment within library space and attempt to reinvent the library "wheel." Oversight of the library is unfortunately likely. Expect reminders of its tradition, holdings, cost-effectiveness, and even presence to be in order—and they may need to be frequent.

Despite potential for competition, the library should not think of standing alone—or necessarily being in the lead. The Web and library success are about community building and multipurposing. Recommendations include parlaying the historical narrative and librarians' traditional persona. Strive to turn potential competitors into allies, or at least the grudging "we're all in this together." Ultimately, assume that newly evolving constituencies are working with the same commitment to institutional success within the same disorienting revolution. One finds that partnerships and enhanced communications are the order of engagement for a variety of offices:

- **Centers for teaching and learning.** The demands of online education spawn specialized training and resource facilities. Expect overlap, but again think Web. The drive is access wherever students and faculty might logically look for them. Ownership is secondary. Reach out for cooperative listings but also to share the library's established expertise in resource sharing.
- **Instructional designers/developers.** Course developers and subject area specialists are natural partners. The developers bring specialized skills in presentations and integrating materials into the classroom. Yet they may be inured to the textbook model and often lack subject knowledge. Librarians can readily partner with subject expertise and superior web skills. The process extends to the promotion of library materials for research methods, cost-effective alternatives to textbooks, and as vital building blocks for enhanced pedagogies.
- **Student advising/recruiters.** These are often large operations within the onlines. They can profit from knowing what the library offers that might attract students as well as from the additional help support and referrals that can come from librarians.
- **Tutorial services.** Online writing labs, media labs, math labs, and other learning support elements are often birthed or sponsored in the library but can take on a life and competitive basis of their own. The library is a logical point of access for such operations as well as for partnerships to exploit its own information literacy tools.

Reputation Management Constituents

Reputation and identity building offer another arena for institutional cooperation and concomitant library sustainability/success. The library positions for long-term engagement. It becomes a native component for building a historical narrative and institutional identity. Several departments could appear as complementary agencies:

- **Alumni offices.** Arrangements with such operations are a natural. The two units share interests in building a positive university tradition and reputation. Although licensing arrangements must be taken into account, online library access is a desirable and among the few initial benefits available for alumni. Such partnerships also act in support of lifelong learning commitments and securing the graduates' return for additional study.
- **Marketing departments.** Those selling the university share common interest in promoting an institutional heritage. They also author and control the main descriptive materials about the school. Such items tend toward high production values but are of short-term marketing interest. News pieces must be constantly refreshed and realia replaced by ever newer tchotchkes. Such content is, however, vital for building the university's documentary heritage and a university archives. With minor negotiations, the enterprising archivist may even succeed in injecting metadata and prepackaging standards for transfer. Other mutually beneficial arrangements may arise. In keeping also with recruiting, marketing will look for

> ### > CRIS in Concert

CRIS approaches are extensible and offer equally valuable guidelines for other classroom support and development units. In this mode, the library and librarians emerge as a nonexclusive node for the discovery of classroom materials with added responsibilities for research/methods support. Librarians become active hunters with emphasis on provisioning upper-division and graduate classes as well as agents in the struggle against textbook dependency and new web-based pedagogies.

As indicated in chapter 8, such directions can spin entrepreneurial options. Librarians are on the lookout for suitable web applications. Information literacy is reworked for tailored program approaches and how those tie (or with correctives for those that don't tie) to the library's holdings. Efforts are constructed in keeping with the departmental learning objectives and measurable rubrics—for example, consideration for time-on-task measurement of library reading assignments. Concern is given for development of web-based pedagogical practices and tailoring to specific disciplinary needs.

blog posts and resources to help tell the university's story. The library and its librarians become useful fodder and partners in the hunt for good copy or commentaries. Such engagement in turn helps secure the library's institutional standing.

- **President's office.** Being close to the top remains the desired tactic in most enterprises. Positioning librarians for research assistance in the university president's offices, or an archivist to help capture the historical legacy, does not hurt. Presidential offices join marketing as major founts for historical documentation about the university. Good relations are a must and vital to the implementation of a university archives.
- **University press.** Beyond their potential for reinventing its operations, libraries have the academic and economic muscle to affect any extant university press significantly. In addition to internal reputation building, they should not shy from cooperative offers for promoting publications through relations with the key market—other libraries.

Administrative Support Offices

The entrepreneurial and developing nature of the onlines invites other forms of institutional engagement. The library may have the opportunity to engage and, hence, further its case for sustainability with an array of administrative offices.

- **Career services.** Overlapping alumni offices and rising under federal pressures, these support units should find library resources and services extremely useful for addressing the job scene.
- **Development/research offices.** Few onlines have as yet embraced research as a major mode. They may also be too raw for endowment drives. Yet

› Internal Identity Building

To act in support of its university's identity, the library has ethical responsibilities and practical opportunities that stretch across staff lines. Online universities, especially those caught in hypergrowth, seem particularly susceptible to psychological estrangement and isolation among employees. Hurried managerial responses can ignore the symbolic power of the university and the importance of building identity over time. Government attacks, economic drives, and the occasional overstep further work against the buffering embrace of established university traditions. The academic library remains a congenial and non-threatening reminder of a vital narrative. In-service training sessions and offers of librarian support may be welcomed calling cards.

such directions are inevitable. The library should be prepositioned to assist and also benefit from support in the hunt for external funding. Indeed, if one is not already present, the library may be able to help launch such an initiative.

- **Financial services.** The library manager should diligently prepare for engagement and communication with finance and accounting, which are frequently the ascendant powers in an online university. Matters, however, can be complicated should the library find itself relegated to second- or third-tier status with little budgetary control.

  In possible point of entry, for-profit financiers may not be fully prepared for library budgetary regimen. The library manager may be able to leverage through explanations of multiyear commitments and bulk purchasing options. If possible, try to isolate library costs as a "direct" expenditure. An automatic student or faculty ratio to librarian is preferred. Items that can be amortized as long-term capital expenses are likely to receive a lower level of scrutiny during budget negotiations.

  CRIS offers other prospects. The library may advance collection development through classroom support. Purchasing is targeted based on course adoptions. With that, the library must prepare to respond to different types of crises. Reading platforms can vary widely and service interruptions intervene. Publishers may pull texts from vendors with little notice. Publisher demands could lead to a fundamental change in costing. They would much favor royalty payments based on individual usage of materials. Libraries would be charged with oversight and student library fees projected as an increasing factor of life.

- **Human resources.** For-profit human resource departments can default to techniques more suitable to mainstream businesses. Libraries provide convenient reminders of university traditions along with options for enhanced internal identification and reputation building.

- **Institutional research.** On one hand, these data-driven operations can find librarians helpful and their databases of significance for qualitative and comparative studies. On the other hand, a "chi-square"-challenged librarian can benefit from assistance in determining and validating metrics as well as in setting up monitoring dashboards.

- **Information technology departments.** IT can fit under more than one category in this analysis. On one hand, support for the library's core information products can now be outsourced. On the other hand, the library is advised to remain abreast of technological changes elsewhere in the university. Assuming the absence of a separate library department and even with outsourcing, IT departments also remain central to integration with the university's virtual operations and authentication procedures. Partnership opportunities are available and particularly important in terms of coordinating for help functions, systems outages, and authentication.

- **Legal affairs.** Opportunities abound for partnerships and support. In addition to engagement in the vagaries of contract law and licensing, libraries should consider promoting their auditing and monitoring functions. Copyright, ADA 508, and higher education regulations offer ripe territory.

> ### › IT Woes
>
> In keeping with frequently heard complaints, relations with IT can prove dicey. A Columbia University type of leadership over campus IT is rare. Some university administrations can even treat the library as a technical, not academic, component and relegate it under an IT department. The virtual library in a for-profit enterprise should certainly not expect its own computer services department and should be prepared for dependence on campus IT services. Security can become a canard and library concerns low-level priorities.

CURRICULAR STRATEGIES

"In any dispute the intensity of feeling is inversely proportional to the value of the issues at stake. That is why academic politics are so bitter." Sayre's tongue-in-cheek indictment exposes the often complicated political situations within the ivory tower. Myth and reality come into sharp perspective when dealing with instructors and departments. Campus politics and community building tactics must be considered. Although the logic of cooperative development remains impeccable, internal situations may reflect uncomfortable isolation. The library joins in the midst of a switch from faculty to administrative dominance. The disruptive forces of the Web can also threaten prior scholarly compacts among various groups:

- Full-time instructors may be physically and mentally alienated from the virtual campus. They require consistent efforts and contributions to

garner as fellow stakeholders and possible coshares in support of academic tradition within the new setting.
- Part-time journeymen offer a subtly different target and likely the majority of the teaching cadre. They too are an off-campus cohort and often work at more than one university. They will require concerted outreach to inform about and engage with the school's library or other support services.
- Department/program directors are the most targetable objects of attention. Given expected workloads and administrative duties, they are also likely the most in need of library intervention. Yet expect them to demand a degree of convincing and ongoing proof of concept.

Partnership Tactics

The mere presence of the library no longer suffices—if it ever did. In the face of Wikipedia and Google, how does the institution engage in branded partnership ventures? Opportunities for chance encounters are few on the virtual campus. Given work schedules and a growing deluge, e-mail messaging is less than effective. Consider research. Professors go directly to the Web. It offers access to myriad resources as well as to other academic libraries that may be more familiar and offer better resources.

Marketing and community development are demanded. Instructors will need reminders and outreach. Most important, the library must actually demonstrate its worth. Engagement may take several forms:

- **Academic mission supports**
  - » *Course guides offer quality and currency assurances on the scope of available materials as research launching pads and for classroom materials.*
  - » *Departmental portals work in tandem with course guides as research launching pads and information literacy toolsets.*
  - » *Program analysis and new program starts provide strategic benchmarking for the insertion of library materials.*
- **Librarian outreach**
  - » *Subject specialist librarians are matched to academic departments.*
  - » *Embedded librarians act as teaching assistants with concentration on information literacy instruction.*
  - » *Librarians, library modules, or both are infiltrated in training for online instructors.*

- **Ancillary supports**
    - » *Tutorial and help services are marketed and extended in support of information literacy and classroom engagement.*
    - » *Web 2.0 sites are monitored for client directions and the active insertion of appropriate information resources.*
    - » *Copyright and ADA 508 audit functions ensure legal compliances.*
- **Student mission**
    - » *The library engages faculty to join a campaign in collective support of their students' financial interests.*

Classroom Challenges

The switch toward the classroom requires heightened understanding of a different instructional environment. Tactics are aimed at advancing the library's participation for the financial good of the student community but also at elevating the quality of online education.

Basics. At this stage of development, librarians can concentrate calculations on two broad classroom classifications:

- **Core competencies/general education.** Universities have developed general education programs to prepare incoming students and account for high school shortcomings. Challenges are magnified for open online universities, with their propensity toward nontraditional students and added burden of adapting to a virtual campus. Libraries have an important role to play in building student success. Information literacy and tutorial/ teaching lab outreach provide gateway tools. The library also has a vested interest in entering the classroom as soon as possible, especially in any mandatory introductory course.

› Facilitating Transition

Success may temporarily hinge on assistance during the move from land-based to online education. Librarians present a useful touchstone. Their established narrative promotes acceptability and lowered threat potential. Librarian web expertise steps forward to help remediate movement in alienating online environs. Tactics involve infiltration into required faculty training courses and the production of help materials. Management adds interpersonal calculations for studied targeting of the most appropriate faculty and departments. Consideration extends to matching factors from age and field of expertise to the recalcitrance or openness of individual professors and top-down mandates.

- **Upper division and graduate.** Higher-level courses are a more obvious and native hunting ground. They are ripe for populating with library-mediated resources and faculty partnerships. Particular notice should be given to subject librarian infiltration, especially in web-based research/ methods classes.

Advancing analysis. Web-based asynchronous teaching brings a wholly different set of instructional challenges yet remains strangely rooted in twentieth-century practice. Nevertheless, the forces of change are clearly in evidence. Analytics and accountability standards are marching to prominence. New technologies daily try to infiltrate the curriculum. The online library can profitably enter these aspects of the changing situation:

- **Lecture loss.** Asynchronous settings are marked by the loss of live lectures and classroom. Such absences remain a telling and unresolved differentiator. Although the skills of the professors remain the key determiner for student success, their main tool is lost. Instead classroom materials rise in importance as the bedrock for the new arena.
- **Research vs. teaching tropes.** Pre-1980s reward structures largely concentrated on research. These have been somewhat ameliorated. The voiced trend is toward classroom engagement and teaching abilities. Online universities heighten such directions. Their business drives, learning outcome metrics, and enhanced in-class oversight push the bar.
- **Textbook dependency.** As noted in chapter 3, publishers have been remarkably successful in securing faculty allegiance to their textbooks. This dependency model works to the economic and, perhaps, intellectual detriment of students. Financial pressures and a different educational environment, however, are advancing to redefine this late twentieth-century orthodoxy.

Pedagogical opportunities. Thanks to its hold on peer-reviewed literature, disciplinary classics, and citation analysis, the library may find openings. Is there a role in dealing with textbook dependency and price inflation? Should the library lobby away from a didactic textbook orientation for a return to the Sorbonne and Socratic methods, which appear well suited to the new medium? If so, how best to curate and promote virtual engagement of "primary" source materials, disciplinary classics, and peer-reviewed literature?

Does it also have other places to play in supporting the construction of web pedagogies? For instance, a "one-size-fits-all" industrial-strength model persists across LMSs. Yet English differs from history, which differs from political science, which differs from mathematics, and so on. Disciplines need decoding; granularity awaits. How does the library orchestrate its inherent prepositioning in reflection of such disciplinary differences? How are such directions integrated with readying collections for a movement beyond books and articles into media, simulations, 3D interactions, and still unforeseen capabilities?

STUDENT-FACING STRATEGIES

Faculty and programmatic needs set the operative directions for the online library, but students are the main audience for service design. The online library must forcefully capture or recapture its pivotal position as the "go-to" place for academic support and the scholarly laboratory for building disciplinary expertise.

> **› Structured Positioning**
>
> Tactical stress is given to "structured positioning." The LMS and virtual campus have replaced the quadrangle. The drive is to become a standard resource in an expected locus within them and a feature for each classroom. The library as link is infiltrated for strategic placement where users might think to look, but also where its information services are needed. Librarians as agents also politely insert themselves and the library's presence in scholarly Web 2.0 hangouts.

With the Web, libraries have lost "build it and they must come" stature. The reverse may be true. As detailed in chapter 4, students increasingly shy away from the facility. APUS internal surveys reveal that students are also more than convinced of their own expertise as web researchers, regardless of the truth of that situation. The power of Google and full-text desires lull into complacency and expectations of simplicity. Also illustrated in chapter 4, the primary audience shies away from the complexities of library databases, Z39.50-based bibliographic searching, and—one projects—semantic web applications. How does the library engage this type of audience?

Marketing. Marketing returns to the fore, albeit in unprecedented and extremely complicated fashion. The nature of an online university and its student body thwarts advertising. Though updatable with a "Notices" section, the library as website lacks a physical lobby for posters and handouts. Institutional drives for metrics and increased reporting demands mean that students are easily oversurveyed. The virtual library does not command notoriety as a "go-to" social space or study arena. Older and nontraditional students also tend to concentrate narrowly and ignore extraneous solicitations.

Given the financial improbability of assigning a librarian to each student, the library requires creative alternatives. Stressing recognition of fiduciary responsibilities should be high on the list. High-touch and personalized services remain on the agenda. Good service stays a major marker for approbation and the all-important building of a repeat customer base—that is, retention and lifelong learning factors. Though mindful of the logistical challenges, online libraries may wish to offer independent, synchronous training sessions and supplemental help modules. Classroom engagement is crucial. Infiltrating information literacy is high on the list along with injections of course embedding. Online librarians also escape the confines of a building. They look to penetrate and establish background presence in places where students and faculty might gather—Web 2.0 communities, for example.

SECONDARY AUDIENCES

In addition to students, aforementioned faculty, and institutional compatriots, online library calculations consider other types of users:

- **Alumni.** Although licensing matters can become legally complicated, alumni access remains a desirable goal. Service extensions help build community identity as well as support lifelong learning and student recruitment/retention for additional study. Such orientation helps the virtual library establish itself as a mainstay with alumni affairs and development offices.
- **Potential students.** The library should consider how it can act as a recruiting draw. Astute applicants and matriculants expect such a place. To many, the library is understood as a distinguishing characteristic and probative mark of excellence. The library narrative thus assists in promoting the future viability of the institution as well as creating a potential sphere for genteel competition among the virtual libraries.
- **Scholarly community.** The virtual library and its librarians offer crucial elements in determining the university's reputation among scholars and accreditors as well as providing a positive element in faculty recruitment. As discussed in the Epilogue, the virtual academic library offers intriguing potential for the promotion/creation of web knowledge centers—the postmodern creation of boundless, interactive zones for enhanced research.
- **Search engines.** Librarians must take note of this new audience. Expect users to employ search engines outside the library's planned navigation. Home-grown assets should be thus tuned to enhance discovery and ensure proper identification—for example, link exchanges and use of the title metatag along with heading levels.

OPERATIONAL TACTICS

Strategic discussions shift toward operationalizing. Ultimately, the range of options defies a single formula. Each university demands its own analysis and selective approaches. These discussions hypothesize for maximizing within a fully virtual, for-profit setting. How can one best operationalize for this new norm? What calculations need to be made for staff, technology, and users?

BASIC SERVICES

The Web fosters an array of new managerial trials and tribulations. The shift to virtual comes with peculiar tradeoffs. The administrator must cope with the diminished or lost intimacies of face-to-face exchanges, physical browsing in the stacks, chance encounters, and socializing. The monumental physical presence of the past undergoes a striking transformation:

- **Remote/global access.** Travel to the campus or library is no longer required. Indeed, the facilities can and should be available to students and faculty anywhere around the world.
- **24/7 self-services.** The prior limitations from set hours are eliminated. Patrons expect to enter at any time of the day or night; moreover, they can complete their business without the intervention of staff, perhaps without even encountering staff.
- **Direct/transparent retrieval of resources.** The two-step process of looking up bibliographic information and then physically hunting on the shelves is gone. Web-age users expect to transit seamlessly to materials.
- **Library as website.** An all-in-one shopping experience emerges, including a mixture of search engine–enabled links to external resources, study services, help features, and on-call librarians.

› The Special Library Juxtaposition

The nimbleness and financial considerations envisioned in this text may be offputting to those inured to the ivory tower and comfort of routine practices. Special librarians may be more welcoming. They have long been susceptible to monetary pressure, information as opposed to genre delivery, and the benefits of entrepreneurial excursions.

MARKETING ONLINE LIBRARIANS

As the client base grows, strategic advancement depends on a critical mass of professionals. Expect to campaign to justify the assemblage of such human resources. Buildup may be slow. Virtual libraries presuppose smaller staffs than a comparable land-based facility. The library is in competition and must not assume anything. Any new position calls for demonstrable figures and a telling narrative. Librarians may need to be "sold" as part of a business case. Accreditation drivers merge with points from the previous chapter and calculated refrains to the 5 Rs.

- **Identity makers.** Librarians offer important and expected signs of excellence. Their absence can be shown to hurt reputation building. Their presence can be branded and exploited for competitive advantage. Moreover, these professionals offer practical respite as intermediaries with the faculty. The librarian as subject specialist brings familiarity and tradition that is less offputting than other classroom support elements.
- **Compliance experts.** Librarians come with defined legal status under copyright and education law. Their presence and involvement can help protect the corporation in a way not available to other nonfaculty employees. The field comes with cachet and valuable trust factors. Librarians can thus readily extend their internal auditing for copyright and ADA 508 issues to broader effect for the class compliance. Similar extensions of skills are available for the blossoming education regulatory arena. Properly positioned, librarians lend credibility to measurement and reporting demands for accreditors and regulators.
- **High-touch intermediaries.** Librarians presuppose interpersonal skills, which are of added value for the virtual campus. They can assist faculty but also help students coping with a readily isolating technological space. Thus, a traditional library skill morphs into a measurable retention and potential recruiting feature.
- **Subject/quality assurance specialists.** In a CRIS model, librarians emerge as subject experts and course support specialists to work with faculty and academic departments. Librarians bring ROI as powerful low-cost engines to ensure currency, but also for quality control and reputation factors with the curriculum. Moreover, such professionals can be marketed as frontline components for the mounting of a new degree option or specialized accreditation visits.

- **Web gurus.** The 5 Rs are on prominent display through librarian web expertise. Tongue-in-cheek comments on either hiring a 12-year-old or a librarian to keep up with the Web can gain traction. They are demonstrable fact. In particular:
  - » *Deep Web.* Librarians are the most knowledgeable for dealing with and exploiting already capitalized resources.
  - » *Open Web.* They are similarly skilled in evaluating and exploiting the myriad "free" resources on the Web.
  - » *Information literacy training.* They are the established specialists for instructing in the new art of web research.
  - » *Technology monitors.* Librarians can add value through ongoing patrol of the evolving technology, such as proactive positioning for Web 2.0.

PERSONNEL MANAGEMENT

Online librarians imply a different set of administrative expectations. The for-profit manager assumes a high degree of control over personnel. For good or ill, unionization and tenure have not entered this scene. Entrenched long-term employees are also presently unlikely. Expect committee demands to also be less or not be in evidence. But the remaining challenges are replete and offputting. Management is stuck in barely chartered waters. Circumstances are radically altered from past practice. Approaches must be redesigned to account for these new circumstances:

- **Flattened organization.** The Web mitigates against twentieth-century bureaucratic units. The information highway and automated services challenge walls and excessive categorization. Dedicated library departments—circulation, government documents, serials—vanish. The medium leads toward flattened and flexible institutions with open flows of communication. Strict top-down controls and deference to authority winnow away. Team controls and consensus building grow, especially for smaller start-up operations.

> **Hiring Delights**

Institutional advantages emerge from the ability to attract and select talent without regard to location. Hiring an outstanding corps of dedicated librarians is an indulgence that can be "sold" as a strategic asset. The group can be marketed and packaged for reputation management purposes as well as to provide vital assets for internal recognition.

› Library Employment Pattern

Commentators also predict smaller staffs at traditional academic libraries. As seen here, the Web's effects may already be in motion. This employment graph from U.S. Census data reflects the positive aspects of post–World War II professionalization but also provides stark evidence of shrinkage that directly parallels the appearance of the new medium.

Number of Librarians

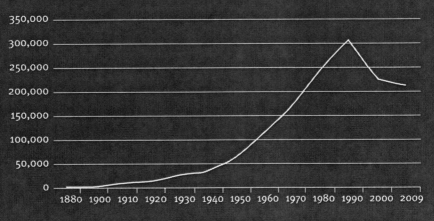

Librarian employment, 1880–2009 (from Beveridge et al. 2011)

- **Remote workers.** Instead of the "desk set" and an array of familiar faces on a nine-to-five schedule, professionals are likely to be telecommuting. Requirements to man regular desks and travel to the library offices are antithetical to online librarianship. They add overhead expenses and remove a significant recruiting draw. Possible professional exceptions feature the library manager, likely vital for in-house political/lobbying at headquarters; and the university archivist (if such a facility is in place), for face-to-face networking and collection development in assembling the school's documentary heritage.
- **Smaller staff.** Given the loss of tangible buildings and materials, the case for reduced professional staff is clear. Shrinkage is even greater for non-professional support staff. Their positions are most affected by the physical losses. Outside of ILL services, paraprofessional activities are reduced to the always important glue of a good office manager/administrative assistant. A virtual library office can be a minimal operation. It needs

only a telephone, mail, and contract support, but even a minor presence offers benefits as a stage for maintaining institutional connections.

- **Part-time over full-time.** Staffing strategies may extend to part-time appointments. This direction is particularly useful for initially building a corps of librarians. Part-time slots are also often easier to secure through budgetary procedures. Such positions join telecommuting as an attractive draw for some applicants, including stay-at-home caregivers and curious world traveler types who would have few other professional opportunities.

Change Management/Identity Building

The onset of online operations and remote workers brings psychological hurdles. On one hand, allowances must be made for the transformation into online librarians. Comfortable research and book tropes vanish. Economic awareness vies for prominence with academic quality. The virtual library is inherently disorienting for those inured to traditional campus life. Communication issues are rife. The absence of physical grounding and anonymity of the Web enhance possible points of rub.

On the other hand, telecommuting offers attractive prospects with disarmingly different managerial challenges. Regular face-to-face meetings are precluded. The wide range of coverage hours means that there is no single collective time when all staff members are together. Group conference calls may need to be arranged by consensus. Bandwidth issues can arise from media engagement. The manager also considers changing telephony options. Is videoconferencing appropriate? What are the telephonic options for VOIP (voice over internet protocols)? What about the use of avatars, Twitter, or future technologies?

Remote personnel magnify identification issues, especially with an online university. The absence of the campus atmosphere is telling on students and faculty, but perhaps more so for librarians. The pomp and circumstance of the university make for a special environment and supportive sense of commitment. Powerful identity/esprit des corps factors have long distinguished librarians and helped compensate for financial shortcomings. Telecommuters, however, are left bereft. Rather than engaging in a daily commuting ritual, online librarians are removed from contact with dedicated "temples of knowledge." They miss out on the ceremonial phasing in and out of staff, or even the holiday party, that comes from a physical location. The virtual cannot pretend to replicate such reinforcing rites.

As suggested, managerial responses are somewhat constricted in cyberspace. One continues to rely on a shared vision of service and professionalism with the staff. Yet, instead of water cooler conversations and wandering the building, the manager deploys from an electronic toolset and e-mail messaging. Tactics blend the old with the new, including consideration for:

- Regularly scheduled virtual meetings as mainstays
- Specialized training exercises as new products and services come online
- Time on the reference desk for a bit of continuity and regularized commitment
- A promotional ladder remaining in order
- Codification of practices and budgetary processes to offer other points of contact
- Annual retreat for face-to-face encounters and group bonding exercises
- Depending on finances, encouraging and supporting conference activities, scholarly endeavors, and entrepreneurial excursions

In theory, the virtual manager will need to become comfortable and embrace collective knowledge. Technological complexity alone defies the idea of a leader who knows all. Expect flattened organizations and smaller staffs but also the onset of a new generation of workers with diminished deference to managerial prestige and autocratic approaches. When group identity takes hold and staffing reaches a critical mass, consider "groupthink" and consensual management decision making. Expect top-down management to evolve into team-based approaches.

Performance Issues

Disciplinary issues are compounded online. There are no simple solutions. Communication hurdles are again a major culprit. Some gleanings may come only from the informal clues in face-to-face meetings. In the online world, the manager and team-based alternatives lose the benefits of direct observance. Humor and nuance are harder or impossible to convey.

In case of individual performance or disciplinary problems, methods revert to the mainstream. Clear prior benchmarks, group pressure, offline comments, the telephone

Growing Pains

As staff expands, the remote manager should expect growing pains. The luxury of more professionals is balanced by the span of control issues and the complications of distance. How to "unflatten" fosters dilemmas. Placing a peer in charge of a group task, especially one that involves performance measures, can lead to grumbling in the ranks.

call, and annual reviews are useful. Single complaints should be investigated, but the loss of physical intimacy accentuates the need for preliminary fact checking. With confirmation of wrongdoing, resolution may be rather simple, but also procedural. A "paper trail" must be started. Consideration should be given to bringing the human resources department into the picture as well as going through the most appropriate communication channels.

Hence, expect to follow a verifiable complaint with a meeting request or comment in writing. In serious matters, try to avoid an active e-mail train or chat sessions; these channels are awkward and privacy can be compromised. You may have better luck by phone in conference calls with additional parties present or, if feasible, in the preferred face-to-face encounter. If the situation remains intransigent, human resources policies need to take over.

Training

Online librarians join their mainstream counterparts in the need for training. Online librarians require special training. This features the addition of working knowledge of the campus LMS. Professional practices are also evolving with alacrity. The onset of a new product or version upgrade can signal a training event as well as a potential building opportunity. Recognize that joint training, with the exception of on-site retreats, is often precluded by telecommuting schedules. Point-of-contact librarians may take the lead for informal sessions and for building or updating help and information literacy fixed resources.

OPERATIONAL OVERSIGHT

Success relies on the dedication of the corps of librarians. As professionals, one expects them to require little oversight. Expected reliability, however, does not suggest complacency. The virtual library requires leadership and oversight. As mentioned in the "Reference" (chapter 6) and "Dashboards" (chapter 7) commentaries, new tools streamline oversight in the world of 24/7 services and telecommuters. The environment also places a premium on reporting and metrics. The manager must conform and take active advantage of these directions to ensure the library's sustainability.

> **› Project Management**
>
> Most work remains routinized. Such activities presuppose initial training regimens and inculcation from group participation but should always be open to fine-tuning. Remote organization for projects is more problematic. The more complex endeavors recommend project management software such as Basecamp or SharePoint.

Documenting and controlling reporting mechanisms are crucial to library advancement. Although evaluation standards remain works in progress, monitoring in the virtual is easier than in analog settings. Every movement can be captured and is susceptible to data mining. The virtual manager's attention divides into two overlapping lines of engagement: reporting and metrics.

Reporting

The lineup for virtual libraries will initially be familiar. User satisfaction surveys are expected and can help inform practice. Quarterly or monthly summaries of site usage, reference services, database searches, and the like should be assumed but also routinized to feed the annual report. The latter is both a marketing and management device. It should be framed for success. The opportunity is to promote services, librarians, and other contributions—but also to frame problem areas carefully for address. Document construction favors business reporting. A lead-in summary is fleshed for ingestion by readers with an affinity for charts and graphs but little tolerance for overblown rhetoric. Moreover, the same accounting joins user surveys as invaluable fodder for accreditation visits and government inquiries.

Metrics-Based Management

It is hard to "walk" around the virtual campus and gain a feel of the operations. The manager of remote workers observes instead by inference and data collection. Benchmarks and performance measures are required. Rather than the overhead of manual reporting, an online setting recommends unobtrusive devices. The operational goal is integrated support of professional work—to provide indicators and guides for honing practice rather than be an end in and of itself. The strategic goal is to gain positive recognition as a productive force within the university.

> **› Traffic Trump Card**
>
> The library should not shy from using successful traffic patterns to build its case in the constant battle against being overlooked. On a virtual campus, library usage measurements will likely stand far above those of competing centers for teaching and learning or other new entrants for student attention.

Operational Tactics

Online operations profitably invest in desktop support tools; with their data-mining abilities, online universities are particularly tuned to scan and monitor operations. Such returns are increasingly on display through electronic dashboards (see chapter 7). Managers are presented tailored sets of key data points. The virtual walk-around takes place through a desktop array. Feeds are tied to selected functions and alert areas:

Classroom materials coordination. The classroom portion calls for specialized monitoring. The manager should stay abreast of the new usage patterns, including areas of success and problems. As suggested in chapter 6, such employ directly affects collection development. Classroom materials, for instance, have much shorter active shelf lives than research volumes. Expect increasing focus and new pricing strategies also to enter the picture.

> **› Classroom Penetration**
>
> At the moment, the library field lacks appropriate impact and ROI indicators. In keeping with this text, a standardized set of metrics for classroom involvement would be of great value. How much time is spent in course-related research? What is the ratio of employ of Deep Web works for undergraduate and graduate instruction? Can we also claim and calculate for vetted open-web infusions?

Article use in the classroom proceeds in a pro forma fashion. In keeping with chapter 7's dark archives entry, the same cannot be said for e-books or pulls from websites. ebrary, EBL, and other e-book providers periodically are forced by publishers to purge holdings. Without monitoring and response procedures, the results can be devastating for classes and CRIS implementation. Recourse begins with mapping of the library materials used in classrooms against "pull" records and related "timeouts" from set period rentals through consortia or other parties. Once problem areas are identified, the library works with faculty to consider appropriate responses—switching texts, alternate vendors, licensing release, temporary electronic copies under fair use extensions.

Scheduling. Usage reports should not stand alone. Their purpose includes guiding staffing levels. With monthly starts, an online university's cycles may emerge with clarity and more addressable patterns than those employing traditional semesters. For APUS, for example, statistics indicate a stress on weekends, with the fourth Sunday accounting for by far the highest traffic. The peak week charting is based on assignment and testing tendencies with eight- and sixteen-week courses. Activities are skewed by the impact of the mandatory undergraduate introduction course. The first level of analysis is equally clear. Given 24/7 library operations, what are the optimum human staffing times in terms of budgeted positions? When does one engage the full 168 hours of potential coverage?

Work product controls. In addition to reference desk duties, online librarians can expect activities with quantifiable end products. In a throwback to Frederick Taylor's scientific management, the library manager needs to work with staff to set rough production guidelines for all products. Those teaching a training course for an online university can expect an end-of-course survey, but time on task is also in the picture for the classroom hours and building a supplemental web page.

Electronic bibliographies are a good example of a chartable product. If one employs a multiyear complete review cycle, production guidelines can be mapped. Matters are not totally straightforward. A simplistic formula that divides number of courses by number of librarians over x years will not work. Some classes are more volatile or their enrollment numbers suggest more repeated address. New courses are added and others removed. Allowance must be given for librarian learning curves. Production should become easier (and the librarian's knowledge enhanced) the more guides are produced for a department.

The manager and the librarian team can employ usage statistics and perceived best practices to advance their operations. Qualitative and quantitative measures enter the picture. Why are some guides or information literacy tutorials heavily used? Equally important, why are some not well used? Which faculty and departments are easy to work with, which are harder, and what can be done about the latter? Such questions are merely a stage one. Once the project achieves basic curricular coverage, planning turns to studied approaches for stage two—the long run. Which courses are more volatile in terms of updating? Which would be most affected by the introduction of a given application?

› Big Data: Predictive Analytics

In 2011 the Bill and Melinda Gates Foundation began funding for a predictive analytics reporting (PAR) framework, the most advanced statistical applications on higher education to date. APUS's Philip Ice is the lead investigator for a "Big Data" project involving hundreds of thousands of records from six universities, which include the exceptional tracking and data-mining capacities of the University of Phoenix and APUS. The initial drive is to create a nationally significant, federated database of student activity. The plan is to uncover patterns of behavior within course activities that are indicative of student dropout, failure, and—conversely—momentum. The goals are to improve systematically the likelihood of student retention and success.

The library challenge with this and related projects is to gain involvement. The drive is to introduce course materials and ideally library assignments/interventions to their proper places in the full-blown educational analysis.

Strategic Reporting

Reporting also involves political/bureaucratic connotations. Given government drives for openness and transparency among for-profits, their online libraries will likely be at the forefront of an emerging culture of assessment. Expect to find it involved with a variety of more sophisticated university-level evaluation instruments, like the Community of Inquiry model or Quality Matters program, but note that such models are insufficient. They tend to overlook the library and course materials.

TECHNOLOGICAL SETTING

This section looks to managerial oversight for the online library as website. Figure 9.1 illustrates a virtual library floor plan circa 2012. What less than five years ago required considerable internal infrastructures and internal staff can now be largely, if not fully, outsourced. Cloud services have rapidly altered and simplified technological matters. Rather than relying on a specialized department and systems expertise, online librarians can fill most of the gaps as part of their general duties. The question is how much outsourcing before the library begins to lose its distinctive nature and financial justification.

Site Development/Construction

The center of attention turns to the look, feel, and ongoing construction of a new creation. Unlike the architect-designed space and fixed walls of its predecessors,

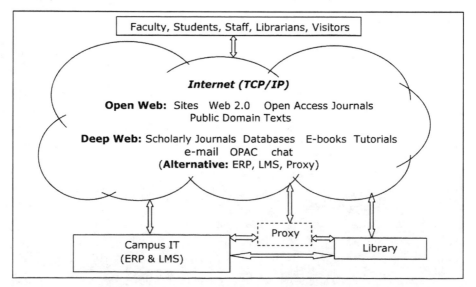

figure 9.1 Technical schematic for an online library, 2012 (Courtesy of the author)

> ### > Minimal Approach
> Mounting a minimally serviceable research library is frightfully simple. Institutional branding can be effected through ebrary, EBL, Books24/7, OverDrive, and others for turnkey e-book delivery—including patron-driven selections and rental options. Book selection readily combines with one of the large academic article database collections from ProQuest or EBSCO. Authentication is handled by campus IT and external agents, or perhaps through the controlled distribution of passwords. E-mail links on the library home page go out to a group (e.g., librarians@university.edu) or to individual librarian addresses. Assuming they are not outsourced, what remains is a library of reference specialists. A single library page wraps up the package. Moreover, OCLC is offering to lift any remaining managerial burdens through its management services.

the online library is constantly evolving and porous. Librarians are partially redefined as construction agents. Their living and never-finished facility comes with an infinite variety of doorways to assets spread across the ether.

Complacency or fixed design has no place in the virtual scene. There is no perfect layout, only a process of constant improvement with periodic review. Design features self-service and transparency, but as augmented by human components. Librarian-based cooperative development must be encouraged, but the manager retains the responsibility to monitor and provide the most cost-effective solutions across multiple components:

- **Core information services.** The heart of the virtual library remains a portal to licensed deep-web resources—the electronic books and scholarly journals in particular. How to best get the clients to such materials remains a challenging question. Access methods are rapidly developing. Relatively new federated searching is challenged by discovery services. Cloud-based housing threatens the ILS. Librarians build tailored course guides and departmental portals, which can exist as independent nodes elsewhere on the Web. How does the manager respond, especially given budgetary limitations?
- **Search engines.** The manager needs to account for external access and internal use of such software agents to the degree possible. The Web's most disturbing element significantly shakes up past library practice and calls into question many of the proposed directions for the field.
- **Supplemental services.** The library should be replete with supplemental web pages. A virtual library is a place where students expect to come for

all sorts of information. Avoid silos. Cooperative access points to other units are in order. The questions are many. What additional services or those fronting for other units are appropriate for branding as belonging to the library site? Where should they be positioned and where else should links appear? What pages from other offices should the library open on?

- **External points of entry.** The virtual library needs to be highly visible. The manager must be constantly alert to attempts to deprecate or bury links beneath layers of clicks. In addition to a prominent link as a major feature of the online campus, keys for success are infiltration into the classroom and the instructor's logon area. Explore the potential for RSS feeds, but also do not ignore the economic setting. Outside visitors may not be able to use the library's facilities, but an "About the Library" page with glossy updates is quite suitable for consideration by the marketing department. The questions are where best to place links and how best to negotiate for placement.

- **Web 2.0.** Social networking also extends the concept of academic libraries beyond the walls. Activity happens in two zones: the library ensures sites in places where students or faculty might reasonably look for its reference and information services; and librarians hunt for and "lurk" as participant observers in campus and related scholarly platforms.

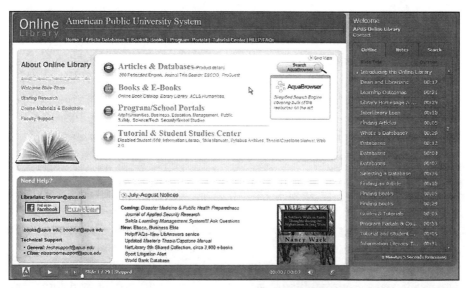

figure 9.2 Virtual library instructional video

> **› Accessible Design**
>
> The virtual library site must be prepared for ADA 508 compliance. In addition to being the right and legal thing to do, such accommodations tend to work to the benefit of all users; they can also help demonstrate library leadership on the campus. Descriptive alt tags for images, scripts for media presentations, and responsiveness to Daisy standards are the norm. Digitization, vendor activity, and WC3's embrace of universal access make for a fluid but addressable situation in terms of textual materials. Expect complications to arise with newer and, especially, interactive modes of delivery.

First-time students and faculty at an online university are expected to come with web facility, but understand that online libraries are among the most challenging sites on the Web. Design is aimed at building familiarity for return visitors. Navigation should be as transparent as possible with a subliminal eye toward memorized pathways. Yet best practice also calls for supplemental resources for the first-time user. The online library comes replete with such introductory options as individualized instructions, training sessions, and instructional videos (figure 9.2).

Technical Support/Staffing

With good system design, technical support should be sporadic. IT and cloud operations oversee ongoing maintenance. One anticipates library engagement to kindle periodically with product upgrades. These may trigger librarian training and user notification procedures. The related focus is the mounting or dismounting of a product and responses to outages or other technical problems. In addition, the library can expect active IT engagement for the following:

- **Dashboards.** IT, an office of institutional research, or a related campus data team may have to assist. Minimal technical staffing and the need to engage ILS data mean that the online library will likely require help in drawing together the disparate resources for a library dashboard.
- **Disaster/service responses.** Management must ensure contacts and contingency responses in the event of loss of service. Librarians are on at all hours and frequently are a main point of contact in the event of technical problems in the library or elsewhere on campus. Staff should not have to think at such times. They need to follow a plan. Measures are predrawn with a checklist for determining the extent of the problem along with notification procedures for technical support and users. Figure 9.3 shows the cover page from one measured set of responses. It includes "idiot-

APUS Online Library
Crisis Response

1-2012 update

Preparatory Steps
Crisis Responses
Campus Down
Library Down
Databases Down
* Many or All
Contact Lists
Librarians
Tech Support
Vendors
Appendices

Cover Sheet

The following is technically part of the Reference section of the Online Library's Procedures Manual. More importantly, it is an active Desktop Guide for Library Staff and resource for Technical Support in event of a crisis. Please note: the document will never be finished. We will update as exigencies arise. Moreover, responders must keep it in a prominent place to ensure operability.

Goals

In case of a service interruption or other significant problem that affect user access, APUS Librarians have two major responsibilities:

1. **Launch Remedial Actions:** Ensure that the appropriate response staff and your fellows are contacted. If response is not forthcoming, you may need to take limited direct action.
2. **Client Remediation:** Equally important reach out to users, especially those that contact us, with information and the offer of extra assistance. Do not try to keep quiet. Our clients will normally understand if they are informed, but will be justifiably agitated if left in the dark.

Preparatory Steps

- Create *Crisis Response* folder in Word.
- Place folder in upper-right corner of your computer's desktop to hold this document

figure 9.3 APUS crisis response cover page

proofing" instructions for placement in a distinct area on the desktop along with the librarian's dashboard.

- **ERP/LMS connections.** Although outsourcing may be an option, expect to rely on campus IT for linkages into the classrooms, but especially for authentication. Such centralized procedures remove the need or can automatically supply the data to a separate library user database.
- **Media/documents server.** Online libraries, especially those with a university archives function, may require their own storage space. Such services could be outsourced or housed on campus by the library or IT. As discussed in chapter 6, they raise overlapping technical and policy issues such as electronic preservation and open access.

- **Proxy server/authentication.** The library, IT, or a cloud-based service will need to house a separate server, EZproxy software, Shibboleth, or other form of authentication.
- **Web security.** The bulk of the online library's security concerns are outsourced with its information products. Still, hacking, denial of service, and viruses are to be expected. The library will need to ensure appropriate firewall and security controls, including backup/restoration schemes. Remote workers pose added threats. Their machines must be part of extended campus security measures, including the delivery of backup machines while infections are purged.

VENDORS RELATIONS

The online library manager can expect to engage in the information marketplace. Rather than relying on the treasure troves of past collections, those online are involved in concerted constructions. The library is built on the fly with still-forming electronic methods of delivery.

As indicated, such matters are heightened with classroom engagement. Though financially attractive, bulk purchasing and focused collection sets do not necessarily speak to properly populated classrooms or a research agenda. The manager has to engage in ongoing study of pricing, DRM, and licensing options. Decision matrices and spreadsheet analysis emerge as a portion of the job.

Matters become complicated too on the political/economic scene. For-profits may be treated as outcasts. They may or may not be allowed to enter consortial agreements. Publishers and vendors may attempt to route them into separate pricing categories. And fear of restraint-of-trade and antitrust violations along with the competitive nature among startups has up to now blocked discussions of cooperative purchasing within the sector.

Isolation, however, does not deny professional and institutional responsibilities to exert economic pressures on the marketplace. The larger for-profits come with built-in advantages and drives. They bring capitalistic intentions and economic muscle as successful web enterprises to such discussions. Academic libraries should also realize their ethical responsibilities to the students. It is time to stand in support of Sorbonne's ideal with open and affordable access as part of the public good. Is it also time to consider library participation in the construction of a distinct educational commons with its own set of intellectual property considerations?

CONCLUDING COMMENTS: AN IDEA OF THE ONLINE LIBRARY

"It has to be more than accreditation." Several colleagues spontaneously erupted with this expression during discussions over the future of academic libraries in the web age. Though a powerful factor, accreditation is not a perfect talisman against marginalization. As an accreditor for the Higher Learning Commission, I am afraid that the bulwark could disappear. Libraries are not clearly stated propositions within many of the accreditation guidelines. Despite ACRL's efforts to align with accreditation standards, librarians are not strongly visible among the higher echelons of the various regional and national accrediting agencies. Indeed, one can search in vain for a mention of the library in the main document currently on the table for accreditation reform—NACIQI's (Jan. 17, 2012) "Higher Education Accreditation Reauthorization Policy Recommendations."

Future sustainability thus requires calculation, action, and studied reinvention for the virtual campus. The Web proffers a shift. The medium not only obviates core concepts from physical storage, it births a new type of university and uncertain future.

Threats to the individual campus library and the field at large are real. Capitalistic forces threaten legal and financial underpinnings. The Long Tail fosters witting and unwitting competition. Search engines and other web applications replace reference activities. Bibliographic functions have been increasingly absorbed by "world libraries," ranging from the commercial of Amazon to the semicommercial OCLC or a JSTOR and nonprofit research libraries. Academic library omission remains far too frequent in these trends and library complacency equally so. Battlefield strategy thus devolves to a pincer movement:

- **Recognition.** The drive is to be seen. The issue is not ability; it is being overlooked and excluded from the opportunity to display the library's wares.
- **Contextualization.** Mechanisms engage on the client territory with language and methods tuned to that setting. Library professional jargon and drives to preserve past goals must be abandoned to pragmatic realities.

Tactics are highly utilitarian. Given a lack of physical collections, virtual libraries act as middlemen consumers and potentially through consortial memberships. Involvement in mainstream advances, from digital preservation to the semantic web, is limited. As with other small to medium-size facilities, their contributions channel through advocacy and financial buy-ins, but with a modicum of skepticism. Those in for-profit, online environments proffer financial counterpoint and question atavisms and inefficient allegiance to print-era practices.

Sustainability requires campaigning and reorientation. Librarians rewire. They market and orchestrate economic, political, and professional prospects within their particular school. Entrepreneurship and bureaucratic sophistication become parts of the quiver. Librarians commit to building a dynamic and flexible enterprise continuously. In addition to the classroom and research, they seek auditing, electronic publishing, tutorial operations, and other emerging web-based information practices.

Library success involves recognition and establishing its own value as a competitive advantage. Secondary positioning involves engagement with units across the institution. The library proactively engages for the school's scholarly reputation, in anticipation of emergent knowledge communities, and in building the foundational chronicle for its school. Internally operations transform and previously unforeseen duties appear. The virtual facility emerges with a selected core from the Deep Web, vetted materials on the Open Web, the prospects of internally produced resources, and involvement in web knowledge communities.

The new model recaptures the narrative of a Sorbonne. Institutionally tailored classroom services and web involvement join research as part of a total mission strategy. The academic library gains a subtly redefined variant in the new age:

Acting as a major hub on the virtual campus with ties to academic and professional communities, the online library engages web information services in support of its university's teaching, research, publications, and identity.

‹ epilogue: musings for the teens ›

> May you be condemned to live in interesting times.
> —*Chinese proverb*

THIS NARRATIVE ENDS ON THE CUSP OF THE "TEENS" OF
the twenty-first century—proximate midstream in the web revolution. While I have been writing, not a day has passed without
a relevant piece of information crossing my laptop's screen. New
applications pop up with frightful regularity. Court decisions
and publisher uncertainties pepper press accounts and trade literature. The world is becoming entrenched within a global web economy and
political scene. Knowledge distribution and the shape of universities continue
to undergo radical transformations. The medium is even altering the means of
human communication. It may join writing and speech in a triad of universal
messaging methods.

Though it is tempting, only a Nostradamus or science fiction writer should
dare prognosticate far into this future. Instead, allow me to indicate a hope,
near-term implementations, and an unfulfilled goal from World War II.

A HIGHER EDUCATION ECONOMIC AND COPYRIGHT ZONE?

Concepts of intellectual property, central to our culture, are not expressed
in a way which maps onto the abstract information space. In an information

259

space, we can consider the authorship of materials, and their perception; but we have seen above how there is a need for the underlying infrastructure to be able to make copies of data simply for reasons of efficiency and reliability. The concept of "copyright" as expressed in terms of copies made makes little sense.

Berners-Lee's (1996) insights on the inappropriateness of copyright speak directly to the academic condition. The Web itself proffers an engaging catalyst. With it goes much of the historical basis for publishers— their financial capitalization of the press and distribution channels. Higher education should embrace the chance to assert control. It needs to extricate itself from the present mire of Dickensian legacies, late twentieth-century opportunism, and antithetical legal implications.

> **Post-Cartesian Web Thinking**

If history is a measure, codification of the Web's effects on human thought will likely push well beyond the hyper-Incunabulum. It took almost two centuries after Gutenberg for René Descartes to coin *cogito ergo sum*. Tim Berners-Lee's 1991 invention is pushing along a similar, albeit accelerated transformational arc. We eagerly await the impact of the first-born web, but expectations are that the post-Cartesian mental update will still take a few generations.

Contradictions are currently rife. Governments and universities that underwrite the research are conspicuously removed from publishers' financial motivations. Unlike public authors and journalists, professors are not intent on profits from scholarly contributions. These fall under a separate academic reward system. Repeated extensions of coverage periods similarly make little sense in the education marketplace. The intellectual contributions that underlie university research and educational information date from an earlier social compact. They reflect an elemental public good that needs to be preserved and asserted.

GOVERNMENT ACTORS

My personal wish list argues for a separate copyright educational zone. Changing the law will require a sophisticated cooperative initiative. Fortunately, government drives are already under way in the United States with singular emphasis on responsibility to share its sponsored scientific research. Matters have gone global. Great Britain with the Finch Report (Finch 2012) and the European Union's "Europe 2020" (European Commission 2012) follow a similar route.

UNIVERSITY ECONOMICS

If implementation is to come, it will require lobbying and the exercise of power from the scholarly and university community. University endowments alone could be marshaled as a determinant force toward differentiating a separate educational/economic zone. The academic library has an added role as a goad. At the micro level, the financial power of academic libraries dwarfs that of the publishing industry in general, let alone the subset that has developed in support of it and now seems willing to compete for students.

> ## › New Publication Sector
>
> The Web, library orientation, and incomparable strength of university technological expertise remove the need for publisher capitalization. Open access, Open Educations Sources, Creative Commons, and HathiTrust-like movements have already built a foundation for disruptive change. An academic combination could readily step to the fore and dramatically redesign publishing for both scholarly and classroom purposes.

The most traditional of secular enterprises no longer needs to be beholden to the private sector. Higher education holds sufficiently mammoth sway on the Long Tail to declare its own economic zone and policies. Even a cursory marshaling of forces from the library niche reveals the unparalleled potential of a university-led coalition:

- **Academic societies.** This situation is complicated. Some associations rely heavily on financial income from research and teaching materials. Yet tradition and duty are in place. The members of even the outliers can be called to task to respond to their primary allegiance to advance the field of study and university affiliations.
- **Nonprofit library economy.** OCLC and its regionals already walk a tightrope of financial allegiance but properly lean toward a separate knowledge community, as do the newer forces of a HathiTrust, JSTOR, and Project MUSE.
- **For-profit library economy.** Database aggregators ProQuest and EBSCO, dependent publishers and agencies from bepress to Scarecrow, and ILS and other support vendors have an interest in academic library sustainability.
- **Student lobbyists.** Students share in both the financial and intellectual directions.

> **> Branding the Library Economy**
>
> Just as the field has succeeded in asserting political power for the public library and intel-
> lectual freedom, advocacy beckons for economic branding. Modern libraries have consti-
> tuted an underacknowledged market force since the nineteenth century. Today they are the
> linchpin for a diverse, multibillion dollar sector at the heart of the Deep Web's knowledge
> economy. This arena is actively stimulating innovation and entrepreneurial advances on
> both sides of the public and private good. The accumulation of old and new is distinguished
> by intensely interested communities and global networks with immense potential.

- **University presses.** The schools and library purchasing power may have
  to pressure for compliance, but university presses must realize the fundamental changes enveloping them—for their own survival.
- **Research libraries.** The nineteenth-century leadership model persists in
  this campaign. The major research libraries will need to be engaged and
  provide leadership for the sector. Smaller college and university libraries
  should join in solidarity and lend their persuasive powers, especially in
  regard to illuminating the case to their members of Congress. Though a
  narrow base, academic library associations bring symbolic value.

This impressive array would certainly welcome other players. ALA and educators of all shapes would likely see the wisdom of cooperative action. The drive
is reasonable compromise. Textbook, trade, and university publishers can make
decent profits, especially if they begin to understand the Long Tail and financial
beauty of lifelong learners. Springer and Wiley are already engaged along such
lines, including offering open-access components. Others may need pressures
and education to be reminded of their ethical responsibilities.

ON EDUCATIONAL TECHNOLOGY

The glasses will have a low-resolution built-in camera that will be able to
monitor the world in real time and overlay information about locations,
surrounding buildings and friends who might be nearby. . . .

The glasses will send data to the cloud and then use things like Google
Latitude to share location, Google Goggles to search images and figure out
what is being looked at, and Google Maps to show other things nearby.

Nick Bilton (2012) of the *New York Times* announced the coming of science fiction dreams for augmented reality and ubiquitous computing. The sensory and physical boundaries of reality would be loosed. Implications of this hyper-charged potential for "anytime/anywhere" education and related library services are immense. They are not alone. The virtual library and university pedagogies have to get in front of such burgeoning technologies as these:

- **Touch screens.** This capacity is being built into all new computers, is part of HTML5, and is featured in the Windows 8 operating system. What virtual "movement grammars" should libraries be considering for navigating their facilities, search, and retrieval?
- **3D projections.** What are similar implications for manipulation beyond two- into three-dimensional space? What are the educational impacts for such fields as geometry and engineering, for gesture-based computing, for the artistic and classroom ability to bring participants together on a "holodeck"?
- **Personal learning environments.** Web delivery has largely been confined to broadcast modes. The medium, however, is well prepared for adjusting meanings in a dialectical session with the user. For education, outcome-based learning through personal learning environments has begun to emerge. With such an approach, individual skills are dynamically mapped against a program of study—assignments tailored on the fly.
- **Voice recognition systems.** In 2012, Apple's Siri opened a new era of familiarity. Yet authentication routines, enhanced language instruction, and personalized dictation were already well on the table. Moreover, voice directions are projected to play an increasing role with enabling the handicapped.
- **Thought projections and eye tracking.** Consider the effects when the blink of an eye or mere thought can cause action. As indicated by Google Glass, the technology is here. Eye-tracking sensors have already been extended beyond the cockpits of fighter jets to multimedia music productions. Brain-wave authentication looms. Experiments look to quadriplegics turning pages with their minds alone.

MULTILAYERED VIRTUAL LIBRARY: TOWARD MEMEX

The virtual library in this text represents established reality at the forefront of online, for-profit universities. Whether its CRIS model extends across the for-profits sector or is partially adopted as a survival mechanism for the mainstream remains to be seen. To be sure, that creation is itself incomplete. The dual-layered institutional approach presented here awaits a third layer to reach long-imagined fulfillment:

- **Layer 1: research laboratory.** A central facility continues to operate as resort for research and a variety of auxiliary services. These are aimed primarily at the curriculum and the identity/scholarly reputation of the university as well as in support of lifelong learning communities.
- **Layer 2: departmental boutiques.** The Web also enables granularity and heightened developmental zones. Interfaces are extracted from the central facility into departmental libraries, which mirror the educational/research contours of the university. Aided by subject specialist librarians, these creations also bring potential for cross-institutional knowledge centers—a new form of the university for the web age.
- **Layer 3: virtual carrels.** Just as Google has helped reinvent practice, virtual libraries have lessons to learn from Amazon. The two layers above remain primarily one-way bulletin boards. But the Web contains barely tapped potential for dialectic with fully responsive, individualized applications. These must be engaged to complete web reinvention.

As envisioned, this third layer of the virtual academic library can act alone or as part of a personalized learning environment. It is realized through virtual carrel functionality. Patrons have access to the gamut of student enrollment and social community activities, but with an emphasis on study and research elements. The space comes with immediate access to supporting software along with writing and information resources. The last are not only available on demand but proffered through active profiling of activities and professional specialization—an interactive learning environment.

One must close by noting that the virtual carrel and parallel hopes for online librarians as a "new profession of trailblazers" are merely expectant brides. Even

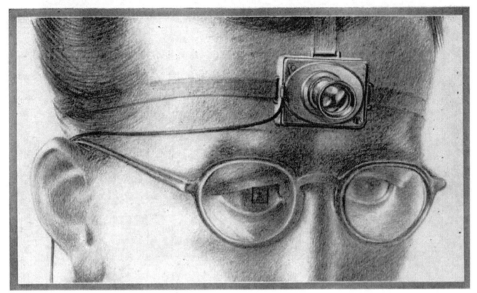

Memex optical input device, *Life Magazine* (1945)

the most advanced of current applications has roots to Vannevar Bush's (1945) landmark "As We May Think." The intellectual fount for the World Wide Web still awaits fulfillment:

> Consider a future device for individual use, which is a sort of mechanized private file and library. It needs a name, and, to coin one at random, "memex" will do. A memex is a device in which an individual stores all his books, records, and communications, and which is mechanized so that it may be consulted with exceeding speed and flexibility. It is an enlarged intimate supplement to his memory. . . . Wholly new forms of encyclopedias will appear, ready made with a mesh of associative trails running through them, ready to be dropped into the memex and there amplified. . . . There is a new profession of trail blazers, those who find delight in the task of establishing useful trails through the enormous mass of the common record.

‹ colophon ›

The work closes with a return to preprint practice. From the cuneiform of the ancient Sumerians to hand-written codices, readers looked to a document's colophon or final strokes to find production details. Those interested in background to this text are similarly invited.

APUS AS SCRIPTORIUM

Reinventing the Library for Online Education is intended to go beyond a "how we did it good" exploration. Yet the end product remains admittedly grounded in eight years of building and running a virtual library at the American Public University System (APUS).

Home is a for-profit, fully online enterprise with two main brands—the American Military University (AMU) and American Public University (APU). Its library story began in mid-2005. As one might guess, the catalyst was regional accreditation. APUS president Wallace Boston joined the recommendations of incoming provost Frank McCluskey. They commissioned a push from the small Online Resource Center toward a cutting-edge and symbolically renamed Online Library.

Thanks in part to library efforts, APUS succeeded. With regional accreditation, the school entered hypergrowth. By 2010, AMU was the largest provider of higher education to the U.S. military. In that same year and after a rigorous national search, Wal-Mart selected APU as its official university. At the time of this writing in the fall of 2012, the student body had grown from around 8,000 at the opening of the online library in 2005 to well over 100,000 registrants in 120-plus countries.

In the words of members of Congress, APUS acts as a "white hat." The fastest-growing for-profit at the time of this writing, the university maintains above-board and transparent practices. It has assumed national leadership in analytics and retains commitment to the humanities along with a duality of quality and affordability—a $250/credit hour basis for undergraduate courses has not been raised in a dozen years. Moreover, APUS continues to support and recognize the centrality of its library as an area of excellence.

ACCREDITATION AND GROWTH

Although more remains to be done, the library has grown more than apace with the university. As the graph indicates, an average of 3,500 monthly visits in 2005 exploded to over 100,000 by 2010. Resources more than quadrupled during that period to runs of 40,000 journals and 150,000 e-books. The staff

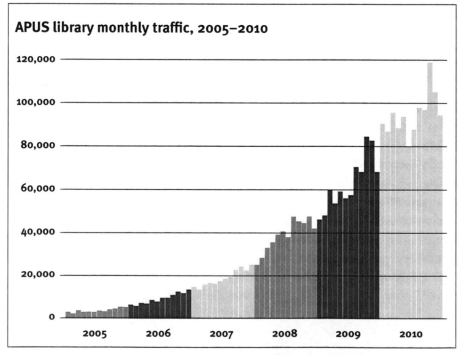

(Created by author from 3Dstats reports)

of professionals expanded from two to twenty-one librarians, with more in the offing. They reside in ten states and Saudi Arabia. Academically outstanding, the cast features five PhDs and averages three master's degrees—collectively competitive anywhere, but also the leading librarian talent among the for-profits and marketed as such.

Growth benefitted from the enlightened support of top management and concerted internal efforts. In July 2005 a hastily drawn "Positioning the APUS Online Library for Academic Excellence" laid out preparations for regional accreditation plus a five-year development campaign. The library staff of two professionals immediately proclaimed leadership in information literacy and propagandized it into a major university goal within the accreditation campaign. The library similarly asserted itself for copyright and ADA 508 compliance as well as in the management of tutoring and plagiarism services. Library exercises were proactively infiltrated into the required introductory course for undergraduates and made part of basic faculty training. A purposively titled Online Library opened on October 8, 2005, with the following vision statement:

> The APUS Online Library strives for academic excellence and professional leadership as part of a new wave of Academic Librarianship. This fully virtual facility is created to provide state-of-the-art research and educational support for the University; moreover, services that are available at any time of the day or night and regardless of geographic location. To these ends, the School has specially committed to professional librarians. Such staff provides personalized relationships, but also advanced subject and Web skills. APUS librarians help ensure competency and currency in Web Information Literacy, information-seeking behaviors, instructional tools, myriad of online resources, search engine applications, and study aids—as well as the display of the University's contributions to the world's knowledge. This complex role is intended to blend in active partnerships with the disciplinary/teaching expertise of faculty. The design is part of an interactive learning community with our students, alumni, and other staff—nothing less than a new idea of the university for the Web Era.

POST-ACCREDITATION AND CRIS ENTREPRENEURSHIP

Thanks to accreditation success, the APUS Online Library reached a position to strike in the afterglow of accreditation and work toward its grandiose hopes.

Library traffic figures were inserted in the university's standard reporting mechanism and serendipitously caught the ongoing attention of the governing board. Rapid negotiations led to three part-time librarians and a full-time support administrator. With that modicum of staffing, attention embraced CRIS strategies. Tactics centered on a long-term electronic bibliography or course guides initiative (now using Lib-Guides software), featuring a three-year review period that harkened to medieval copy cycles. If we could prove these ongoing quality and currency devices, library sustainability would be ensured and the university manifestly improved.

> ## Recognition
The APUS Course Guides project surfaced to modest acclaim as I write in 2012. IMS Global Learning Consortium, the international Common Cartridge standards organization, recognized it with a Gold Innovation Award, and the National University Technology Network singled it out with an Honorable Mention prize.

The library also seized other opportunities. In particular, APUS was continuing distance education practices with the mail-delivery of printed texts. Textbook and shipping inflation joined with the then budding availability of digital books for our opening. In late 2006, a second white paper proposed an electronic

APUS library opening and online librarians, 2011 (APUS staff photographer)

course materials (ECM) initiative. The ECM plan sought engagement through a tripartite structure, one that remains among the most sophisticated responses to textbook inflation and for the creation of web pedagogies:

- **Electronic bookstore.** Initial attention was given to the "low-hanging fruit" of transitioning textbooks. The library created the ECM office with separate staffing. The latter orchestrated controlled conversions from print to electronic formats. The inchoate textbook marketplace proved complex and negotiations complicated. Negotiations were strengthened by the rapid growth and increased clout of the university.
- **Online library/Open Web.** The second and overlapping phase called on library deep-web holdings and librarian expertise in validating open-web resources as course materials. Librarian subject specialists were selectively added in targeted support of the university's degree programs and enrollment formula. Tactics stressed definable ROI but also the unprecedented quality and currency assurances that could come from librarian involvement.
- **E-press.** The third leg extends analysis toward a reinvention of the university press. From a CRIS perspective, university presses and their overlooking of course materials made little senses—doubly so for a sector in deep financial trouble made little sense. The response was to launch an APUS ePress in early 2011. Monographs and scholarly journals (including

> **Virtual University Archives**

With a physical base in hand, the APUS library also took the opportunity to push to the next level. It engaged a librarian/archivist to extend to another phase of web reinvention. Our electronic university archives steps forward with multiple goals.

- **Dark archives.** The new office fills an immediate role in quasi-preservation/disaster preparation operations to ensure the steady flow of electronic course materials.
- **Documentary heritage.** The archives respond to the challenge of building long-lasting internal identification for faculty, students, and staff and set groundwork for the rise of an alumni network in a new institution.
- **Reputation management.** Archival programs and related web projects can highlight and help legitimate the achievements of the university and faculty to the scholarly community, but also as part of future marketing ventures.

an underwriting arrangement with the Policy Studies Organization and Wiley) are factored for reputation management purposes. The focus, however, is on the classroom. APUS ePress is aimed at improving the classroom with uniquely web-based publications that will go beyond the textbook to a new generation of course materials.

SUMMARY, AND NO GOOD DEED REWARD

Electronic advancement brought an ironic benefit. In late 2010, President Boston called with an offer from Lt. Gen. (ret.) Richard Trefry. The general asked about our interest in owning the library of the Association of the U.S. Army. The answer was yes—but we would need a "real" library. Boston committed to a state-of-the-art facility within an environmentally gold standard building in Charles Town, West Virginia. The new special library focused on military studies and history and officially opened as a campus landmark on September 26, 2011.

THE SCRIBE

Like all men of the Library, I have traveled in my youth; I have wandered in search of a book, perhaps the catalogue of catalogues; now that my eyes can hardly decipher what I write, I am preparing to die just a few leagues from the hexagon in which I was born. Once I am dead, there will be no lack of pious hands to throw me over the railing; my grave will be the fathomless air; my body will sink endlessly and decay and dissolve in the wind generated by the fall, which is infinite. I say that the Library is unending.
—*Jorges Luis Borges, "The Library of Babel"*

With this book, the scribe wraps up a long and varied career. At the time of writing, I have the good fortune of serving as dean of libraries, electronic course materials and APUS ePress as well as vice president with APEI, the NASDAQ-listed corporate owner of APUS. In addition, I enter a two-year appointment as ALA's library representative on the U.S. Commission to UNESCO. Other bona fides begin with 1960s-era training as a data-processing specialist and systems analyst in the U.S. Army. Education includes an MLS from the University of Rhode Island. A dual doctorate in history and American studies from Indiana University in the mid-1970s featured perhaps the first punchcard-produced dissertation in the field of history.

My professional career in libraries and archives began in 1980 at the New England Library Board and moved to head special collections at what is now the University of Louisiana–Lafayette. That was followed by a decade as a professor at the University of Maryland and Catholic University along with visiting professorships at the universities of Illinois, Perugia, and Puerto Rico. The 1990s brought a return to administration including directorships at the Amistad Research Center at Tulane University, Mid-Hudson Public Library System, and in the early twenty-first century the Reuther Labor Library at Wayne State University.

Side ventures extend to development teams for HyperTIES, the first DOS-based hypertext program, and Sirs-Mandarin's M-3 ILS. A variety of consultancies and advisory boards involve such institutions as Books24/7, Bowie State University, Cengage's MindTap Board, CourseSmart's Internet2 Assistive Advisory Committee, ebrary, National Agricultural Library, New Orleans Jazz and Heritage Festival, URI's Harrington School, and the World Bank/IMF—along with "oracle" duties for the American Association of Museums. Professional commitments extend across a half-dozen associations, most notably ALA with chairing its Web Advisory Committee, CALM (archival, library and museum joint committee), and Intellectual Freedom Roundtable.

Selection in 1999 as an MCI "Cybrarian of the Year" reflected my early engagement of the Web. A sample of other recognition includes ALA's Justin Windsor Prize, J. Franklin Jameson Fellowship at the Library of Congress, Fulbright Scholarship in Italy, URI alumnus of the year, APUS's Etter Award for Creativity, and IMS Global's Gold Innovation Award. Eleven book-length productions feature *Creating Virtual Libraries* and *Building Digital Archives* for Neal-Schuman, with Mary Lee Bundy *Activism in American Librarianship,* the award-winning *The Management of Oral History Sound Archives,* and with Philip McNair *Finding Success for Returning Veterans and Active Duty Students.* Journal publications range to over one hundred scholarly articles. Apropos of this text, related editorial directions currently involve coeditorship of *Internet Learning,* an open-access journal in collaboration with Oxford University and the Policy Studies Organization for the Wiley Publishing suite.

‹ bibliography ›

This book leans heavily on web resources. Those cited below were retrieved between July 2011 and October 2012. See also the "webliography" that follows this bibliography.

AAUP American Association of University Presses. Feb. 2007. "Statement on Open Access." www.aaupnet.org/images/stories/documents/oastatement.pdf.

———. March 2011. *Sustaining Scholarly Publishing: New Business Models for University Presses.* A report of the AAUP Task Force on Economic Models for Scholarly Publishing. www.aaupnet.org/images/stories/documents/aaupbusiness models2011.pdf.

ACRL Association of College and Research Libraries. Jan. 18, 2000. *Information Literacy Competency Standards for Higher Education.* www.ala.org/acrl/standards/ informationliteracycompetency.

———. 2010. *Value of Academic Libraries.* Chicago: Association of Research Libraries.

———. Oct. 2011. *Standards for Libraries in Higher Education.* www.ala.org/acrl/ sites/ala.org.acrl/files/content/standards/slhe.pdf.

Adema, Janneke. 2010. *Overview of Open Access Models for eBooks in the Humanities and Social Sciences.* http://project.oapen.org/images/documents/open accessmodels.pdf.

ALA American Library Association. 2012. "E-content: The Digital Dialogue." *American Libraries,* May/June. http://viewer.zmags.com/publication/f8ac9caa#/f8ac9caa/1.

ALA Presidential Committee on Information Literacy. 1989. Final Report. Chicago: American Library Association. www.ala.org/acrl/publications/whitepapers/presidential.

ALA Presidential TCE Task Force. Jan. 2011. "Traditional Cultural Expressions Task Force Report." American Library Association. Access via http://wo.ala.org/tce/2011/01/28/tce-task-force-final-report/.

Allman, William. 2012. "Accidental History of the @ Symbol." *Smithsonian Magazine,* Sept. www.smithsonianmag.com/science-nature/The-Accidental-History-of-the-at-Symbol-165593146.html.

Anderson, Chris. 2004. "The Long Tail." *Wired,* issue 12.10 (October). www.wired.com/wired/archive/12.10/tail.html.

———. 2005. "The Origins of 'the Long Tail.'" *Wired Blog Network,* May 8. http://longtail.typepad.com/the_long_tail/2005/05/the_origins_of_.html.

Anderson, Rick. 2011. "'Librarians'"—An Endangered Species?" *The Scholarly Kitchen,* Aug. 25. http://scholarlykitchen.sspnet.org/2011/08/25/librarians-an-endangered-species/.

Aptara. 2011. "Uncovering eBooks' *Real Impact,* 2009–2011." Access via www.aptaracorp.com/home/survey.

ARL Association of Research Libraries. Oct. 2009. "ARL Strategic Plan, 2010–2012." www.arl.org/arl/governance/strat-plan/index.shtml.

———. 2010. "Strategies for Opening Up Content." *Research Library Issues.* April. Access via www.arl.org/news/pr/RLI-269-17may10.shtml.

———. 2012. *Code of Best Practices for Fair Use in Academic and Research Libraries.* January. Access via www.arl.org/pp/ppcopyright/codefairuse/code/index.shtml.

———. 2012. *Guide to the Library and University Expenditure Data.* February. Access via www.arl.org/stats/annualsurveys/eg/index.shtml.

Authors Guild, Inc., et al. v. HathiTrust, et al., Oct. 10, 2012. United District Court, Southern District of New York. www.scribd.com/doc/109647049/HathiTrust-Opinion.

Battles, Mathew. 2003. *Library: An Unquiet History.* 2003. New York: Norton.

Beagle, Donald. 1999. "Conceptualizing an Information Commons." *Journal of Academic Librarianship* 25(2): 82–89.

———. 2006. *The Information Commons Handbook.* New York: Neal-Schuman.

Benedict of Nursia. *Holy Rule of St. Benedict (Regula Benedicti)* (ca. 530). www.ccel.org/ccel/benedict/rule2/files/rule2.html.

Berners-Lee, Tim. 1991. "Qualifiers on Hypertext Links." Access via www.w3.org/People/Berners-Lee/1991/08/art-6484.txt.

———. 1996. "The World Wide Web: Past, Present and Future." Aug. www.w3.org/People/Berners-Lee/1996/ppf.html.

———.2006. "Linked Data." W3C, July 27. www.w3.org/DesignIssues/LinkedData.html.

Berners-Lee, Tim, James Hendler, and Ora Lassila. 2001. "The Semantic Web." *Scientific American,* May 17. www.scientificamerican.com/article.cfm?id = the-semantic-web.

Beveridge, Sidney, Susan Weber, and Andrew A. Beveridge. 2011. "Librarians in the U.S. from 1880–2009: An Analysis Using 120 Years of Census Data." *Social Explorer,* OUP Blog, June 20. blog.oup.com/2011/06/librarian-census.

Bilton, Nick. 2012. "Google to Sell Heads-Up Display Glasses by Year's End." *New York Times,* Feb. 21. http://bits.blogs.nytimes.com/2012/02/21/google-to-sell-terminator-style-glasses-by-years-end/.

Bledstein, Barton. 1978. *The Culture of Professionalism.* New York: Norton.

Borges, Jorge Luis. "The Library of Babel" (1941). http://jubal.westnet.com/hyperdiscordia/library_of_babel.html.

Bosch, Stephen, Kittie Henderson, and Heather Klusendorf. 2011. "Periodicals Price Survey." *Library Journal,* April 14.

Boston, Wallace. 2010. "Measuring Student Retention at an Online Institution of Higher Learning." PhD diss., University of Pennsylvania.

Bradford, Alexandria. 2011. *Learning at a Distance.* U.S. Department of Education. http://nces.ed.gov/pubs2012/2012154.pdf.

Brandt, Richard. 2011. *One Click: Jeff Bezos and the Rise of Amazon.com.* New York. Portfolio.

Brown, Karen, and Kara J. Malenfant. 2012. *Connect, Collaborate, and Communicate: A Report from the Value of Academic Libraries Summits.* Association of College and Research Libraries. www.ala.org/acrl/sites/ala.org.acrl/files/content/issues/value/val_summit.pdf.

Brown, Laura, Rebecca Griffiths, and Matthew Rascoff. 2007. *University Publishing in a Digital Age.* ITHAKA. Access via http://quod.lib.umich.edu/j/jep/3336451.0010.301?rgn = main;view = fulltext.

Burgess, Jean, and Joshua Green. 2009. *YouTube: Online Video and Participatory Culture.* New York: Polity.

Bush, Vannevar. 1945. "As We May Think." *Atlantic Monthly,* July 1. www.the atlantic.com/magazine/archive/1945/07/as-we-may-think/303881.

Canfield, James Hulme. May 1902. "The College Library." Outlook 71.

Cassiodorus, Senatorus. *Institutiones Divinarum et saecularium litterarum* (ca. 562). Access via www2.idehist.uu.se/distans/ilmh/Ren/bibl-cass-vivarium.htm.

Casson, Lionel. 2001. *Libraries in the Ancient World.* New Haven: Yale University Press.

Center for History and the New Media. 2010. *Hacking the Academy.* http://hackingtheacademy.org.

Chait, Richard, and Zachary First. 2011. "Bullish on Private Colleges." *Harvard Magazine,* Nov.–Dec., 36–39.

CHEA Council for Higher Education Accreditation. 2010. U.S. Department of Education Final Regulations on Program Integrity and Student Aid. *Federal Update,* Nov. www.chea.org/Government/FedUpdate/CHEA_FU13.html.

Christensen, Clayton M., Michael B. Horn, Louis Soares, and Louis Caldera. 2011. *Disrupting College: How Disruptive Innovation Can Deliver Quality and Affordability to Postsecondary Education.* Center for American Progress: Washington, DC. Access via www.americanprogress.org/issues/2011/02/disrupting_college.html.

Clark, Mathew P., and Roger C. Schonfeld. 2011. *S+R Library Survey 2010: Insights from U.S. Academic Library Directors.* ITHAKA. Access via www.sr.ithaka.org/research-publications/us-library-survey-2010.

CLIR Council on Library and Information Resources. 2010. *Transforming Research Collections for 21st Century Scholarship.* Washington, DC: Council on Library and Information Resources.

Committee des Sages. 2011. *The New Renaissance,* European Union, Brussels. http://ec.europa.eu/information_society/activities/digital_libraries/doc/refgroup/final_report_cds.pdf.

Cormier, Jeff. 2010. "Xplana Launches Free, Online, Collaborative Educational Tools." *The Next Web,* Aug. 10. http://thenextweb.com/socialmedia/2010/08/10/xplana-launches-free-online-collaborative-educational-tools.

Cornell University. n.d. Cornell Electronic Course Content Copyright Guidelines. http://copyright.cornell.edu/policies/docs/Copyright_Guidelines.pdf.

Cornell University Library. 2000–2003. "Moving Theory into Practice: Digital Imaging Tutorial." www.library.cornell.edu/preservation/tutorial/intro/intro-01.html.

Courant, Paul N. 2006. "Scholarship and Academic Libraries (and Their Kin) in the World of Google." *First Monday* 11:8. http://firstmonday.org/htbin/cgiwrap/bin/ojs/index.php/fm/article/viewArticle/1382/1300.

Courant, Paul, and Matthew Nielson. 2010. "On the Cost of Keeping a Book." In *The Idea of Order: Transforming Research Collections for 21st Century Scholarship.* Washington, DC: Council on Library and Information Resources.

Coyle, Karen, and Diane Hillman. 2007. "Resource Description and Access (RDA)." *DLIB,* Jan.–Feb. http://dlib.org/dlib/january07/coyle/01coyle.html.

Creaser, Claire, and Valerie Spezi. 2012. *Working Together: Evolving Value for Academic Libraries.* Sage Report, June. http://libraryvalue.files.wordpress.com/2012/06/ndm-5709-lisu-final-report_web.pdf.

Crow, Raym. January 2009. *Campus-Based Publishing Partnerships: A Guide to Critical Issues.* SPARC, Jan. Access via www.arl.org/sparc/partnering/guide.

———. 2009. *Income Models for Open Access: An Overview of Current Practice.* SPARC, Sept. www.arl.org/sparc/bm~doc/incomemodels_v1.pdf.

Dames, K. Matthews. 2012. *Decision Summary: Publishers v. Georgia State University.* http://copyright.syr.edu/publishers-v-georgia-state.

Darton, Robert. 2010. "The Library: Three Jeremiads." *New York Review of Books,* Dec. 23. www.nybooks.com/articles/archives/2010/dec/23/library-three-jeremiads.

Davidson, Cathy N. 2011. *Now You See It: How the Brain Science of Attention Will Transform the Way We Live, Work, and Learn.* New York: Viking Press.

Davis, Denise. 2011. *Trends in Academic Libraries, 1998 to 2008.* Chicago: American Library Association. Access via www.ala.org/research/sites/ala.org.research/files/content/librarystats/academic/ALS%209808%20comparison.pdf.

Davis, Jinnie, Mignon Adams, and Larry Hardesty. 2011. "Academic Libraries in For-Profit Schools of Higher Education." *College and Research Library* 72(6). http://crl.acrl.org/content/72/6/568.full.pdf+html.

De Bury, Richard. Philiobiblion (1345). Trans. E. C. Thomas (1909). London: Chatto and Windus. Excerpt at http://historymedren.about.com/library/text/bltxt philbib19.htm.

Derrida, Jacques. 1998 [1967]. *Of Grammatology.* Baltimore: Johns Hopkins University Press.

De Rosa, Cathy, et al. *College Students' Perceptions of Libraries and Information Resources*. Dublin, Ohio: OCLC, 2006.

Dewey, Barbara. 2004. "The Embedded Librarian: Strategic Campus Collaborations. *Resource Sharing and Information Networks* 17:5–17.

Dublin Core Metadata Institute. n.d. "About Us." http://dublincore.org/about-us.

Duke, Lynda M., and Andrew D. Asher. 2011. *College Libraries and Student Culture: What We Now Know*. Chicago: American Library Association.

Education Advisory Board. 2011. *Redefining the Academic Library: Managing the Migration to Digital Information Services*. Access via www.eab.com/Research-and-Insights/Academic-Affairs-Forum/Studies/2011/Redefining-the-Academic-Library.

Eisenstein, Elizabeth. 1979. *Printing Press as an Agent of Change*. Cambridge: Cambridge University Press.

Electronic and Information Technology Accessibility Standards. Dec. 21, 2000. www.access-board.gov/sec508/standards.htm.

European Commission. July 17, 2012. "Towards Better Access to Scientific Information: Boosting the Benefits of Public Investments in Research" [Europe 2020]. European Union. http://ec.europa.eu/research/science-society/document_library/pdf_06/era-communication-towards-better-access-to-scientific-information_en.pdf.

Fiels, Keith Michael. 2011. "ALA meets with AAP." *American Libraries,* Sept. 26.

Finch, Janet. June 2012. "Accessibility, Sustainability, Excellence: How to Expand Access to Research Publications." Research Information Network (Great Britain). www.researchinfonet.org/wp-content/uploads/2012/06/Finch-Group-report-FINAL-VERSION.pdf.

Fitzpatrick, Kathleen. 2011. *Planned Obsolescence: Publishing, Technology, and the Future of the Academy*. New York: New York University Press.

Foster, Nancy Fried, and Susan Gibbons. 2007. *Studying Students: The Undergraduate Research Project at the University of Rochester*. Chicago: Association of College and Research Libraries.

Gallagher, Kelly. 2011. "Overview of the College Textbook Market Academic Year 2010," in BSG's Making Information Pay for Higher Education. www.slideshare.net/bisg/bisgs-mip-for-higher-ed-gallagher-kelly.

Garrett, J., and D. Waters, editors. 1996. *Preserving Digital Information*. Report of the Task Force on Archiving of Digital Information. Commission on Preservation and Access and the Research Libraries Group. www.oclc.org/resources/research/activities/digpresstudy/final-report.pdf.

Ginzburg, Carlo. 1992. *The Cheese and the Worms: The Cosmos of a Sixteenth-Century Miller.* Baltimore: Johns Hopkins University Press.

Glaser, Barney G., and Strauss, Anselm L. 1967. *The Discovery of Grounded Theory: Strategies for Qualitative Research.* Chicago: Aldine.

Gleick, James. 2011. *The Information: A History, A Theory, A Flood.* New York: Pantheon.

Goldstein, Daniel. 2010. "Library, Inc." *Chronicle of Higher Education,* October 17.

Greenstein, Daniel. 2009. "Libraries and the Academy." ITHAKA's Sustainability Conference. Reprinted as "Strategies for Sustaining the University Library. 2010. *Portal: Libraries and the Academy.* Access via muse.jhu.edu/journals/pla/summary/v010/10.2.greenstein.html.

Guthrie, Kevin, Rebecca Griffiths, and Nancy L. Maron. 2008. *Sustainability and Revenue Models for Online Academic Resources.* ITHAKA, May. Access via www.sr.ithaka.org/research-publications/sustainability-and-revenue -models-online-academic-resources.

Guy, Bradley, and Eleanor M. Gibeau. 2003. *A Guide to Deconstruction.* Deconstruction Institute. www.deconstructioninstitute.com/files/learn_center/45762865 _guidebook.pdf.

Hanson, Cody, and Heather Hessel. Sept. 2010. "Discoverability: Phase 2 Final Report." University of Minnesota Libraries.

Harley, Diane, et al. 2010. *Assessing the Future Landscapes of Scholarly Communication: An Exploration of Faculty Values and Needs in Seven Disciplines.* Berkeley: Center for Studies in Higher Education, University of California–Berkeley.

Harris, Michael H. 1995. *History of Libraries in the Western World,* 4th ed. Metuchen, NJ: Scarecrow Press.

Hilderbrand, Lucas. 2009. *Inherent Vice: Bootleg Histories of Videotape and Copyright.* Durham, NC: Duke University Press.

Hobbs, Renee. 2010. *Copyright Clarity: How Fair Use Supports Digital Learning.* Chicago: Corwin, NCTE.

Howard, Jennifer. 2009. "In Face of Professors' 'Fury,' Syracuse U. Library Will Keep Books on Shelves." *Chronicle of Higher Education,* Nov. 12.

———. 2010. "Overdue at the Library: Good Guides on How to Use It." *Chronicle of Higher Education,* June 29. http://chronicle.com/article/Overdue-at-the -Library-Good/66086/.

IMLS Institute of Museum and Library Services. 2008. *InterConnections: The IMLS National Study on the Use of Libraries, Museums, and the Internet.* http://interconnectionsreport.org.

International SGML Users' Group. 1993. "SGML History." Accessed via http:// xml.coverpages.org/sgmlhist0.html.

Internet Archive. 2011. "In-Library eBook Lending Program Launched." *Internet Archive Blogs,* Feb. 22. http://blog.archive.org/2011/02/22/in-library -ebook-lending-program-launched.

Jackson, Sidney. 1974. *Libraries and Librarianship in the West,* New York: McGraw-Hill.

Jobrack, Beverlee. 2011. *Tyranny of the Textbook.* Lanham, MD: Rowman Littlefield.

Kaufman-Wills Group. 2005. *The Facts about Open Access: A Study of the Financial and Non-financial Effects of Alternative Business Models on Scholarly Journals.* Association of Learned and Professional Society Publishers. Access via www .alpsp.org/ngen_public/article.asp?id = 200&did = 47&aid = 270&st = &oaid = -1.

Kelley, Michael. 2011. "How the W3C Has Come to Love Library Linked Data." *Library Journal,* Aug. 31. www.libraryjournal.com/lj/home/891826-264/ how_the_w3c_has_come.html.csp.

———. 2011. "Library of Congress May Begin Transitioning from MARC," *Library Journal,* May 26. www.libraryjournal.com/lj/home/890784-264/library_of _congress_may_begin.html.csp.

Kieft, Robert, and Lizanne Payne. 2010. "A Nation-Wide Planning Framework for Large-Scale Collaboration on Legacy Print Collections." *Collaborative Librarianship* 2(4): 229–233.

Kohrman, Rita. 2012. *Curriculum Materials Collections and Centers: Legacies from the Past, Visions of the Future.* Chicago: American Library Association.

Kolowich, Steve. 2011. "Academic Publishing and Zombies." *Inside Higher Ed,* Sept. 30. www.insidehighered.com/news/2011/9/30/planned_obsolescence_by_kathleen_fitzpatrick_proposes_alternative_to_outmoded_academic_journals.

———. 2011. "High Enrollers." *Inside Higher Ed,* Feb. 3. www.insidehighered.com/ news/2011/02/03/college_enrollments_keep_booming_especially_at_for_profit _institutions.

———. 2012. "Smaller Servings for Libraries," *Inside Higher Ed,* Feb. 21. www .insidehighered.com/news/2012/02/21/library-budgets-continue-shrink -relative-university-spending#ixzz1n2K5bBRt.

Kountz, John. 1992. "Tomorrow's Libraries." *Library Hi Tech* 9:39–50.

Kuh, George, and Robert Gonyea. July 2003. "The Roles of the Academic Library in Promoting Student Engagement in Learning." *College and Research Libraries* 64(4): 256–282.

Kuhn, Thomas. 1962. *The Structure of Scientific Revolutions.* Chicago: University of Chicago Press.

Kvenild, Cassandra, and Kaijsa Calkins, editors. 2011. *Embedded Librarians: Moving Beyond One-Shot Instruction.* Chicago: American Library Association.

Lankes, David. 2011. *The Atlas of New Librarianship.* Chicago: Association of College and Research Libraries.

Lavoie, Brian, and Lorcan Dempsy. 2010. "Rethinking the Boundaries of the Academic Library." *Next,* Dec. www.oclc.org/nextspace/017/research.htm.

Ledeen, M. A. 1999. *Machiavelli on Modern Leadership.* New York: St. Martin's Press.

Lessig, Lawrence. 2008. *Remix: Making Art and Commerce Thrive in the Hybrid Economy.* New York: Penguin.

Levien, Roger E. 2011. *Confronting the Future.* Chicago: American Library Association. Access via www.ala.org/offices/sites/ala.org.offices/files/content/oitp/publications/policybriefs/confronting_the_futu.pdf.

Lewis, David W. 2007. "A Strategy for Academic Libraries in the First Quarter of the 21st Century." *College and Research Libraries* 68(5): 418–434.

Library of Congress. 2011. *Preserving Our Digital Heritage: The National Digital Information Infrastructure and Preservation Program 2010 Report.* http://digitalpreservation.gov/multimedia/documents/NDIIPP2010Report_Post.pdf.

Lippincott, J. K. 2006. "Linking the Information Commons to Learning." In *Learning Spaces,* ed. Diana G. Oblinger. *EDUCAUSE.* http://net.educause.edu/ir/library/pdf/PUB7102g.pdf.

Lyrasis. Sept. 2011. "Everything I Know about eBooks I Learned from My Librarian." www.lyrasis.org/Resources/Articles/eBooks%20part%201.aspx.

Malpas, Constance. 2011. *Cloud-Sourcing Research Collections: Managing Print in the Mass-Digitized Library Environment.* Dublin, Ohio: OCLC Research.

Maron, Nancy L., K. Kirby Smith, and Matthew Loy. July 2009. *Sustaining Digital Resources: An On-the-Ground View of Projects Today.* ITHAKA. Access via www.sr.ithaka.org/research-publications/sustaining-digital-resources-ground-view-projects-today.

Martin, Randy. 2011. *Under New Management: Universities, Administrative Labor, and the Professional Turn.* Philadelphia: Temple University Press.

Mason, Matt. 2008. *The Pirate's Dilemma.* New York: Free Press.

McCluskey, Frank, and Melanie Winter. 2012. *The Idea of the Digital University.* Washington, DC: Policy Studies Organization.

McGovern, Nancy. 2012. *Aligning National Approaches to Digital Preservation.* Educopia Institute. Access via http://educopia.org/sites/educopia.org/files/ANADP_Educopia_2012.pdf.

McLuhan, Marshall. 1962. *The Gutenberg Revolution: The Making of Typographic Man.* Toronto: University of Toronto Press.

Michalko, James, Constance Malpas, and Arnold Arcolio. 2010. *Research Libraries, Risk and Systemic Change.* Dublin, Ohio: OCLC Research. www.oclc.org/research/publications/library/2010/2010-03.pdf.

Mullins, James, et al. 2011. *Library Publishing Services: Strategies for Success Research Report Version 1.0.* Purdue University, IMLS. http://docs.lib.purdue.edu/cgi/viewcontent.cgi?article = 1166&context = lib_research.

NACIQI National Advisory Committee on Institutional Quality and Integrity. 2012. "Higher Education Accreditation Reauthorization Policy Recommendations." 2nd draft, Jan. www.insidehighered.com/sites/default/server_files/files/NACIQI%20Policy%20DRAFT%201-17-12.docx.

Network Development and MARC Standards Office. 1999. "Guidelines for the Use of Field 856." www.loc.gov/marc/856guide.html.

Newman, John Henry. 1858. *The Idea of a University.* National Institute for Newman Studies. www.newmanreader.org/works/idea/.

New Media Consortium and Educause. 2012. *Horizon Report: 2012 Higher Education Edition.* Access via www.nmc.org/horizon-project.

New York Times. 2010–2011. "Your Brain on Computers." Article series. http://topics.nytimes.com/top/features/timestopics/series/your_brain_on_computers/index.html.

North, Ada. 1885. "A Western University Library." *Library Journal* 11.

Oakleaf, Megan. 2010. *Value of Academic Libraries: A Comprehensive Research Review and Report.* Chicago: Association of College and Research Libraries. www.ala.org/acrl/sites/ala.org.acrl/files/content/issues/value/val_report.pdf.

OCLC. 2011. "Perceptions of Libraries, 2010," Dublin Ohio: OCLC. www.oclc.org/reports/2010perceptions.htm.

Phan, Tai., et al. Dec. 2011. *Academic Libraries: 2010 First Look.* National Center for Education Statistics. Access via http://nces.ed.gov/pubsearch/pubsinfo.asp?pubid = 2012365.

Pope, Barbara Kline, and P. K. Kannan. Jan. 31, 2003. *An Evaluation Study of the National Academies Press's E-publishing Initiatives: Final Report.* National Academies Press. Access via www.aaupnet.org/resources/mellon/nap/index.html.

Pritchard, James P., editor. 1969. *Ancient Near Eastern Texts Relating to the Old Testament.* 3rd. ed. Princeton, NJ: Princeton University Press.

Rothstein, Edward. 2009. "Typography Fans Say Ikea Should Stick to Furniture." *New York Times,* Sept. 4.

Rouse, Mary A., and Richard. 1991. "The Early Library of the Sorbonne." In *Authentic Witnesses: Approaches to Medieval Texts and Manuscripts*. South Bend, IN: University of Notre Dame Press.

Samuelson, Paul A. 1954. "The Pure Theory of Public Expenditure." *Review of Economics and Statistics*. 36(4): 387–389. DOI:10.2307/1925895. JSTOR 1925895.

SchlagerBlog. 2009. "The Problem with Reference Publishing." *SchlagerBlog,* May 3. http://neilblog.schlagergroup.com/2009/05/03/the-problem-with -reference-publishing/.

Schonfeld, Roger C., and Ross Housewright. 2009. *What to Withdraw? Print Collections Management in the Wake of Digitization.* Ithaka S + R. www.sr.ithaka.org/ research-publications/what-withdraw-print-collections-management-wake -digitization.

———. 2010. *Faculty Survey 2009: Insights for Libraries, Publishers, and Societies.* Ithaka S + R. www.sr.ithaka.org/research-publications/us-faculty-survey-2009.

Schottenloher, Karl. 1989. *Books and the Western World.* Trans. William K. Boyd and Irmgard H. Wolfe. Jefferson, NC: McFarlane.

Seneca, Lucius Annaeus. De Tranquillitate Animi (ca. 60), xi. Excerpt and translation in www.newadvent.org/cathen/09227b.htm.

Shannon, Claude. 1948. "A Mathematical Theory of Communication." *Bell Systems Technical Journal* 27. http://cm.bell-labs.com/cm/ms/what/shannonday/ shannon1948.pdf.

Sheiber, Stuart M. 2009. "Equity for Open Access Publishing," *PLoS Biology* 7(8). www.plosbiology.org/article/info%3Adoi%2F10.1371%2Fjournal .pbio.1000165.

Silverstein, Michael, and Neal Fisk. 2003. *Trading Up.* New York: Penguin.

Simpson, Carol. 2005. *Copyright for Schools: A Practical Guide,* 4th ed. Chicago: Linworth.

Sinclair, Bryan. 2009. "The Blended Librarian in the Learning Commons." *College and Research Libraries News.* http://crln.acrl.org/content/70/9/504 .full.pdf + html?sid = de78dd95-5138-4f4b-8b3e-38b023c03c5f.

———. 2012. "GSU Library Promotes Open Access to New Faculty." *Library Journal,* Sept. 13. http://lj.libraryjournal.com/2012/09/opinion/backtalk/gsu -library-promotes-open-access-to-new-faculty-backtalk/.

Snead & Co. Ironworks. 1915. *Library Planning, Bookshelves, and Stacks.* Jersey City, NJ: Snead. See at http://books.google.com/books?id = 3VUAAAAAYAAJ& pg = PP1#v = onepage&q&f = false.

Sparrow, Betsy, Jenny Liu, and Daniel Wegner. 2011. "Google Effects on Memory: Cognitive Consequences of Having Information at Our Fingertips." *Science,* Aug. 5. www.sciencemag.org/content/333/6043/776.abstract.

Spiro, Lisa, and Geneva Henry. 2010. "Can a New Research Library Be All Digital?" *In The Idea of Order.* www.clir.org/pubs/reports/pub147/pub147.pdf.

Stanley, Hiram M. 1889. "University Library Buildings." *Library Journal* 14.

Stielow. 1990. "Librarian Warriors and Rapprochement: Archibald MacLeish, Carl Milam, and World War II." *Libraries and Culture* 25.

———. 1999. *Creating Virtual Libraries.* New York: Neal-Schuman.

———. 2002. *Building Digital Archives.* New York: Neal-Schuman.

Stuart, C. 2008. *ARL Learning Space Pre-planning Tool Kit.* Washington, DC: Association of Research Libraries.

Suber, Peter. 2012. *Open Access.* Boston: MIT Press.

Sun Tzu. *The Art of War* (300 BCE?). Access via http://suntzusaid.com.

Thomas, Lisa Carlucci. 2010. "Going Mobile." *Library Journal,* Oct 15. www.library journal.com/lj/ljinprintcurrentissue/886987-403/gone_mobile_mobile _libraries_survey.html.csp.

———. 2012. "The State of Mobile in Libraries 2012." *Library Journal,* Feb. 7. www.thedigitalshift.com/2012/02/mobile/the-state-of-mobile-in-libraries -2012/.

Trithemius, Johannes. [1492]. *De Laudem Scriptorium [In praise of scribes].* Excerpted at http://misc.yarinareth.net/trithemius.html.

UNESCO and Commonwealth of Learning. 2011. *Guidelines for Open Educational Resources (OER) in Higher Education.* Commonwealth of Learning. www.col .org/PublicationDocuments/Guidelines_OER_HE.pdf?mid=56.

Universities UK, Research Information Network. 2009. "Paying for Open Access Publication Charges." Access via www.rin.ac.uk/our-work/research-funding -policy-and-guidance/payingopen-access-publication-charges.

U.S. RDA Test Coordinating Committee. June 20, 2011. *Report and Recommendations of the U.S. RDA Test Coordinating Committee on the Implementation of RDA—Resource Description and Access.* www.loc.gov/bibliographic-future/rda/ source/rdatesting-finalreport-20june2011.pdf.

Vaidhyanathan, Siva. 2011. *The Googlization of Everything.* Berkeley: University of California Press.

Vesey, Lawrence. 1965. *The Emergence of the American University.* Chicago: University of Chicago Press.

W3C World Wide Web Consortium. November 3, 1992. "Tags Used in HTML."
www.w3.org/History/19921103-hypertext/hypertext/WWW/MarkUp/Tags
.html.

———. 1999. "Web Accessibility Guidelines." www.w3.org/TR/WAI-WEB
CONTENT/#Guidelines.

Waltham, Mary. 2005. *JISC: Learned Society Open Access Business Models.*
www.marywaltham.com/JISCReport.pdf.

———. 2009. *The Future of Scholarly Journals Publishing among Social Science and
Humanities Associations.* National Humanities Alliance. www.nhalliance.org/
bm~doc/hssreport.pdf.

Waters, Don, and John Garrett. 1996. "Preserving Digital Information: Report of the
Task Force on Archiving of Digital Information." Washington, DC: Commission
on Preservation and Access and Research Libraries Group.

Waters, Peter. 1975. *Procedures for Salvage of Water Damaged Library Materials.*
Washington, DC: Library of Congress. http://cool.conservation-us.org/bytopic/
disasters/primer/waters.html.

Weber, Max. 1978 [1922]. *Economy and Society.* Berkeley: University of California
Press.

Williamson, Charles. 1923. *Training for Library Service.* New York: Updike.

Wittfogel, Karl. 1957. *Oriental Despotism: A Comparative Study of Total Power.*
New York: Random House.

Wortham, Jenna. 2011. "Shorter E-books for Smaller Devices." *New York Times,*
Feb. 12, Sunday Business.

Zipf, George Kingsley. 1949. *Human Behavior and the Principle of Least Effort.*
Boston: Addison-Wesley.

‹ *webliography* ›

In addition to cited publications listed in the bibliography, the following sites were consulted and may be referred to within the text.

Academia.edu (scholars' journal storage and registration area). www.academia.edu

ADL (Advanced Distributed Learning). www.adlnet.gov

ALA OITP, Policy Briefs. www.ala.org/ala/aboutala/offices/oitp/publications/ policybriefs/index.cfm

AltMetrics Manifesto. www.altmetrics.org/manifesto

American Association of University Presses. www.aaupnet.org/index.php

Arizona State University Libraries, The Library Channel. http://m.youtube.com/ profile?gl = US&hl = en&client = mv-google&user = librarychannel

Bath Protocol. www.collectionscanada.gc.ca/bath/bp-current.htm

Book Business Magazine. www.bookbusinessmag.com

Book Industry Study Group. www.bisg.org

California Digital Library (CDL). www.cdlib.org/services/publishing/ ucpress_ebooks.html

CERN Web Information. http://Info.cern.ch

Chronicle of Higher Education. http://chronicle.com

CLOCKSS (Controlled LOCKSS). www.clockss.org/clockss/Home

Connexions (Rice University sponsored e-Press). http://cnx.org

Copyright Alliance. http://copyrightalliance.org

Corpus Thomisticum. www.corpusthomisticum.org

Creative Commons. http://creativecommons.org

Daisy Consortium (handicapped accessibility). www.daisy.org

Deconstruction Institute (building trades). www.deconstructioninstitute.com

Digital Public Library of America. http://cyber.law.harvard.edu/research/dpla

DOAJ (Directory of Open Access Journals). www.doaj.org

Dublin Core Metadata Institute. http://dublincore.org

Educators List (Second Life). http://educators@lists.secondlife.com

Educause. www.educause.com

Equella (Pearson). www.equella.com/home.php

ERIAL (Ethnographic Research in Illinois Academic Libraries). www.erialproject.org

Factual. www.factual.com

Fister, Barbara. Library Babel Fish (blog). www.insidehighered.com/blogs/library
   _babel_fish

Huffington Post, Libraries in Crisis. www.huffingtonpost.com/news/libraries-in
   -crisis

IMS Global, Common Cartridge Specifications. www.imsglobal.org/cc

Index Thomisticus. www.corpusthomisticum.org/it/index.age

Indiana University Press. www.iupress.indiana.edu

Inside Higher Ed. www.insidehighered.com

Internet Archives: The Wayback Machine (Brewster Kahle). http://archive.org/
   web/web.php

ITHAKA. www.ithaka.org

Lessig (blog). www.lessig.org/blog

Library Bureau, History Page. www.librarybureau.com/aboutlegacy.html

Library Copyright Alliance. www.librarycopyrightalliance.org

Library Journal. www.libraryjournal.com

Library Works. www.libraryworks.com

LOCKSS. www.lockss.org/lockss/Home

MacArthur Foundation, Digital Media and Learning. www.macfound.org/site/
   c.lkLXJ8MQKrH/b.946881/k.B85/Domestic_Grantmaking_Digital_Media
   _Learning.htm

Minnesota Population Center (IPUMS). www.ipums.org

National Center for Educational Statistics. http://nces.ed.gov

NDIIPP (National Digital Information Infrastructure and Preservation Program).
   www.digitalpreservation.gov

OCLC. www.oclc.org

OCLC Research. www.oclc.org/research/default.htm

OCLC WorldShare Platform. www.oclc.org/worldshare-platform

Online Journal of Distance Learning Administration (OJDLA). www.westga
   .edu/~distance/ojdla/

Open Content Alliance. www.opencontentalliance.org

Open Discovery Initiative, NISO. www.niso.org/workrooms/odi

Orange Grove (Florida). www.theorangegrove.org

Professional Scholarly Publishing Association. www.pspcentral.org

ResearchGate. www.researchgate.net

ROAR (Registry of Open Access Repositories, University of Southhampton).
   http://roar.eprints.org

Scholarly Societies Project. www.scholarly-societies.org

Section508.gov. www.section508.gov

Sherpa/RoMEO. www.sherpa.ac.uk/romeo/index.php

Sloan Consortium. http://sloanconsortium.org

SPARC (Scholarly Publishing and Academic Resources Coalition). www.arl.org/
   sparc

Teaching Online Pedagogical Repository (University of Central Florida). http://
   blended.online.ucf.edu/effective-practices/teaching-online-pedagogical
   -repository/

The Pirate Bay (from Sweden, the world's top bit torrent site for pirated materials).
   http://thepiratebay.org

Three Percent (University of Rochester blog on translations). www.rochester.edu/College/translation/threepercent/

University of Michigan Press. www.press.umich.edu/ebooks

University of Pittsburgh D-Scribe Digital Publishing. www.library.pitt.edu/dscribe/search.php

U.S. Department of Education, Common Educational Data Standards. https://ceds.ed.gov/Default.aspx

U.S. Department of Education, Integrated Postsecondary Education Data System (IPEDS). http://nces.ed.gov/ipeds

W3C Semantic Web (wiki). www.w3.org/2001/sw/wiki/Main_Page

W3PLE (Personal Learning Environment). www.w3ple.org

Web History Center. http://webhistory.org

WebKit (HTML 5). www.webkit.org.

Wikipedia. http://en.wikipedia.org/wiki

World Public Library. http://worldpubliclibrary.org

World Wide Web. www.w3.org

‹ index ›